The Manual
Survival Guide for
Visual Artists

The Manual Survival Guide for Visual Artists

Edited by Noel Kelly, Niamh Looney & Jason Oakley

Contributors: Annette Clancy; Dr. Tina Fiske; Flannigan Edmonds Bannon; Sarah Glennie; Kevin Kelly; Noel Kelly; Niamh Looney; Jacinta Lynch; Fred Mann; Kerry McCall; David McConnell; Jacqui McIntosh; Paul O'Neill; Alan Phelan; Sarah Pierce; Gaby Smyth & Company

Visual Artists Ireland
The Representative Body for Visual Artists in Ireland: providing practical support in all art forms

First Printing: 2015

ISBN 978-1-907683-13-8

Visual Artists Ireland
Central Hotel Chambers
7/9 Dame Court, Dublin 2
Ireland

 www.visualartists.ie
www.visualartists.org.uk

The Sculptors Society of Ireland t/a Visual Artists Ireland is funded by the Arts Council /An Chomhairle Ealaíon, The Arts Council of Northern Ireland, Belfast City Council, and Dublin City Council.

Contents

2

The Business of ART

Making art and making an art career are two different things. A professional artist is responsible for the day-to-day business of their career such as financial management, applying for grants and funding, documenting work marketing, promotion, researching opportunities, and a list of other tasks. These areas are not always covered within the education system so, while highly educated and skilled, many visual artists are not prepared for the reality of life after art college.

As an artist led organisation Visual Artists Ireland is keenly aware that artists are pressed for time, trying to fit their art making into daily lives that juggle family, work and other commitments. We hope this manual will provide you with some of the tools to make the most of the opportunities that come your way, whether it be pursuing a post graduate course, getting a studio, entering juried exhibitions, initiating your own projects or getting representation through a gallery. But, don't forget… you should never rely on an opportunity finding you. It is very much you creating them for yourself. VAI is there to assist you with the many services and information channels that we offer to professional visual artists in all art forms.

Noel Kelly
Chief Executive Officer – Visual Artists Ireland

Keeping it Practical

Art Handling

Basic Principles of Art Handling

The objective of good art handling is to move artworks from one location to another in a way that no damage occurs to the work. Basic care and common sense will usually be enough to achieve your objective. If the works to be handled are of a delicate nature more than ordinary care and attention is required. Works created in the studio need to be prepared and carefully packed for safe transportation to a gallery or museum.

Good handling is fundamental to the long-term care and preservation of a work of art. The moment the work is being moved from the studio to the gallery is the time when it is at its most vulnerable. The work might well be handled by the artist themselves or by a transporter. In both cases it is best that basic principles are adhered too. Common sense and care are the watchwords here. Know the weaknesses of the work and plan your moves in advance. When moving art out of a building make sure that door widths and heights are known in advance and have the move well prepared in advance. If the work is large consider making it in parts that can be easily disassembled. You may have to move it on your own. If working with others ensure that they too are aware of the delicate nature of the work.

There are a wide variety of artworks made today and even something as seemingly straightforward as a DVD needs similar attention. It's important to impart to any movers or shippers that you need the work to be handled properly. This might mean requesting that the work is transported in the correct orientation i.e. that they follow the arrows on the box or crate. Simple things like this makes sure the work gets handled properly.

Preparing and Packing Artwork for Transport

When preparing a work for transport it is a good idea to write out a condition report before packing the work. Damages and repairs can be noted, and when the work is returned to you any further damages can be seen. Examples of condition report forms can be obtained online or you could make up your own to suit your work.

Most condition reports follow a similar format containing detailed artwork information first – name of artist, artwork, materials, size, date; the travel information, destination, duration of exhibit – followed by a description of the object in question. This will generally focus on the surface condition of the work in text and is often accompanied by a small diagram locating the items described. The language used can be quite tricky – words like "accretion" or "scratch" can have several interpretations and applications. These often need clarification. For a glossary of these terms

11

see Conservation OnLine which hosts comprehensive information for many media.

This task within a museum context is done by the Registrar or Conservator who will have specialised training. For those not trained in museum practices, it is good practice to include a straightforward consignment note, listing the work details along with any major flaws (scratches, missing paint, uneven surfaces, etc). Documentation is always important should something go wrong and insurance has to be called on. A copy of the condition report should travel with the work so that the gallery can form an agreement with you as to the condition of the work when it arrives.

It is also advisable to have the work transported by a reputable freighting company that has established art handling experience. Express courier services can treat art works in a slipshod manner as they may not be mindful of the delicate nature of the piece. Many prefer not to ship art because of the difficulty in assessing value after damage. Sometimes, however, there can be no option if speed is required. In this case, good preparation and packing is imperative. These companies prefer to carry small document sized packages but a small drawing, photograph, painting or DVD, once carefully packaged can generally survive the rough treatment that a package gets through any postal or courier service.

Packing

There are a number of important things to look out for when packing an artwork for transport even if you are delivering it yourself. The packing should provide adequate protection for the work while it is being transported. This should include protection from pressure, moisture, knocks, vibrations and dramatic climate changes. There are a number of ways that this can be done. Firstly aim for the highest standard of packing and transport that your budget will allow. It is ideal if you can wrap the work and put it into a crate. For short trips it can be wrapped in poly sheeting and bubble wrap protective corners or even blankets. Poly sheeting can be obtained in various thicknesses from hardware suppliers. For small quantities uses plastic drop-sheets which can be purchased from any DIY shop. Bubble wrap is best purchased in bulk – as a roll from any office supply company like Viking or Albany. It can also be bought by the metre in Evans Art Supplies off Capel Street in Dublin. Hardware mega stores like B&Q only sell it in small quantities and it is enormously expensive.

If transporting 2D work via lorry or truck it is wise to strap the work securely to the truck itself. A sheet of firm card to cover the surface can be useful. Several sheets can provide protection between each work while they are stacked together in the truck. It is advisable to oversee the loading and unloading of your work so that you can alert people to how it should be handled. Avoid clutter in the vehicle and all items travelling with the work should be properly tied down. Always label the work, clearly noting if it contains glass and which way up it should travel. 2D work is safest if it is placed in the direct line of travel. This helps to ensure that the work absorbs the least vibration across its surface.

If a crate cannot be sourced and the work is delicate, the next best thing is to make your own crate. Try to incorporate as many of the features found in museum cases such as water proofing and internal foam lining. Museums use an inert foam called Plastazote which can be purchased from UK suppliers like Conservation by Design. Polystyrene is often used – this does not have as much give but may be the only material available.

Cardboard sheeting and boxes are often used for national shipping. This offers basic protection along with the bubble-wrap and blankets which shippers usually carry in the trucks. For international shipping a tougher box is always more advisable and plywood makes a good lightweight solution, offering a hard puncture proof surface (for the most part). Triple strength cardboard can be a solution for lightweight non-fragile artworks but only as a last resort.

Soft Wrapping

Works for short trips can be wrapped in poly sheeting with the addition of padded corners or edges. The wrapping of artworks is best done in a clean area preferably on large tables which have a padded surface, if possible. Ordinary tables can be covered in bubble wrap or blankets. Make sure the packing area is free from any fixings, tools or screws. A clear area on the floor can also be used. It is important not to over wrap artworks. Small delicate works can be damaged by the application of too much packing material. For example, when unpacking, excessive packing material can obscure the work and the removal of tape can put pressure on parts of the work that may be delicate.

Before wrapping make sure that all parts of the work are sound and remove or tighten any loose fixings. Loose fittings and bits can act as missiles during a bumpy ride in a truck. Some prefer the use of acid free tissue paper as a protective layer over the work before the poly sheeting is put on. A number of factors need to be considered before deciding to place any packing material directly onto the surface of an unprotected work particularly a painting or a photograph. Firstly the surface should be completely stable, dry and durable as materials can adhere to the surface and/or the surface could be abraded by the movement of that material on the surface while in transport. It is best if the packing material does not rest directly on the surface of the work. If the work has a very delicate surface a travel frame should be used. Ideally, artworks should be packed in conservation standard materials if they are to be stored for any length of time.

Conservation standard materials are considered inert which means that they contain no substances that could be harmful to the work. These are, however, expensive and can be only purchased in the UK from companies like Conservation Resources, Conservation by Design and Preservation Equipment. The least an artist on a limited budget can do is use correct materials on the inner most layer which is in contact with the artwork or if contact is inappropriate, that there are sufficient spacers or padding.

If the work is framed and the frame is raised above the surface of the painting, unbleached cotton tape can be stretched across the painting. This will help to keep the poly sheeting from sagging onto the surface. Make sure to position your tape where it will not put pressure on any vulnerable part of the frame. Place the lengths of tape so that it divides up the picture surface evenly. Use slipknots as these are easily removed and reused. Tie the knots on the back of the work towards the edge so that no loose bits of tape rest on the painted surface. Use lengths of folded acid free tissue to protect the frame from any abrasion caused by the tape.

Measure the work and cut the poly to fit. Place the poly sheet down and lay out the cotton tape and folded tissue and then position the picture face down onto the packing material. Use thick low tack vinyl tape if possible to seal the poly sheet on the back along one edge to avoid putting pressure on the back of the canvas. It is always a good idea to put a tab on the beginning of the tape so that it can be removed easily afterwards. This is both a courtesy to those doing the unpacking as well as good practice as some delicate works can be damaged while tape is being scratched off. If the work is glazed it is best practice to use specialized glass tape to protect the work from glass shards in case of an accident. Some works contain specialised low-reflective coated glass and should not be taped. Works in chalk or pastels should not be glass taped as removal of the tape may lift particles of the pigment from the work. If the packing material is opaque always mark where the top is. If there are delicate bits on the work, mark those positions on the packing material so handgrips can be placed elsewhere. If the work is not being placed in a crate the corners may need protecting. Bubble wrap is often used for this purpose and works well on most small light works. If the work is heavy a dense foam is used as bubbles have a habit of bursting just where the protection is most needed.

Moving and Handling Sculptures

The same advice applies to sculpture as outlined above for 2D works. Sculpture covers a wide selection of art objects. It is important to know the various weaknesses of each material or construction before the handling and moving is considered. Delicate parts that may break off should have additional supports added for protection. The delicate parts should also be clearly marked on the outside of the packing. Objects constructed from porous material or delicate surfaces should be handled with gloves. If working with gallery staff you should insist that they wear gloves or provide your own for their use. While moving small objects it is best to place them in a padded container. It is then possible to move the object about without putting any strain on it.

Handling Large or Heavy Sculptures

The frequent combination of great weight/size/vulnerable or unorthodox structures and sometimes fragile surfaces means that handling large

14

sculptures is especially difficult. As an artist or art handler it is sometimes wise to let a specialist lifting team handle the job. The operation of cranes and hoists is a specialist task. It is however important to keep a presence there and be vigilant as the lifting team will not always be as mindful of the delicate nature of the piece as you are.

It is necessary to know the weight of a work that is unusually heavy. It is possible to guess the weight even if the work is too awkward to weigh. Most materials have a definable weight and the overall weight can be worked out by measuring the volume of the work. It is important to know the weight of the object that you are dealing with as this has to be checked against the Safe Working Load of the equipment that you are using. Often the movement of large sculptural pieces is regarded as an event in the life of a gallery or museum and careful planning is essential. Apart from the artwork the personal safety of the handling team and the suitability of the building that is going to house the work needs to be considered.

Installation of Artworks

When preparing for an exhibition it is helpful if you can get a detailed floor plan of the gallery in advance. This plan should contain information on all aspects of the space such as the placement of windows, doors and any other fixture that may intrude on the space. It is advisable also to know where the invigilator/information point will be during the exhibition run. It can be very frustrating to install an exhibition only to come back when the show is open to the public to find an information table with staff sitting in an inappropriate place in the exhibition.

Individual galleries use different systems for hanging work. Often it depends on how the walls are constructed. The general principles of installing remain the same. Always plan ahead to ensure all installation needs will be met. Any unusual fixings or material that will be needed should be ordered in advance. While installing try to keep a clean and orderly environment so that the work is clearly seen at all times. If the gallery has an installation team, work closely with them on the installation. Insist that the work is sited correctly and not placed in any danger of being exposed to heat or moisture.

In the situation where the gallery has no installation team, basic DIY skills are usually enough to get you through the installation. Unless the works are small, it will be necessary to have some help while installing an exhibition. It is good to have a plan of how an installation should look. This cuts down on unnecessary moves and avoids nasty repairs which follow moves especially when fixing works directly onto the walls. As some unplanned moves are the norm it is helpful to have a pot of paint left over from the wall painting as colour matching later is nearly impossible. Fit brackets to the work and try to select ones that can cope with the weight of the work as lengthy spells on a wall can weaken frail brackets. Different wall types require different methods for mounting work. The construction of load bearing walls, ceilings and floor areas are best left to specialised building firms.

15

Wood / Plaster Combination

The combination of a solid wood base with a plasterboard surface is usually standard in galleries. This surface is ideal for fixing screws directly into. Make sure that the screw used is long enough to reach the wood below the plaster. These walls can easily be repaired during installation or afterwards.

Plaster Masonry

Walls that are entirely made from plaster require the use of plasterboard raw plugs. Sometimes it is possible to 'find' the timber structure behind the plasterboards and screw directly into that but it is limiting your options for spacing works. If a work is particularly heavy then you will need to 'find' those timbers as the weight of the object could rip the plaster board off. In some instances it may be necessary to put in re-enforcing behind the wall. There are a range of plugs and expansion bolts specially to hang works on concrete or stone surfaces

Common Risks to Works not Handled Properly

The principle risks to artwork not properly handled range from minor chips from frames to major loss (i.e. gouge or missing part) of the artwork. If a work is extremely fragile and not properly handled it may be crushed or broken by inappropriate handling methods. If it is not properly installed it could fall from the wall and be destroyed. Likewise if a work is incorrectly packed it could be badly damaged by any accident that occurs during transport. In seemingly more robust works frequent knocks and bumps can undermine the basic structure therefore making it deteriorate more rapidly over time. In the situation where work is left against heaters or is allowed to remain in damp conditions damage can occur very rapidly. Bad packing with contaminated materials can also result in permanent damage to works. If bubble wrap comes into direct contact with a slightly wet painted surface, for example, it can leave an impression which is difficult to remove afterwards. The bubbles should always face out. Sticky tape placed anywhere on the work should be avoided as the tape will draw dust and leave marks on the work. Works on paper need to be protected from excessive light and also kept free from contamination by non-conservation standard materials.

To summarise, always try to plan the movement of artwork in advance. Protect it adequately to make sure that you minimise the potential damage to the work while in transit. Use good quality packing materials and packing techniques. Try to use a specialised art transport company to move the work.

By Kevin Kelly with additional text by Alan Phelan

Importing and Exporting Your Work

Introduction

The transportation of works of art can be a complicated and costly business involving a variety of factors such as art handling, packaging, customs' paperwork, shipping and insurance. Museums and larger galleries often employ the services of a variety of companies with expert knowledge in each area, and extraordinary measures of care are taken in order to protect priceless works of art. When art movers Rock-It Cargo transported Da Vinci's *Lady with an Ermine* in 2003, the painting, crated complete with a homing device, was flown with its own seat in first class and two armed guards on either side. It is not only the old masters that get armed protection. All works valued at over €15 million are required to have armed escort. For the 2006 Ned Kelly exhibition at the James Joyce House of the Dead in Dublin, the shipment of artefacts, including Ned Kelly's suit of armour, required a police escort from Australia and then a Garda escort to its destination in Ireland.

For most artists, the transporting of their work is a less dramatic affair, but one riddled with pitfalls nonetheless. Reasons why you may want to transport your work could include selling to an overseas client, participating in an exhibition or competition or sending a piece of your work as a gift. In general, if you are represented by a gallery they will look after transportation of work. If you have been invited to participate in an exhibition or art fair by a gallery or organisation then the consensus is that it is their responsibility to organise and pay for transport. Always ask the gallery or organisation involved for as much information and advice as possible if they expect you to organise transport from your side. This also applies to entering competitions or open submission exhibitions. Competitions such as the BP Portrait Award usually provide clear guidelines about collection points and details of how to send your work. For less well organised events it is always worth contacting the organisers directly for advice.

Choosing a Shipping Company

On the high end of the scale, art movers listed on the ICEFAT website: www.icefat.org (The International Convention of Exhibition and Fine Art Transporters) are experts in their field, offering a wide range of services including packing, storage, insurance and customs and security expertise. Irish company Maurice Ward & Company Ltd. are ICEFAT members and regularly handle the shipping of artworks provide a personalised service depending on your requirements.

Gereon Krebber, a German artist based in London, has exhibited extensively throughout Europe and often arranges transport himself. "To keep costs down, I usually try to find a transport which is already scheduled and where they offer the remaining space at a discount rate," says Krebber. Krebber tends not to use art specialists. "They are too expensive," he says. "Furniture and freight forwarders usually work alright – especially if you know them. Krebber currently exhibits with a gallery in Cologne and uses a company that drives on a weekly basis between London and Cologne. "You can phone up and say – do you have a bit of space available?" he says. "Within the centres I think it is still possible to get a good deal." Krebber usually ensures that he transports his work on pallets: low, portable platforms on which goods are placed for storage or moving. "There are some thumb rules, "he says. "On pallets is cheaper. The faster, the more you pay."

Before deciding on which transport option to take, it is advisable to get recommendations from artists, curators and local galleries both at home and in the country to which you are shipping. Get a range of quotes, and provide the shipper with details such as the size and weight of work, when it needs to get to its destination and access details for the venue. Your choice of transport will depend on how fast you need to get your work to its destination, how much money you are willing to spend, and how much time and effort you are willing to commit. Transporting by road and sea is cheaper, but by air is quicker. Depending on your experience and where you are shipping to, it may be advisable to consider the services of a reputable shipping agent.

Factors to take into consideration:

How fragile is the work and how will it be handled in transit? Who will be supervising the loading of work?

Will you (if exporting work) or the person on the other end (if importing work) provide packaging? How much does the shipping company charge for packaging?

If you are shipping outside the EU what documentation are you required to complete and how much will the shipping company charge to co-ordinate this for you?

Courier Companies

Using a courier company can be a fast and reliable method of shipping work provided your work is adequately packed. Parcels have a track and trace number which makes it easy to confirm that they have reached their destination. The simplest way to send work by courier is to choose a company that sends one off shipments without the need for opening an account. Both DHL and Fedex have this facility, whilst TNT only deals with company accounts. Most courier companies will not open an account for an individual unless registered as a business. Fedex is an exception, but opening an account requires your credit card details going through a credit check, and then filling out a form. This can take time; so if you are in a hurry to send a package, send it as a one-off shipment.

Not all courier companies will transport works of art. Many view artwork as high risk, and companies such as UPS and TNT refuse to ship it. DHL and Fedex will ship works of art, but require documentation including:

- An independent proof of value before pick up, e.g. the value of the work printed on headed paper from a gallery or auction house.
- Insurance documents for the value of goods. The courier company that you are shipping with will provide these documents if you take out insurance with them. If you do not require insurance then you need to state this in a document.

There can be confusion as to whether you are required to provide this information or not when talking with courier companies. It is important to remember that most courier companies are not experts in sending art and that you will be dealing with unpredictable factors such as how knowledgeable the representative is that you are speaking to and their interpretation of your definition of what it is that you want to ship. The mere mention of the word 'artwork' can make some companies assume that you are trying to send the equivalent of the Mona Lisa and immediately complicate matters. A clear description of what you are sending, using simple language – e.g. a framed drawing that I have made – can make the process easier and cut down on unnecessary costs.

Nevertheless, some artists have found it costlier to send works labeled 'artwork' than normal goods. Others have found it complicated to obtain a valuation of their work and have chosen to not declare that their package contains artwork. For example, artists have sent crates of paintings and labeled them 'catalogues' or 'materials'. Others have sent drawings under the guise of documents. This is a high-risk strategy. If anything happens to your package, you will only be covered for the contents that you stated it held. It is also inadvisable to wrongly label your package when sending work outside the EU, as all packages are subject to the scrutiny of customs and will be x-rayed.

Documentation required for sending by courier – outside of the EU:

If importing or exporting artwork outside of the EU, an awareness of customs procedures and documentation is essential to ensure that your shipment reaches its destination. When sending work within Europe no customs documentation is required to be completed. However if sending outside of the EU you will be required to complete either a Commercial Invoice if the work is to be sold or a Pro-forma Invoice for non-commercial shipments. Essentially these documents are the same and you can either use invoices provided by the courier company or make your own based on their templates.

Whether you will be charged VAT and duties on your package depends on whether the work is being temporarily exported or permanently exported. For example, a painting that is being sent temporarily for an exhibition to the USA technically is not liable for VAT and duties, whilst a work that has been sold to a client outside of the EU is. Goods travelling outside the EU will go through customs and customs officials will decide, based on the documentation provided whether VAT or duties are due. If VAT and duties are due, the courier company will pay on your behalf. By default, the receiver of the package will be required to pay any costs covered by the courier company on delivery. Most courier companies allow you to pay estimated VAT and duties by prior arrangement so that the receiver will not be charged.

Importing and Exporting within EU

If shipping within the EU, no specific customs documentation is required. "Once you are travelling within the EU and the item is a work of art originating within the EU then it is not under any form of customs controls," says Ken Mills of Aquaship. "It can move in what is called 'free circulation'."

Importing and Exporting to outside of the EU

Custom's rules and regulations are set by bodies such as the European Union, the World Customs Organisation and national governments. All carriers are legally bound to comply with these rules. Packages and shipments going outside of the EU will pass through customs and must be accompanied by customs documentation. This is usually in the form of a Pro-forma Invoice, Commercial Invoice, Single Administrative Document (SAD) or ATA Carnet. Based on this documentation, the customs team overseas will decide whether any customs duty, excise duty and VAT are liable on the package. In general terms, a Commercial Invoice is used for goods that are to be sold, a Pro-forma Invoice for non-commercial goods. Further details about ATA Carnets can be found in the next section.

VAT and Duties

Goods are liable to VAT at the same rate as applies to the sale of similar goods within the country they are entering. This varies for each country. In Ireland, the rate is 21%.

Your liability for VAT and duties on work that is to be shipped depends on whether it is being temporarily or permanently exported. For example, a painting that is being sent from Ireland temporarily to an exhibition in the USA technically is not liable for VAT and duties, as long as Ireland is its country of origin and that it is returned within a certain time limit. For goods being temporarily imported into the EU the time limit is two years, but varies outside of the EU. If in any doubt of time limits it is advisable to contact customs in the country that you are sending work to for clarification. If a work which has been temporarily exported to an exhibition or art fair outside the EU is subsequently sold, then VAT and duties will now be due to be paid. For the main this will be handled by the gallery or organisation showing your work, however if you sell work whilst outside the EU, customs within that country should be contacted for details of how to pay any VAT and duties that you may be liable for, as this varies from country to country.

A piece of work that has been sold to a client and that has to be shipped outside of the EU, for example from an online sale, is liable for VAT and duties. It is important to factor these costs when giving a quote to a client before shipping. VAT and duty payments are due at the point of customs clearance and are usually covered by the company that you have chosen to ship your package. By default, the receiver of the package will then be charged any costs covered by the shipping company on delivery. Most shipping companies allow you to pay estimated VAT and duties by prior arrangement so that the receiver will not be charged.

Whether temporarily or permanently exporting goods, it is always advisable to follow the law. Wrong paperwork can result in fines, delays to your package being delivered and extra charges for storage whilst it is waiting to be cleared by customs. If in any doubt as to whether you have all the necessary paperwork, contact customs either in Ireland or the country to which you are sending goods to.

Documents and Gifts

Documents are usually allowed to pass through customs without any duties and taxes being applied, but this may vary from country to country. Gifts sent from one private individual to another up to the value of €45 are exempt from VAT and duty. Whether sending documents or gifts, a Pro-forma Invoice is still required stating the contents of your package, country of origin, estimated value and reason for export. You can either use documentation provided by your shipping company or make your own invoice.

Carrying Work in your Suitcase to Countries Outside of the EU

Many artists choose to travel with their work, carrying it within their suitcase. Legally if you are carrying work which is to be sold outside of the EU, it must be declared in the Red "Goods to Declare" Channel, or Red Point in the customs area of the airport on arrival at your destination where any VAT and duties due will be collected. Even for works which are not intended for sale – e.g. samples of your work to show a potential client or gallery – it is advisable to carry relevant documentation. This could be in the form of an invoice stating the contents of your package, the country of origin, estimated value and reason for export. Any other documentation, such as letters of invitation if participating in an exhibition, documents showing when the work will be returned, or letters confirming meetings if showing your work to a gallery, will all help if, on the off chance, you are stopped going through the "Nothing to Declare" channel at customs. Similarly if you are returning back to Ireland with work in your suitcase from a previous journey, keep copies of the original invoices created for taking the work out of Ireland alongside new ones stating the reason for bringing the work back.

ATA Carnet

An ATA Carnet is an international customs document that can simplify customs procedures for the temporary movement of goods to countries that are signatories to the ATA or Istanbul Convention. Goods brought into a country on a carnet are exempt from Customs duties and VAT under the condition that they are re-exported within a specified timeframe. Carnets are valid for up to one year and can be used for unlimited exits and entries into participating countries. Carnets can contain multiple vouchers, which allow items listed to move between numerous countries, so may be an option, for example, if organising a touring exhibition that will travel to more than one country. Additional items cannot be added to a carnet once it has been issued.

Carnets can be used for commercial samples, professional equipment, and goods for exhibitions and fairs. They are not intended to be used for works which are to be sold, however if this happens you may be liable for VAT and duties. "You need to check your tax liability," says Noel Kelly, Curator with Temple Bar Gallery & Studios, "because if it's coming in from America and you've sold it here, even with the carnet you are now liable to the revenue commissioners for tax."

A carnet is not required for goods originating in the EU that are temporarily imported to or exported from another EU country. So where can you obtain a carnet? "There is one national, guaranteed organisation in every country, "says Richard Brown Export and Consular Manager for the Dublin Chamber of Commerce, "and we're the one for Ireland." Carnets are issued by the Dublin Chamber within 2-3 days and currently cost €120 for Dublin Chambers members and €200 for non-members. There is also a 24 Hour Service, costing €180 for members and €260 for non-members. Non-member companies will have to supply a Certificate of Incorporation or Certificate of Registration of their Business Name. In addition, you are required to complete an application form supplied by the Chamber, provide an itemised list of goods being carried abroad and a bank guarantee or bank draft, which is calculated at a set percentage, based on the kind of goods being carried and where those goods are going. If you require a carnet, talk with your shipping agent. They may co-ordinate the necessary paperwork on your behalf. Whilst most courier companies such as UPS and Fedex do not generally work with carnets, some do, so it is worth enquiring with their customer service. Overseas artists requiring a carnet should contact their local chamber of commerce or equivalent.

Packaging

Whether using a specialised fine art shipping agent, courier or general removals company, correct packaging will limit potential damage that could occur to your artwork during transit. At the top end of the scale, companies such as Constantine and Momart will work with you to create a bespoke packaging solution. But what if you have limited funds and are transporting your work using a non specialist fine art shipping agent?

Berlin based artist Ulrich Vogl, whose works include fragile, large scale, engraved glass panels, transports his work using crates which he constructs himself. "It is important for the crates not to be heavy but stable", says Vogl. "I use a frame construction and only very thin panes of wood to fill the space in-between. The object inside should neither be pressed nor able to move around. If you screw the cover and the box together, it gives you extra stability." Using screws rather than nails also makes crates easier to open and close and limits the potential of damage to work. "Besides bubbles wrap I use isolation tubes (that are used to isolate hot pipes) to keep the wooden frame from being damaged" says Vogl. "For Frames with glass", he adds, "it is good to put tape over the glass so that if the glass breaks the pieces stick together and do not destroy the artwork inside the frame."

Artist Gereon Krebber also builds his own crates for both transit and storage of his often massive sculptural works. "I do recommend crates, in terms of when you have pieces that travel without you," says Krebber who builds his crates from plywood. "Bubble wrap is still the best for padding," he adds, "but you need some kind of Styrofoam to fill the hole."

Packaging Tips:

Whilst building your own crates can be cost effective, especially if your work is unusual in shape or use of materials, for some works, sturdy cardboard packaging with good padding will suffice.

Unframed drawings can be safely transported if sandwiched between two pieces of plywood to avoid being bent.

If sending more than one painting, they should be packed surface to surface, frame to frame.

Ensure that your painting is dry well in advance of your deadline for shipping.

Due to changes in temperatures and depressurized environments during the shipping process, bubble wrap should not be placed directly on the surface of a canvas as it may leave marks. A layer of cardboard packing between the surface and bubble wrap will prevent any damage.

Protect from damage and shocks caused by movement and pack your work to endure being dropped, bent and pressed against. Assume that your package will be dropped several times in transit and that heavy objects will be placed on it.

Clearly mark your address and telephone number on the outside of the package so that if it gets lost, or is wrongly delivered you can be contacted.

Include correct handling procedures, and a packing plan to assist the person sending your work back to you.

Customs and Excise Regulations Related to Packaging

If sending work to a destination outside of the EU, you should ensure that your packaging complies with customs and excise regulations for that country. "Any article of wood going into the United States has now by law to be heat treated," says Ken Mills of Aquaship. "The same rule prevails in Australia and China. Ireland and the EU have not adopted that policy yet but I imagine that that is not too far down the line." Exemptions to this rule include manufactured wood, materials such as fiber board, plywood, and veneer. Stretchers and frames are not considered packaging so do not fall under the Wood Packaging Materials (WPM) regulations. Specialist art shippers should be aware of this issue and advise you accordingly. If sourcing your own packaging, companies such as Precision Box Company Limited and Atlas Box & Crating Co. manufacture heat treated timber crates to order.

By Jacqui McIntosh

Managing My Work: Video and New Media Artworks

Introduction: Letting go or holding on?

There are many common misconceptions regarding the archiving and documentation of technology-reliant artworks, particularly in relation to those works that are taken to be intentionally ephemeral.

Often in relation to web art, performance, or interactive-based work, there is the sense that such works should be allowed to 'go', that trying to 'hold on' to them is a contrived gesture that at worst undermines the original intention of the work, and at best can only represent a part of it.

'Archiving' is a loaded word: it is often negatively bound up with notions of 'fixing', 'preserving' or 'freezing', or with an approach that places too much emphasis on materials, components, and their durability etc.

Archiving does often connote a sense of 'completion.' It is also seen as something that institutions, curators, archivists, or conservators are concerned with rather than being the preserve of artists themselves.

Philosophical issues aside, there is the simple fact that artworks, which are reliant on technologies, typically require close management if they are to remain viable or displayable beyond their initial incarnation.

Remember, most technology-based works or installations have to be 'dismantled,' and comprise of numerous disparate parts. This makes 'the work' quite vulnerable. Those 'parts' are rarely dedicated to one work, where many artists will re-use some of parts in other works. The best, most well-intentioned memory is fallible when it comes to recalling installation specifications, and technology is in a constant state of upgrade as formats become incompatible, data becomes unreadable and equipment wears out.

All of these factors have bearing upon the integrity of your work, and upon your ability (or the ability of others) to re-install it as per your preferences into the future.

Consider the following scenarios:

I made a video work for Glasgow, and now I want to restage the work in a gallery in Berlin. But the only copies I have now are not in good condition, and they don't give the picture quality that I wanted.

A curator has asked to loan a media work that I installed two years ago in Limerick. She seems to remember it differently from me. I have some slides of it somewhere I think.

I loaned a video installation to a gallery in Cork, which I was not able to install myself. I thought it was pretty obvious how it should be arranged from the photograph that I sent them. But they did it wrong, and it was installed incorrectly for three weeks.

Managing Your Work

Simply put, 'managing' your work means putting in place certain documentation and back-up practices. These will help you safeguard the conceptual, visual, or physical integrity of your work.

If you document and archive your work, you can help:

- Ensure its correct display, even by others, to your specifications.
- Ensure that its integrity is maintained, to your intentions.
- It is important that you make realistic choices; choices that will keep your work safe and easily accessible, and which will also be cost effective for you.
- Depending, of course, on the nature of your work, there are those aspects of 'managing' your work that you should undertake frequently 'as routine'. There are other aspects that are more 'on demand' – but it is worth developing some idea of how you would deal with them in advance.

'As routine'

- Backing Up
- Display documentation

'On demand'

- Making display copies
- Certificates of Authenticity
- Maintenance Statements

The following sections will focus on these aspects more closely, providing tips and further reading.

Formats and Backing Up

If you work with some form of technology – be it digital video or an Apple 280c Powerbook, backing up or making archival copies of your work is vital.

It is a good idea to distinguish between an 'archival' format, and possible formats your work will be copied onto for 'display' purposes. It is also important to distinguish between, and decide upon, types and number of copies, i.e.

- At least one that will be 'archival', and not used for making copies
- At least one that is 'archival', but from which copies can be made
- Copies for display

You will have to make choices about formats, which will be informed by a number of factors, such the nature of your work, but also *importantly*, economic considerations. Do some research on formats (about prices, accessibility, durability, playback quality), and take good specialist advice where possible before deciding.

Tips & advice for Video

Back up and store your work in a way that you can get to it easily.

Currently, most industry specialists suggest digital tape formats such as Digibeta or DVCam for backup/archival purposes. However, it depends on your original working format: there is less loss when you dub within format, but something mastered on Digibeta, and transferred to DVCam will suffer loss during that process.

Always retain two master versions in whatever format your work was originally formatted on.

DVDs are cost effective, giving you good sound and image quality. However, they can be difficult to move to other formats. It is a good idea to archive the Splits (the MPEG2 and sound files) on a hard drive, because they can then be used or modified more easily, for different sync units, or compilations.

Compression: Ask about data-rates. You can have a very poor image resolution with a high data-rate compression, and it can affect playback on some players. Other factors such as the type of compressor used can also be influential.

Hard Drives: Watch storage capacity vs. file size. With some computer systems there can be an issue with storing files that are larger than 2GB.

Hard Drives: Good, reliable portable hard drives are relatively inexpensive now, and are becoming indispensable. As they can be very large, you might feel tempted to store lots of material on a single, large capacity unit. However, hard drives do fail, and it can become difficult or expensive to get material off once they do. They can be dropped/damaged, so where affordable it is best to invest in a number of hard drives that you can dedicate to raw footage, to edits, and Masters respectively.

On the whole, backing up your work on multiple formats is the key: Back up projects onto hard drives, but also keep copies on tape (DVCam or Mini-DV) and on DVD.

Keep your masters safe, in a dry place where there is not going to be fluctuations in temperature or moisture.

Always store tapes of whatever kind standing vertically. Do not stack tapes horizontally, as this can damage the tape.

Once you have played a tape through, do not immediately rewind, as these changes the tape tension. Rewind it just before you next play it back. This is better for the tape tension.

FACT, who are based in Liverpool, offer a number of services for artists. For instance, they operate MITES – The Moving Image Touring and Exhibition Service, and a Digital Mastering Service. They offer telephone and on-line support, and they have also developed a manual that is available to those who attend their new tool courses, or those hiring equipment.

Installation Notes / User's Manual

Many purchase or commission agreements require a set of installation notes as part of the negotiated agreement. For the artist, they are an important means by which to communicate the keys factors about the work's display and functioning.

Remember: video and new media work will exist for periods of time in a 'de-installed' state. They do not themselves suggest to any future re-installer how they should be reassembled. Some aspects of how any given work is installed may appear to be self-evident. Some will not be. It is best not to take this for granted.

Installation Notes give you the opportunity to make sure all aspects of the work are explained, so that it can be correctly and appropriately installed to your preferences by other parties.

There is no template for Installation Notes. They have to best meet the needs of the work, and the information the artist wants to communicate.

However, there are some general principles to follow:

- Name of artist
- Document Type (i.e. 'Installation Notes'; it is also worth prominently noting that these must stay with the packed work)
- Details of work (Title, date, duration (running time) and other details of 'performance', materials, dimensions where applicable, exhibition history)

- Images and schematic drawings (video still, or screen shot, or installation view)
- A description of the intention of the work, including a description of it as installed (noting a preference for any one particular installation of the work)

All equipment and spatial specifications, including:

- -List of all equipment requirements
- -List of all spatial requirements
- -Instructions on how to make exhibition copies of video/digital elements
- -Instructions on how to install/position playback equipment
- -Instructions on how to cable equipment
- -Instructions on how to calibrate projector/or monitor/image quality
- -Instructions on how to set lighting/projection conditions
- -Instructions on how to position furniture, objects, and other artefacts
- Instructions of how to build or modify gallery/display space (including any false walls, colour of walls etc)

Making copies for display

I have been invited to show a video piece in a small exhibition in the US. It will run for three months. What do I supply for it?

I have sold a video installation, and want to stipulate how exhibition copies should be made from the masters that I have supplied

When works are displayed or sold, it can be difficult to maintain some control over how, where and when copies are produced, and the formats on which your work is displayed. It is worth considering how much involvement you would like to have in such matters, and how and where you might communicate any specifications or stipulations.

Some notes

The primary display format at the moment for video works is DVD.

Some artists still like for their work to be displayed using analogue formats such as laser disk, but increasingly galleries and museums are replacing analogue systems with digital.

Remember, display copies will be run for up to 8 hours a day, sometimes 7 days a week for intensive periods. They will be subject to wear and tear.

So, choose a format that gives the image quality that you want, and which can deliver that quality for the longest time before having to be replaced.

Most venues will have playback equipment or preferences for the format that you supply on, and will let you know. If you have specifications, they may require that you supply hardware or playback equipment yourself.

28

Make sure you communicate all your specifications for looping, syncing etc. in Installation Notes. This will help ensure that future display copies of your work can be made as close to your preferences as possible.

It is well worth also considering the following:

For an exhibition running time of 3months, it is a good idea to supply two DVDs.

Tapes often have an optimal running time of 2-3 weeks before they need to be changed for fresh copies.

For a longer show, you might also want to send a contact, so that the venue can make more if required.

Make sure EVERY copy you send out is clearly labeled 'Exhibition copy only. Not For Sale. Return to the artist.'

Remember to have the contact returned to you after the show is concluded. Also request that any display copies are returned to you, or are destroyed.

There are factors such as the quality of playback equipment, or of technical support, that will influence how your work is installed.

If the venue is in the US, you also have the issues of PAL/NTSC standards problems. There is also SECAM too. This will be the case whether you are using DVDs or tape formats. Also, make sure they are not region coded.

A lot of DVD players can play both PAL and NTSC, but it is important to check that the monitors/projectors can as well. Some services, such as MITES, can author disks on NTSC, some in the UK don't.

Certificate of Authenticity

A Certificate is an indispensable way of stating categorically what a work comprises. The Certificate of Authenticity must stay with the work if it is subject to further sale.

There is no one template for a Certificate. It will be informed by the specific needs of the work, and also perhaps by certain aesthetic considerations on the part of the artist. However, here are some general principles to follow:

- Name of artist:
- Document Type: (i.e. 'Certificate'; it is also worth prominently noting that this certificate must stay with the work)
- Details of the work: (title, date, materials, duration, dimensions)
- Image: (video still, or screen shot, or installation view)
- Edition:(if applicable)
- Work comprising: (I.e., this certificate, installation notes, 1 x 60 minute digibeta master tape)
- Relevant notes: (i.e., installation notes are based on such-and-such exhibition; issues of replacement for

hardware or playback items; issues of re-formatting or transfer)

Maintenance Documentation

What is the difference between 'Installation Notes' and 'Maintenance Documentation'? Aren't they the same thing?

No, not necessarily.

Sometimes clauses are added to Installation Notes or a User's Manual, with regard to possible malfunction of equipment, or the need for replacement. These are often particular to the timeframe of a particular exhibition or installation.

However, there is much to support the idea of dealing with issues of maintenance, particularly in the longer-term, under separate cover from installation notes, and in a proactive (rather than reactive) manner.

Variables

Video and new media works typically rely on numerous variables (power supply, network feed, equipment maintenance, cleaning etc) in order to continue functioning correctly over periods of time. Often different variables influencing the working of a piece will be the responsibility of a chain of different parties. With works in public situations, those parties may be subject to change.

It is always best to clarify those variables, the individuals responsible for each of them, and what should occur if problems arise, and if individuals change.

Variability

Jill Sterret, Head of Collections and Conservation at SfMoMA, has noted: with new media works, 'there is this inherent variability. Keeping an artwork alive over the long-term calls for mediating this variability, and it puts key aspects of decision-making in the hands of the collector or steward of the work.'

Technologies change rapidly. Contexts change. Analogue is giving way to Digital. Actual hardware or software is superseded, but also, more broadly, cultural transitions take place (i.e. from fax to email to SMS) that make certain types of work seem 'out-moded.'

All of these elements incur losses to the work, of different kinds and to different degrees. With video or new media works, the integrity of any one work has to be managed through those kinds of changes.

Therefore, it is important that you expect and plan for malfunctions, contingencies and change

Is it important to my video installation that it is shown with CRT projectors? How might I feel about exhibiting it with LCD projectors? Would it become a different work?

Could my work be re-created using newer technology? Would I be happy with the fact that it could look quite different?

What happens if there is a loss of Internet connection? Or even loss of power?

For works that are reliant upon a power supply or a connection, it is important to consider options or possibilities if either of those sources is disturbed. Sometimes, solutions can be built into the work itself. In a recent on-line discussion, Craighead and Thomson noted about their work, 'we have a series of strategies in place so that even if the computer is not replaced and network connections are lost, something can still happen that looks 'graceful.' The bottom line for us is if mains power is lost, as we have no other means of running the screen.' Similarly, Matt Gorbet noted of his installations, 'We like to design in layers, so that if a network connection is someday no longer maintained, or LED brightness fades, the piece itself will not appear 'broken.'

For further perspectives on technology reliant works, change, and maintenance, see 'Public Art and Permanence' Theme of the Month July 2006 on the CRUMB discussion list. It is archived athttp://crumb.sunderland.ac.uk

Maintenance Statements

There is no template for a maintenance statement or for maintenance documentation. The type of statement or documentation will be dependent upon the specific work in question, the context [whether the work is in a private or public collection for instance], and the needs of the individuals involved in the future care of the work.

However, it is vital that your wishes, as the artist, are represented in any decision-making process about the future of a work you have made. Typically, where you are available, you must make it known where you require to be consulted in all maintenance or re-formatting matters.

Maintenance documentation does NOT necessarily replace actual consultation where you are available. However, maintenance or re-formatting/re-creation issues may arise on occasions that you are not available. Maintenance documentation will be invaluable for those who are placed to make decisions about the future of your work.

You may feel that it is impossible or undesirable to hypothesise possible future problems with your work. However, it is possible to state how you feel about certain aspects of the work, i.e. its appearance, functionality, or 'cultural relevance', and how they might fare under certain changes (i.e. different OS systems, etc.)

A maintenance statement is an excellent way to present:

31

- Your preferences for courses of action, i.e. exhausting all available supplies of items
- Your 'philosophy' regarding aspects of the work and possible changes to them (i.e. is colour change ok from one OS system to another)
- Any ideas you might have with regard to future re-creations of the work
- Any preferences you have for potential approaches, i.e. emulation, migration etc.
- If /how you would expect changes, or changed states to be acknowledged
- Your 'bottom line', i.e. when you think that changes would indeed lead to the work becoming 'another work

The presentation of preferences and recommendations regarding the future maintenance of works varies from work to work, and artist to artist. Some artists supply formal documents that include information about carrying out repairs, or replacement of parts. Others supply more simple philosophic statements, or even a letter outlining preferences. It is important that these statements represent, as accurately as possible, your current thinking, whilst not forcing you to be definitive to a degree that you might find uncomfortable or even untenable in the future. Your attitude or preferences with regard to any one work may change or adapt over time. It is worth putting in a clause in any maintenance statement that you supply that you retain the right to revisit (and possibly revise) your opinions at a later date.

Further Reading

TechArchaeology Special Edition, Journal of the American Institute for Conservation, 40, 3, 2001

Medien_kunst_net, Dortmund, 404: Object Not Found: International Congress concerning the Production, Presentation and Preservation of Media Arts, 19-22 June 2003, conference

Wijers, Gaby, Ramon Coelho, and Every Rodrigo, The Sustainabilty of Video Art: Preservation of Dutch Video Art collections, Amsterdam: The Foundation for the Conservation of Modern Art, 2003,

Frieling, Rudolf and Wulf Herzogenrath, 40YEARSVIDEOART.DE – Part 1 Digital Heritage: Video Art in Germany from 1963-the Present, Hatje Cantz Verlag, 2006

Besser, Howard, 'InterPARES 2 and the Electronic Café International: Aging Records from Technology-based Artistic Activities,' presented at AIC, Electronic Media group, June 2004.

Richard Rinehart, A System of Formal Notation for Scoring Works of Digital and Variable Media Art, 2003, p. 2.

Frohne, Ursula and Mona Schieren, Jean-Francois Guiton (eds.) (2005) Present Continuous Past(s): Media Art. Strategies of Presentation, Mediation and Dissemination. Vienna: Springer- Verlag.

Besser, Howard (2001). "Longevity of Electronic Art."

Bruce Altshuler (ed.) (2005) Collecting the New: museums and contemporary art. Princeton: Princeton UP.

Depocas, Alain, and Jon Ippolito, Caitlin Jones (eds.) (2003).*Permanence Through Change: The Variable Media Approach.*

HorizonZero issue 18. 'Ghost' (November/December 2004) The Banff New Media Institute.

By Dr. Tina Fiske

Tina would like to acknowledge the advice and help of the following people: Alison Bracker, Clare Mitchell, Paul Cameron, Russell Henderson, Jon Mack, Susan Collins, Jon Thomson, and others.

Organising and Managing Projects

Introduction

Undertaking a self-managed project successfully can be difficult. Being aware of some of the pitfalls and following a few basic principles can make a real difference to the success of a project. 'Organising / Managing Projects' is intended as a basic guide which you can use as a touchstone at any stage in the evolution of your project.

A little like planning a journey, you need to decide where are you going, how you are going to get there and what you will need along the way to make your journey a comfortable, satisfying, successful and safe one. So using this analogy let's consider...

Vision – Where are you going?

Having a strong sense of where you want your project to take you is the best way to begin. This does not rule out the fact that changes will occur along the way, as this will undoubtedly happen, but what it does secure for you is a sense of a vision or driving force behind the project. A vision is necessary as a banner under which you, and in the future others, will operate as your idea moves forward. A vision provides a sense of cohesion and a united purpose. It should be inspirational, ambitious and motivating. It should make venues want to be involved, draw sponsors in, excite stakeholders, unite partners and motivate a team towards achieving a common goal. Your vision should be specific, motivational and achievable.

Key words in your vision statement might be – *exciting, promoting, extensive, progressive, showcasing....*

From your vision statement you can formulate goals or objectives, which will focus you towards achieving your vision. These become targets to aim for and should spring directly out of your vision statement. If your vision is "to be the most exciting xxxx, showcasing Ireland's premiere xxxx", then how are you going to do that? Your goals or objectives will tell you how and will put you on the path to achieving your vision. For example, "targeting xxxx segment of the population, sourcing xxxx artist or drawing together xxxx community to engage in the experience". Goals and objectives begin with active verbs and demonstrate an intention to do something. You can have as many goals or objectives as you wish but approximately five would be a sufficient number to work towards.

Task - Can you write down one/two sentence(s) describing your aspiration for your project? This will become your vision. Can you then draw from this, how will you achieve this vision? Write 3-5 achievable statements, all beginning with an active verb about how you will achieve it. These are your goals and objectives and you should refer constantly throughout the planning process to both your vision and your goals/ objectives to see if you are staying on the path you had initially envisaged for yourself.

Managing Change

Your project will change during its realisation and that is to be expected so don't be alarmed if what you imagined, works out slightly different to what you had envisaged. Elements necessary for the general infrastructure of your project might actually lead to changes or alterations within the project. These 'elements' could include your sponsors, venues, commissioning bodies, resources etc. Once external factors become enlisted, they influence the outcome of events and should be expected and assimilated into the main body of the project.

No two projects are ever the same and that is because the situations and factors surrounding each creative endeavour can never be repeated in exactly the same way again. However, anything or anyone who fundamentally shakes the nature of your project and alters it beyond your initial ambition should not be allowed to do so – unless you feel it is for the better and they have your complicit agreement to do so. Managing this uniting of forces and securing of resources can be a very difficult period and will be fundamental in forming the basis of your project. You should tread carefully, research, consult as widely as possible, and feel the fear of this new endeavour. Tolstoy once said "the greater the risk, the greater the reward" so be prepared to take risks but make sure they are calculated, researched and supported (financially or otherwise).

So while it is important to be inspirational, it is also important to be realistic – aim high but ensure to match your ambitions with what is realistically achievable. Your goals will keep you on course.

Planning – How Are You Going to Get There?

This brings us to consider what is realistically possible. How do you determine this? Consider what is really achievable and what you can access and legislate for. In other words, how much financial, physical or human help (resources) do you need to make your idea happen? How easy are they to access? How do you get to them? Within what timescale do they need to be drawn down? Each of these things will substantially affect how your project pans out and this is where you need to keep asking yourself, what am I doing, why am I doing it? If you can answer these questions readily, it will be easier for you to communicate your concept and easier for people to understand your concept and get behind your idea. For example, if one of your goals is to engage the local community in an artistic experience, what do you need to do this? What money do you require? What suppliers or team do you need around you? What administration, marketing? This is the beginning of considering your resources, your budget, your stakeholders, your marketing, and your operational plan. Some of the aspects of planning are:

People – People make ideas happen. They are creators, developers and implementers of projects as well as the engagers with a project. A project or event without people would be a solitary activity and a personal endeavour. Therefore you need to consider who you will need to make your project happen as well as consider who your project is for, i.e. your audience.

Communication – this is the beginning of your marketing campaign. At least in the sense that you are starting to inform those around you of your idea and what you need to make it happen. You will need to be able to communicate in a written, verbal and electronic way and so if you have managed to distil your concept into a maximum of two sentences, you can get to the heart of the matter swiftly and then build on this as and when you need to.

You need to consider who are the people you need to communicate with (known as your stakeholders)

How you are going to communicate with them-, do you need a mobile?

Have you got a land-line with an answering machine, do you need an email address or a website?

Do you need someone else to take on this role?

Stakeholders — are anyone who has a claim or 'interest' (not in the passing sense, more in the 'involvement' sense) in your project. They will be your audience but they will also be your funders, your 'backers' – as in supportive creative team or individuals – , your venue or site manager, your technical crew or suppliers, potential press etc. Consider what you need to tell them and if you need a system to be established in order to communicate with them – this could be as simple as twice monthly meetings, a phone call each Monday morning or setting yourself up with headed paper and an email address. If you are drawing down money from a funder or sponsor you should also consider the following:

Do you need to keep them informed of your activities and to what extent?

What are their expectations?

Consider what they are hoping to get out of the involvement with your project. What does their money 'get' them? They are not doing you a favour but engaging in a contract for exchange of goods. Write to them and tell them what you are prepared to offer them for their money. See if this is acceptable or does it need to be negotiated.

What form will this communication take – should it be formal or casual? Should there be an established timescale of meetings? Or friendly chat over cups of coffee?

Start keeping a paper trail (don't forget to print out emails) so you can easily look back and see what exactly was agreed and when.

This project (and your next one – keep an eye to the future) can live or die on stakeholder relations and you need to become adept at people and information management. You may also need to communicate with your stakeholders before and after your project. The relationship doesn't occur simply 'on the night' but right through the planning, operations and post project experience.

Task - Who are your stakeholders? Draw up a list of each individual involved in the project and try and establish what they will 'get out' of the project but also what they are prepared to 'put in'. Is there anyone in particular who carries a great degree of authority over your project? How will you communicate with them? What information do you need to feed them? How much control to they want/are you prepared to give?

Resources = Resources are often referred to as 'physical', 'financial' and 'human'. You will need to scope and secure the resources required in the realisation of your project in order to activate and implement your concept or idea. In other words, if you think of human resources as the people you will need, physical resources as the equipment you will need and financial resources as the money you will need. How much will you need of each of these things?

Human Resources ⸺ try to imagine all the people you will need in order to make this project happen. There may be a cost involved, begin to research this. There might also be a requirement for you to have your idea or budgets or sponsors approved by a particular committee or individual. Try to find out whom the decision maker is and how they intend to make their decisions. If you have deadlines to meet and their approval is required for these deadlines, make sure you communicate your needs to them. Effective project management is very often about the sharing and management of information in the most effective way. Beware of lack of information and misunderstandings as these can drastically undermine the project and alter the outcome in a way that you will not be happy with.

Physical ⸺ physical resources can be the technical equipment needed to make the work or they can be the venue and all things contained therein – seating, reception area for tickets, catalogues or press releases, or simply bare walls and a roof with heating. Think about the kind of location that would work best for you. Draw up a list of possible requirements you might have, physical as well as your estimated financial bottom line and source a venue that meets these needs best. To say you need a 'venue' is to imply a number of things are required within that venue like lighting or heating or phone lines and insurance. This is known as a resource hierarchy and be careful that when you say you need a space for X or a place to site Y, that what you have in your head as implied within that space, is guaranteed as part of that space. Do not take anything for granted! Otherwise, you could end up with many extra costs for hire equipment or insurance or transportation, etc. Have a face-to-face meeting with the site or venue owner/manager and consider all the possibilities and requirements from both sides. If you want to hang material from the rafters, does it need to be fire retardant? If you want to have 100 people at the opening, how are you going to accommodate them? If you want to project on to a particular wall, how much light pollution do you need to legislate for? Brainstorm for questions and consider all possibilities. This is the beginning of your risk management plan and the operational process to implement your vision.

Financial – financial resources are usually the resources that people worry about and focus on the most. This is because of the scarcity of this resource for creative projects in this country. This is where you may need to be at your most creative and think laterally about where you can access finance. Financial support comes in many shapes and forms. It can be by way of grants from organisations or corporate subvention, private patronage, support in kind or some related commercial activity which will bring in cash flow. Be careful not to alter the shape of your idea to fit into funding criteria. There is always a way to get money or support if the idea is good enough and in the right place at the right time.

Task – How much financial, physical or human resources do you need to make your idea happen? How easy are they to access? Within what timescale? Estimate what they will cost. Can you separate each of these out and form a written plan for your project? Be realistic. Make sure that the resources you can access, achieve the goals you have outlined.

Creating a budget

Write everything down that you imagine you will need – people, objects, materials, equipment, website development, invitations, press, couriers, trains, accommodation, your time, other people's time, postage – and try to estimate the cost as best you can. It doesn't matter if the figures are not exact at this stage. Then write down all the possibilities for income generation. These can be very basic such as sponsorship from local business to larger public subsidy grants such as the Arts Council or local arts office. Consider if you can include some revenue aspect to your project – catalogues or handouts, parking or limited edition pieces. Somehow, you need the two figures (income and expenditure) to balance.

Scoping a budget (and this is what you are now doing) begins with forming a basic idea of what is needed. From here, you can make phone calls, ask questions and begin to develop your budgets in an informed way. You will develop a trail of budgets so number or date them, in order to keep track of your most recent one. It doesn't matter that your figures keep changing, this is normal and this will continue to happen until the end of the project. Create an archive of all budgets.

Some things to remember:

Consider cash flow -will you have received money in time to spend it and when you need to?

Keep a profit and loss sheet – a record of money going in and out according to dates.

Separate your own money from that of the project, either by way of a separate bank account or simply on paper

Keep receipts for everything

Remember to ask if VAT is included (and at what %)

Beware if the project takes longer to realise than expected as there may be possible price increases

Make sure you include contingency – your financial cushion in case something goes wrong or was not considered as initially required. Contingencies can be anything from 5-15% and should be calculated on your subtotal figure.

Cost your own time; include this in the expenditure part of your budget. You can simply detail it as 'artist fee' or as a 'production expense'. Then, if you decide not to be paid for the project, you can enter this personal support in the income part of your budget. So along with arts council grant, sponsorship or patronage you can write 'artist fee' or 'production support'. Make sure to write exactly the same figure, demonstrating that there was a cost to the project that became support-in-kind, personally donated by you.

NB: Always include support-in-kind in your budget. Do not ignore it. Even though money is not changing hands, it still counts as a form of sponsorship.

So now you have given your project some definition. You have a sense of what it feels like, might taste like and what it hopefully will look like. You still have some way to go to actually doing it but you are well informed, well prepared and ready to execute the task in hand. There are a couple of other things you still might need to consider...

Marketing

So far, you have initiated your concept, developed your idea and scoped your budget and now you are about to begin realising it. Consider; do you have all the systems and resources in place, in a way that you are happy with? In the journey of your project so far, are you satisfied that you have the right mix to make your project happen? All successful projects have something unique about them. In marketing terms, this is considered your USP – your unique selling point. What element of your project is the USP?

A focus on marketing does not imply a shift away from artistic integrity; it is simply a way of communicating to those whom your project is aimed at. The marketing and publicity of an arts project often requires maximum affect on a minimum of budget. Therefore, much creative thinking needs to be utilised. To market a project effectively with little to no budget for promotion, you need to use your self-belief to sell your product and therefore, think laterally about all marketing possibilities.

You need to be passionate about what your concept is in order to market it. You need your audience to believe that you believe and you need to preserve that initial spark and 'sell' or 'promote' your project at every opportunity. You will have to be innovative and focused and understand why you are doing it and whom you are trying to reach. You do not want to try to set about attracting everyone but should focus on whom you need to reach – focus on a particular group or age range or type of person – try to define who this person is. Also:

Will you target the press so that they reach your audience?

Will you go straight to your audience, or are you marketing to the critics and not the public?

Is critical acclaim and coverage more important than bums on seats?

Where will you focus your energies with a small budget to achieve maximum effect?

Marketing a cultural product (experience) is about your reasons for existing as an artist and the values you place on your creative endeavour. Ultimately you need to consider the mediation of this and any tangible experience (catalogue, flyer, leaflet, ticket stub, CD) you can give the 'engager' or 'individuals in the audience' to take away.

Development of a marketing strategy — A project's 'concept definition/vision' is often the essence of what is being marketed and in this sense marketing an arts project, becomes the mediation of what it is you do, why you do it and whom you do it for. So, take your vision and supplement this with a list of potential benefits, which this project can bring to your potential audience. Would it include social activities, promotion of individual artists, promotion of a chosen medium, raising awareness of societal issues or sharing of an individual's valuable experience or ideas. Formulate these benefits into sentence format and incorporate the following information. You should now be able to say:

- Who you are
- What you are doing
- When you are doing it
- Where you are doing it
- Why you are doing it

This will form the basis of your press release and is known as the five W's. All press releases should contain this information early in the body of the document. Always avoid jargon and superlatives in your press release and try to make it sound as interesting as you can. No one wants to read a list of facts and the press will thank you for making their job easier. Don't forget to include all your major sponsors and a contact name or address for further information.

Information Dissemination – How you are going to disseminate this information? Will it be via email, as leaflets, handouts, press releases or will it take another form? It is hugely important that whatever your chosen medium for information dissemination, that you establish clear and consistent messages. In this way, awareness will be created and a profile established. For one off projects, it can be particularly difficult to gain a 'market presence' or create audience awareness and so the answer might be to link yourself to a more established event, activity, organisation or individual on which you can 'hang' your own clear and consistent message.

Be clear and concise – perhaps rehearse a verbal description of your project with a colleague and ask them in turn to relay back to you their interpretation of your project, as they understand it. Do you need to develop the messages you are sending out?

Above all, be creative and engaging in all your dealings with all those interested in your project. Think about what it is they want and how it is you are going to deliver it to them – particularly with regard to the press – and follow up on anyone who has expressed an interest and wants more information.

Task ‑ Consider who it is you are trying to reach and what it is you are trying to say. Can you expand on the concept vision that you outlined early on and expand on the information you have now gathered about where your project will be, when it is happening, where and why? How will you get this information out there and who needs to know about it? Draw up a checklist for whom your project exists, It might be artists, the interested public, arts managers, arts officers, students, children, local community and so on. These are the individuals you want to target. How will you reach them? What will this cost?

Risk – A safe journey?

Creating awareness around risk is key. Never underestimate what can go wrong. If you don't plan for problems, when they arise, you will be unprepared. You have to be able to anticipate the problems in advance and take action to avoid the problem. This is known as risk management. Considering what might crop up is half the battle to solving it. If you have considered the problems before they arise, you will have an idea about how you can militate against them or legislate for them.

Risk management ― There is uncertainty in all projects and risk management is the process by which this uncertainty is managed. If at the beginning of the project you carry out an initial risk assessment, you will be armed with foreknowledge of the potential risks. You should adopt the thinking that if anything can go wrong it will go wrong. Think as laterally as possible.

Evaluate potential risks — make a list of all possible risks and balance them with possible actions. You have to consider just how serious a threat they may be to the project and what can be done in order to minimise their impact on the success of your project. Derive an action plan (or contingency plan) to contain the risks. Promptly resolve any issues arising from risks that happen. Carrying out a comprehensive risk assessment would mean thinking of anything that could go wrong to hinder the project's progress. Include all perspectives – the sponsors, the stakeholders, the audience, the artists and the creation of the artwork itself. Test the validity of any risk by asking: what is the impact on cost; does it have an impact on the schedule; does it have an impact on the project's quality and objectives?

If an identified risk carries a real and serious threat to your project, take steps in the early stages of your project lifecycle to offset this risk. For example, if the foundry want a 30% deposit on work to be carried out (and you weren't expecting this), consider your cash flow and when and how you will access any monies. Identify which of these can be drawn down or accessed for the date you need them (applying financial resources to the problem). Or, could you negotiate with the foundry for a lesser deposit or a 'slipped' deadline (moving the date by when they need the money). A second example might be that the public art committee keep asking for changes to your agreed proposal. This is taking a lot of time, energy and commitment on your part to keep up with their comments. What do you do?

Establish one point of contact on the committee who will feed you the real information as to what the committee are trying to get at.

Use clear and precise language in all your conversations (verbal and written).

Keep a paper trail of all conversations so there is no confusion – date all conversations. This is a valuable and simple method of information retrieval and will place you in a more confident position if a problem arises.

Establish who the decision maker is on the committee.

Establish a deadline beyond which you can make no more changes.

Establish a percentage or level of change that you are prepared to go to and not beyond, as compromise of your idea is beginning to occur.

The list of risks from any project is a source of valuable learning data for future projects – this is known as 'knowledge transfer'. Current projects can inform future projects and form the basis of this project's risk management information. Therefore, even if the risks don't occur you have created awareness within yourself and others involved in the project as to what may go wrong and you can bring this knowledge forward into the next project.

Task ‑ Try and identify five possible real risks to your project idea, anything that could seriously undermine your concept. What do you think you need to do, or whom do you need to talk to, to lessen the threat of these risks. Do you need to create a greater financial contingency (more money), slip your deadlines, do you need to access more support in kind (e.g. standby equipment on loan) or do you need to confirm the venue's marketing strategy to guarantee an audience take up of tickets.

Health and Safety Statements ― are borne from risk assessment. They increasingly form part of any activities (cultural or otherwise) that involve engaging with the public in any shape or form. You need to be able to write one, or at the very least feed into one, so if you have considered your risk management strategy, you are well on the way to being able to create a Health and Safety statement.

Operations – The Final Realisation of Your Project

The actual doing, the arrival at your destination. Finally, you have got here. The 'doing' will end up as a 'blip' in the lifecycle of the project, if you have planned correctly, as much of your energy and time has been spent in the detailed preparation of your project. This is not to underestimate the energy that will be needed to actually 'do' your installation or event but to say that it should run effortlessly and without incident as you have prepared for all eventualities- everyone knows what is happening, what their role is and what to expect. You're 'doing', in other words, should be a 'real live' version of your vision combined with your objectives.

A useful tool for operations management is a 'call sheet'. Used comprehensively in the film and TV industry, it is a list of what is happening, when, where, who is expected to be there, what their movements are and what their contact details are. It has a certain application within the creative and cultural industries and could be especially useful for 'live' performances but it depends on the nature of the event or project and it is for you to decide what information you (and those involved) need to have to hand on the day.

In the moments before your project becomes a reality, you should engage in a checking exercise – do you have all you need, does your project team, does everyone know what is taking place and do you and those involved have all the equipment required? It can be useful to hold a pre-project meeting and circulate this information in both a verbal and written format. In this way, everyone is 'briefed' and has a feel for what is happening. If you do not feel able to engage in this exercise, you could suggest it to an administrator involved in the project and see if they feel it would be useful. In addition, make sure you have organised some formal and/or informal documentation of your project- this is valuable future reference information.

42

Task - Check and recheck all aspects of your plan. Do you have all you need and do all the bits fit to make your initial vision a reality? If anything is missing, you will need to act fast.

Evaluation – A Satisfying and Successful Journey?

You can finally breathe easy again, the project has completed its lifecycle and the journey is over, but and it's a big but, there is still a little more to do...

In the post project administration and evaluation stage, you need to tie all your loose ends up and complete the finishing touches. These can include balancing the books, drawing down final stage payments, lodging money to the bank, finalising any outstanding bills, sending thank you letters to each person involved in the project who brought about its realisation. Sponsors and funders will expect a report (sometimes this can be formal, sometimes informal-check in advance which is expected of you) on the outcome of the project and this report might need to include all press garnered and monies acquired. Do you need to update your website with a post project rundown, images, thank you's? Consider what you will do with your documentation – archive, post marketing campaign, sponsors reports, website?

Legacy Management and Knowledge Transfer — All projects are unique, no two are the same and this means that the experience learnt on this project can feed forward into the next one. Therefore, management of stakeholder relations as well as keeping track of all correspondence, audience profile, budgets, press relations, developing a risk management plan, press coverage and documentation, will help you go forward into the next project with a well informed document for you to look back on, when you start your next idea...

By Kerry McCall

Re-entering the Visual Arts?

Many times we receive telephone calls from artists who have taken time out from their practice and even if this is only for a very short time, they feel that the art world has changed, and in some extreme cases appears to have left them behind. There is a certain sense of fear in these conversations, and even with the most experienced of artist there is a sense of helplessness. Based on these conversations we have prepared this basic guide to "Re-entering the Art World"

Our first piece of advice is "Get up to date on what is going on." This is a simple matter of research and following the news. A good place to start is by subscribing to Visual Artists Ireland's eBulletin service and the Visual Artists Ireland News Sheet. Both of these, with our website, on-line presence and Smartphone App, offer the most up to date information of what is current in galleries and other venues around the country, as well as offering opportunities for artists such as calls for submissions and other forms of supports and revenue generation. Using this information it will be possible to see what different types of galleries are showing, and potentially which of them will be interested in your form of work. Don't assume anything. Go to their exhibition openings and get to know them in person. It is really obvious to gallerist and curators who have engaged with the space before making a proposal, and those artists who are simply scatter gunning galleries for exhibitions.

The jobs and opportunities also provide a good guide to the expanse and the limitations of what is out there. Use them to build a realistic picture of what the art world is offering. Looking back through recent archives and keeping up to date will also start to show patterns that will help to know when to step back in again. There is also an immense wealth of handy hints, information articles, and advice on how to protect yourself from being taken advantage of.

The next piece of advice given is to "Get up to date with technology." It is important to make it easy for people to find out more about your work and how to contact you. No matter what opinions may be held about having an email address, and we hear many, get one NOW. As part of our membership services we have a directory that artists can join and provide a place to give some information about your work, as well as a place that people looking to make contact can use while at the same time maintaining a level of privacy (keep in mind that spam merchants love unguarded email addresses).

A website always appears to be a daunting task. But keeping it very simple with the basic information of background, examples of work, and a simple statement on practice are the minimum and most important content. Simple, clean and clear are the key tenets. Like any good exhibition, the website is your shop front on to the world. So, it is not a place to put every piece of work ever made. Instead it should have selected samples of recent works, and where pertinent highlights of past work. A good hint is to get help from a fellow artist or curator in terms of selecting the works to be shown, and also to ensure that the images used are composed so that the works are clear and unambiguous. Some installation shots can also give a level of engagement. There is much assistance to be found in this, including a regular professional development workshop run by VAI on presenting your work.

So, with an email address, a clear website, registration in the VAI directory, and a clearly prepared statement about practice and work, the next steps are to look into what social media can do. This has become more important in contemporary society, and as can be seen from VAI's wide ranging presence, there are many ways to get a message out, as well as create opportunities of networking with fellow artists. Like it or not sites like Facebook and Twitter is a great way to keep people up to date, and also to see what is going on with other artists around the globe. Remember to "Keep it professional", and give people a reason that they want to come back and subscribe to your updates.

This brings us to our next point, "Network with fellow artists and art world professionals." Everywhere we go in Ireland we hear the same thing: "I feel isolated, I'm not part of the crowd, I don't know what is going on!" There is really no excuse for this anymore. Apart from the regular networking events that VAI holds around the country, there are many formal and informal artists groups that can be a great way of building a local support and information network. Being an artist can be one of the most solitary professions, and keeping a positive attitude and the creative juices flowing can be hard. But through these local groups, and also the annual Get Together event that VAI holds, it is possible to find other artists who are more than willing to talk about their work, share experiences, as well as understanding that key point "You're not alone".

We also get asked for advice on artistic direction. VAI runs peer critique groups on a regular basis throughout the year. We advise artists not to be afraid to put themselves forward for these, and have found several groups who have met through a peer critique session and have maintained a supportive contact with fellow artists afterwards. The VAI offices meeting room is available in Dublin, but having some artists do reciprocal studio visits can pay many dividends when there is a level of professional appreciation and trust.

Let's assume that all of the above have been done, and that the habit of regular studio time is in place... the next big question is "how do I get my work out there? How do I get curators to notice me?" Frankly, if there were any simple answers to this then we would write that book and live off the royalties. But, there are some very simple steps that increase the possibility. Why not consider "Curating yourself!" There are lots of local opportunities to be found in places such as small museums, interpretative centres, and local galleries. These may be places that would like to engage with the visual arts and will find it interesting to have an exhibition or simply have blank walls that they are looking to use.

Also, in the eBulletin there are often calls for submissions that are a good way to get curators to see your work. Selection panels often contain key decision makers that use them for their active research. Even if you are not successful, curators sitting on the selection panel will get to see your work.

Another good option is to put together a carefully edited and documented group of works and indicate their availability through the VAI website Exhibitions for Touring feature. Just remember that it is key to "Present yourself with the highest level of quality and professionalism." Review, edit, review, edit and get advice from friends on how your proposals look. Assume that the selection panel will never have heard of you and check that your submission gives them the best clear picture of your proposal.

It is almost too obvious to say, "Approach galleries and curators." But, this simple act can be expensive, and may not yield results without some careful consideration. Using the research above, find out places that show the type of work that fits best with your own practice, and start from there. Make sure that you have a clear statement that can be easily understood. One of the most remarkable things at a recent VAI networking event that included curators was the number of artists who came with no images of their work. This left a lasting bad impression. So, get some advice on presenting yourself, and also do some practice run with other artists and friends.

Lastly, when you have had successes "Celebrate them." This is not just that glass of wine shared with friends after an opening. Make sure that you update the general public with them. Share them through your online presence. If there are any curators who have asked to be kept up to date and then make sure that they know that you have a show on, or that your work has been written about. Never assume that people are out there looking to find out what you are up to. Instead, have a mailing list of people who you know want to be regularly kept up to date on what you are up to.

So these are a few simple steps. By its very nature this article is short and not fully inclusive, but it is good with a number of simple first steps for re-entering the art world.

Summary

- Don't despair; you are not alone
- Do your research, including the extensive self-help and advisory articles in our Resources Section
- Get an email address
- Become a member of Visual Artists Ireland
- Subscribe to VAI's eBulletin and Visual Artists News Sheet (delivered to your door if you are a member of VAI)
- Look out for networking events and make a point of going
- Develop a professional looking website and web presence
- Use to the web to increase your professional network
- Look at what VAI professional development workshops and peer critique sessions are suitable for you to attend (members get big discounted rates on these)
- Maintain contact with like minded people that you meet at these events
- Look for local opportunities to show your work
- Apply for the opportunities advertised in the Visual Artists' News Sheet and eBulletin that are suitable for you
- Be prepared for refusals, but use them to learn by asking for feedback
- Target galleries and curators that you feel will be interested in your specific work after researching carefully what they show (there's no point in offering

your paintings to a curator who only shows moving image etc.)
- Be professional at all times and have a clear statement about your work, and professional images in electronic format
- Use the supports that VAI offers members to their best advantage
- Be careful out there, there are a lot of unscrupulous people around at the moment. Use your VAI membership to get advice on who and what to avoid using our help line +353 (0)1 672 9488 or info@visualartists.ie
- Above all, remember that it is about making work and the rest is just the business surrounding it, KEEP AT IT.

By Noel Kelly

Self-Organisation as a Way of Being

A Personal Example

When I returned to Dublin in the late 1990s from living and working outside of Ireland, I realised that there were limited opportunities for me to show my work, to curate exhibitions and to activate the network of people I had established whilst away. There was limited infrastructure available for operating on a continual basis as an artist working on a curatorial basis and making-exhibitions with other practitioners. I felt restricted in what I could do on a daily basis and in what I could offer as a host for potential moments of exchange with others.

As a means of widening my existing network and creating a space for these moments to happen, I founded MultiplesX in 1997 with fellow artist Ronan McCrea. MultiplesX was initially meant to be an intermediary solution to having our own gallery space. After numerous formal and informal conversations seeking support by means of funds or exhibition space, eventually Temple Bar Gallery, with the support of its curator at the time Vaari Claffey, and the design firm Language became the central components in the organisational structure of our initiative. MultiplesX facilitated a space in which I could extend invitations to a large number of artists and curators over a relatively short time-span. MultiplesX eventually became a vehicle through which I could mobilise my thinking and speaking beyond the limitations of the subjective, and often isolationist, "I" towards a more empowered position of the "we".

As a non-for-profit organisation we commissioned, organised and curated exhibitions of Irish and international artist's editions at regular intervals in the foyer at TBGS and the works were distributed widely through catalogues designed by Language. We also had regular touring exhibitions of the works in Ireland, the UK and Europe, which further extended our network of artists, curators and critics. As a self-organised initiative, it began as a way of dealing with a lack of exhibition space, limited opportunities and a restrictive critical space around what I was interested in doing as an artist whose practice was shifting towards the curatorial. It also helped me to self-generate a network of curators, artists and practitioners with whom I have remained in contact with and continue to collaborate with on a regular basis. Rather than waiting around for invitations from others to take part in projects, I was able to do the inviting myself in the knowledge that such relationships could facilitate further moments of exchange in the future. MultiplesX also helped me to learn a wide range of administrational and organisational skills such as writing funding applications, handling artworks, writing press releases, consigning works, insuring works, packing and transporting works, dealing with artists, gallerists, collectors, curators, and critics and generally introducing a greater level of professionalism into my overall artistic and curatorial practice. It was my earlier self-initiated projects in the early 1990s that also enabled me to consider MultiplesX as a possibility.

Although many of MultiplesX objectives, such as establishing a market for emerging Irish art alongside an Irish market for established international artists who were not represented by Irish galleries was not to happen, and may have been badly timed, but many of the skills, experiences and the network I emerged with after MultiplesX I carried with me into my first institutional post as gallery curator in London Print Studio between 2001-03 and I have been able to continually call upon the artist, curator and critic contacts I established during this time and I continue to work with and share an expanding cultural network with many of the participants. Like any self-initiated project either before or subsequently, all has continued to provide a space of learning and development, often in some unexpected ways, but it is it at the stage of self-organisation that such projects become more expansive when they are more than just self-enterprise by initiating and supporting the involvement of others in what one does.

Self-initiated Projects: The First Stage of Self-Organisation

Self-initiated projects are the first stage in configuring a world through which we wish to be read. By making connections between what we do and what others do, we can begin to enable pluralist forms of exchange. Initiators start with and from a position of desire for a space of readership, as well as production that is temporarily unavailable to them. There is recognition of an absence, which the initiator wishes to make visible. By bringing this appearance into the present an organisation begins to be formed beyond the individual position. As Mika Hannula has argued:

Self-organisation is a so-called third space. It is a peculiar concentration of time and energy in a particular place where the interests of the participants in that context are debated, constituted, defined, clarified and defended. It does not belong to either A or B, but is constructed spontaneously through the interaction between A and B. It is a meeting point at which both sides have found the capacity to listen to each other on the others terms. It is based on acknowledging interaction that seeks to

48

negotiate a sustainable compromise for existing alongside one another, not as a unity, but in a plurality.

Self-initiated projects are the life-blood of culture, i.e. culture as understood in both *material* production and as a *symbolic* system of that production. Self-organisation is about making things happen on one's own terms alongside like-minded positions. An artist, curator or writer who initiates projects with others is self-directing notions of both "commonality" and "connectivity" in relation to how they wish to position what it is that they do and how they wish it to exist in the world. These two central terms begin to function as inherent qualities within one's own work: common to the general idea of practice as a form of self-positioning alongside other like minded positions and connected to the belief in the potentiality of these other like-forms of practice as part of the same critical discourse. As Anthony Davies, Stephan Dillemuth and Jakob Jakobsen have claimed in their co-penned essay *There is no Alternative: The Future is Self Organised*, self-organisation is, amongst other things, " a social process of communication and commonality based in exchange; sharing of similar problems, knowledge and available resources."

As a shared space for discussion, self-organisation enables a directed vocabulary to take place around what one does. Every exhibition becomes a contingent moment in an on-going evolution of one's practice over a longer period, where such momentary events function as self-regulated research tools for establishing continuous links between one's practice as a space of negotiation beyond the individual position, and hopefully adds to the flow of a more agile and self-empowering culture without the restraints of, or the necessity for, a more fixed institutional structure.

From Conversation to the Formation of a Position

The artist Douglas Gordon once said that "exhibitions are an excuse for a conversation", but what Gordon's casual remark implies is that any moment of public display can initiate a potential space of dialogue between interested parties that only the event can set in motion. What Gordon is highlighting is a necessity for dialogue to move things forward, without which artistic practice remains in a self-imposed vacuum. Self-organised projects are the difference between waiting for those moments of exchange to be initiated by outside forces instead of producing such moments one-self.

Conversational modes of exchange are not without their own formal restraints or limitations. In fact, exhibition-moments such as the private view or the after-opening pub session can end up as the most formal of all discursive exchanges – with or without the alcoholic lubricant. Conversations are the first stage of exchange in a necessary move towards more formalised critique and modes of participation through which the potentiality for engagement with different publics, divergent readerships, and diverse audiences can be widened beyond the mere convivial space of chatting. The transformation of the space of discourse into forms of exhibition, public events, publications, public discussions, reading groups etc., also enables the configuration of a useful social network for the initiator as well as activating a potential space for that network to be called upon again in the future and for it to continue to grow over time.

From Invitee to Initiator:

The invitation to take part in providing this text began with an email followed by a conversational form of exchange. It was my ambition to maintain this mode of exchange for as long as was possible during the writing process and instead of just saying yes to the invitation and following instructions, I wanted to initiate an organisational process through which I could involve other voices instead of mediating solely on my own behalf. Having been given the opportunity by Visual Artists Ireland to write a text about organising one's own projects, this potential "exhibition moment" became a further opportunity for me to activate an exchange between myself, and a number of other potential contributors.

The primary space of discourse that was set in motion between Visual Artists Ireland as the inviter and me as the invitee became a secondary space of initiation, opened up by the invitee. In turn, I asked twenty practitioners whose work is often conditioned by self-organisational principles to respond to five rather oblique but loosely formulated questions:

Why should we organise or initiate our own projects?

What are the benefits of self-initiated projects?

Is there a difference between taking part in self-organised projects and those that have been initiated by others?

What is self-determinism?

What is alternative cultural practice?

Their more than generous responses operated as the foundation for this text and wherever possible, their words are mediated here. Somewhat unsurprising, every respondent looked at self-initiated projects in a positive light, but perhaps a little less so was a certain sense of suspicion towards any fixed notion of what form these projects could take. In many ways what for some may be organised due to an urgent necessity, for others it may be in the guise of self-enterprise and an alternative conduit to the market, the establishment and so on. As Pavel Büchler put it:

They can (but by no means necessarily do) manifest that things can be done differently in the face of concrete social, cultural or material situations. It goes without saying, then, that self-organisation is particularly meaningful where it is conceptually integral to the work, project or practice, rather than being merely a strategy for the dissemination of autonomous artworks or an exercise of entrepreneurial enterprise.

There is Always an Alternative

In 2005, Dave Beech and Mark Hutchinson curated the exhibition and publication 'There is Always an Alternative' at temporary contemporary gallery space in Deptford, South London, which then toured to International 3 in Manchester. The exhibition proposed an alternative story of the period of artistic activity in the UK during the early 1990s – an alternate history to both the dominant yBa story and its leading counter-narrative aligned to DIY artist-run spaces such as City Racing and Bank, of which both temporary contemporary and International 3 are natural descendants. Instead of offering any grand narrative, Beech and Hutchinson were proposing that they are many number of personal alternatives to what passes as dominant cultural history, one of which was told through their hand scribbled notes on the walls next to each artist's work exclaiming how they had met the artist, what they were doing at the time and how they ended up working together.

'There is Always an Alternative' was not an alternative exhibition history in itself, but a proposition for the endless alternative accounts that make up cultural history. Without their initiation, such a narrative would remain untold, but it also enabled Beech and Hutchinson to insert their own practice into some meaningful framework for themselves without waiting for it to happen elsewhere. This need for a self-production of a discourse around one's own practice is, "vital to control some aspects of the manifestation and dissemination of the artwork in the loosest and widest possible sense," and controlling this discourse at some level seems to be central to both Ele Carpenter and Ian Rawlinson position also, where they relate the ownership of one's own ideas to the regulation of its reception where, "the artistic principles of the work are contextualised, but not compromised in the process," or when artists "are able to control the context in which the work is received to a greater extent through self-initiated projects...[and] the absence of an over bearing institutional agenda can allow some room for forms of production and distribution unavailable elsewhere".

This urge to speak on one's own behalf in a self-generating manner is again mirrored in Pil and Galia Kollectiv's experience:

The best motivation for self-initiated projects is the desire to contextualise one's work. In the wake of the death of the author, we must ensure that viewers get the best reading conditions. By placing our work alongside not just related or similar work, but work from other disciplines altogether, we can create and more importantly dictate or at least influence the new meanings that emerge from the juxtaposition.

The Doing is of Fundamental Importance

Self-initiated projects express an urgency to replace a lack of discourse around certain issues as well as providing a less corralled version of the process of one's own cultural operations. Likewise, by initiating organisational activities, an artist, curator or writer expresses what Annie

51

Fletcher called a, "need to see and discuss artistic practices or to manifest an idea through art which is not being manifested elsewhere" which can open up the possibility for a multitude of short-lived alternative perspectives as well as facilitating a more horizontal critical space for a shared enquiry between participants. Self-initiated projects also deduct the effects of an over-reliant culture, dependent upon our existing fixed institutional structures and conventional critical frameworks – a dependency upon more bureaucratic organisations such as public governing bodies, state commissioners, public-funded museums or established commercial art galleries. As Pavel Büchler argues, such projects also "differ from those initiated by institutions to the extent that they are expressions of an individually perceived sense of necessity, urgency or responsibility." These initiatives are all urgent and particular to each initiator, and can come in infinite guises, ranging from the artist who takes on a commission in order to fund a new body of work, to the curator who organises a show with a group of artists at a local market stall, to the writer who regularly writes letters to existing art magazines because of a lack of publishing outlets and eventually self-publishes them as a zine.

For each of the fore-mentioned artist, curator, or writer, they may only wish to continue this type of work for a limited period before they move toward their eventual goal. It is the doing that is of fundamental importance, within which certain previous unknown possibilities can open up. In many ways all cultural projects, regardless of their resistant origins, have an uneasy and habitually co-dependent relationship with established institutional structures and will often necessitate their support at a future stage in order to move things forward. It does not naturally apply that all self-organised projects are necessarily better than those initiated by institutions, but they do mediate some cultural discrepancy at a given moment in time for at least one member of that culture. This does not mean that such activities provide any concrete alternative to existing power structures, but they do propose that there is every possibility that the existing infrastructures are not to everyone's satisfaction and that there is always another space in which things can be done differently. Alternatives can be expressed as a drive toward a more constantly shifting field of cultural production as was echoed in an earlier text by Büchler, when he proposed that being an artist means:

[...] Not doing different things than others do, but doing things differently [and] modern society needs creativity, critical imagination and resistance more than it needs works of art. It needs artists with their own ways of doing things more than it needs the things that they make. It needs the artists for what they are, rather than what they do, then it is in the sense in which artists are producers of culture rather than of discrete artefacts which characterise this culture.

An example of Büchler's approach to thinking about artists for what they do rather than what they make is apparent in an attitude of hospitality that often emerges in his projects, such as the book *Conversation Pieces*. This was produced to accompany his exhibition at Tampere in Finland, 2003, when he commissioned nine practitioners including John Stezaker, Simon

Morris, Tim Brennan, Sharon Kivland and Will Bradley to produce a piece of writing that was in dialogue with his work but only to use it as a magnifying glass or optical lens for their own practice. The texts vary in style and approach, but central to each is how the writers use the provided context to produce extensions of their own practice and not merely respond to Buchler's work. It is a non-prescriptive invitation that acts as a contemplative trigger for each of the contributors to reflect on their own work. The texts becoming a means of exploring their own ideas, and the invitation as an excuse to produce something new for themselves. There are infinite examples of such projects based on varying modes of the hospitality principle, where there is always a two-way exchange between host and guest.

Some Notable Initiatives

Closer to home, numerous initiatives such as Via, Four Gallery, Feint zine and Pallas have all taken hospitality as their central organising principle for accommodating local practice. Other variations on the theme of hosting have included Sarah Pierce's The Metropolitan Complex, Dublin, where she holds informal meetings between local practitioner's to discuss their concerns as a way of understanding her own and publishes the proceedings in a newspaper; Do Something For Floating IP at the artist-run space Floating IP in Manchester, 2004, where the artists Dave Beech and Graham Parker simply asked artists to do something for them as a way of kick-starting their programme, but without limitation and all responses were exhibited, in order to grasp the general direction of their own organisation or the first exhibition at The Colony Gallery space in Birmingham, when All at Once, 2006 was initiated by Paul McAree and Mona Casey, whereby all artworks proposed as part of an open submission where accepted regardless of merit, as a means of establishing an artist network for the organisation, and temporary contemporary (Jen Wu and Anthony Gross, London) have always taken an open curatorial approach to their expansive exhibitions, without being tied down to an overarching or restrictive thematic and accommodating as many artists as is within their expanding local and now international network.

Conclusion

Self-organisation is about undoing certain historical preconceptions of any set notion of what roles an artist, critic or curator can take on. As Dave Beech claims, "it is about doing things on your own terms" and "taking control of the means of distribution" that have an impact on the work, which can provide a mode of resistance to art's institutions and to resist the conventions that artists make, critics and curators display. Self-organisation also offers an alternative to art's institutions from which they can learn and adopt, although at a different speed of engagement. If everyone waited for supportive assistance, the progress of culture would be at a relatively fixed rate, whereby the inherent distribution of power would be maintained as a certain level from the top down. As David Blamey states:

It is important that some artists and curators organise their own projects. The art world relies upon independent producers to challenge its power base just as democracy flourished with a measure of dissent. As new ideas and practices are assimilated into the mainstream the prevalent culture of agreement is protected and the power base maintained.

For James Hutchinson, the existing framework for cultural activity is always shifting around and it is up to the artist/ curator to recognise gaps in the existing cultural framework and to generate new conventions for operating, which in turn can be subverted further in a constantly shifting environment. Hutchinson describes these gaps in culture as "alternative space", and he claims that "once the gap is filled, it becomes part of the existing framework for other artists/curators (i.e. institutionalised)... and the gaps change all the time and new gaps form" which can never be completely filled at any one time. Similarly, for Liam Gillick, the benefits of self-initiated projects is in the acknowledgement of culture as having certain gaps or can be expressed as having the "potential for absences; modes of refusal; excess or lack of mediation; use of new spaces, geographies and proximities; avoidances of the validating processes of official culture" and that self-organised projects can "question the established mediating structures that develop around cultural activity with specific instrumentalised aims that might run contrary to the critical potential of art now."

As well as gaps in culture there are always gaps in one's personal knowledge. By establishing a way of working in the world that employs knowledge producing attributes learnt through self-organised projects one can begin to think of those gaps in our culture as opportunities for, rather than obstacles to, our own self-education. As David Goldenberg described the effects of his first self-initiated projects on the whole development of his later and more established practice:

Later self-initiated projects were seen as a possibility for developing a project completely on my own terms. While I treated the construction and formulation of a project as an extension of my practice and thinking, where staging a project allowed the possibility for working through ideas for assembling and staging the different components of an exhibition – in other words, a project is a reflection of a complex understanding of how an exhibition is constructed and how one element is dependent on all the other elements. This led to a type of critical practice that tested out available positions and the limitations of the construction of the exhibition. This blurring of roles, where the artist and curator merge, and a meta-understanding of staging a project was developed, and corresponded [with an] understanding of [how] the methodology of a contemporary practice [could] provide the critical tools to dismantle and deconstruct the ideological construction of the traditions of modern art.

Many of the responses to my questions mirrored Homi Bhabha's well worn statement, that "in every emergency, there is an emergence." What Goldenberg self-determining response demonstrates is not just how self-initiated projects are a necessary tool during periods of emergency in one's career, but also how out of such self-organisations can emerge a more complete practice, which also benefits from being more skilled, networked and well-informed.

Self-initiated projects are about projecting onto a desirable future for yourself and others. From initial idea to eventual completion, self-organised projects increase one's understanding of the complexities of the processes and stages of its development. Alongside the knowledge that is gained through these experiences, one can begin to configure in one's mind how even the institution of culture itself is more of a long-term construction rather than a short-term fix.

By Paul O'Neill

Kindred Spirits: Studios & Residencies

A Practical Guide to Setting Up Studio Space

Introduction

Few artists can afford the expense of owning their own studio, particularly at the start of their careers. Working with a group of artists can be a viable economic alternative with the additional advantage of shared information, expertise, facilities and resources. Setting up a studio in Ireland today is a tricky business. Property prices are at a premium and even if you find a space, holding on to it may not be that simple. This practical guide is intended to equip practising artists with some general information and advice needed to set up a studio group.

Getting started

Before you start looking for a space to develop, it is worth spending some time thinking about the type of studio you need. A great way to start this process would be to read artist Alan Phelan's text, 'I'm thinking of getting a Studio'.

Although it may take time to find the space that's right for your needs, your budget will often determine the level of compromise between what you want and what you can afford.

You may have to respond quickly to an opportunity that arises unexpectedly, or you may have the time to research a variety of possible spaces – in either case having a relatively clear idea of what you really need from a studio will focus your search when looking for space. If you are planning to work with a group of artists there are some basic questions you may wish to consider in advance.

- Who is involved?
- Can we trust each other?
- Are there particular facilities or resources needed to develop work?
- What is affordable?
- How much time do I personally want to invest in the process of operating a group studio?
- Do I want the responsibility of managing a group studio or do I just want to concentrate on my own work?

It is worth considering these issues before you start, as they will impact on the kind of studio space you will create. Even though you may share similar interests with others in the group and you may be the best of friends, your needs may conflict with theirs depending on the type of work you do. If for example you work with chemicals and industrial equipment, you will have different needs from someone that works with photography, paint, digital equipment or whose practice is primarily research based. Dust, sound, smells and noise can be disruptive features of a shared working environment. It is possible to find solutions to these problems when designing your space so as to accommodate a range of work practices, however this will depend on the budget you have available and the time provided in your tenancy agreement to develop the studio.

Responsibility

Whilst a degree of flexibility is necessary, the sustainability of the project will also depend on the group's ability to manage the studio effectively; how decisions are made and how the fundamental issue of managing responsibility for the project is dealt with. Consider whether you would prefer to share this with a group, perhaps go it alone or within a partnership agreement. Either way you will need to consider the long-term legal and financial implications of managing a group studio and how to balance the time needed to run the space with time for your own studio practice.

Research

Visiting other studios will give you a sense of what is possible and the opportunity to learn more about what is actually involved in running a studio. An excellent way to test your ideas in advance is by talking through your project with someone who has either found solutions to problems or discovered mechanism's to deal with some of the challenges you may encounter. Valuable information can be gained from the experience of existing studio groups. The legal and financial responsibilities for a studio workspace take effect from the very start of the project. Contracts have to be signed, bills have to be paid, common areas need to be kept in order, studios need to be allocated, rubbish needs to be disposed of, things need to be fixed and conflicts need to be resolved.

Other issues might include:

Health & Safety – By law, the studio is required to ensure the personal safety of anyone using the space and that adequate measures have been taken to enable people to exit the space in the event of an emergency.

Having suitable insurance policies in place for Public Liability is essential.

Monitoring bank statements and recording the studio bank a/c transactions can be time consuming work, yet elementary to any studio's survival.

Corridors and common areas often become unofficial 'storage' areas, which can be an on-going headache, as the studio artists' output inevitably expands.

Cleaning up after artists that move out and chasing after any unpaid rent is not fun.

Talk with other artists about their experiences with studios both good and bad, in order to establish a direction for your project and to assess potential problems in advance. Knowing what doesn't work as well as what does, can be useful information when deciding the structure of your studio.

Group dynamics

When deciding to set up a studio, there are several options open to you, each with its own particular benefits and risks. You may decide to work with a group of other artists, with just one or two partners or perhaps on your own. In many ways setting up a studio can be like setting up a small business – you need to know who your partners are, the level of commitment they are willing to invest in the studio and their ability to take responsibility in a group venture.

The scale of your project and the length of tenancy available to you will inevitably influence a number of key decisions, both in terms of the physical space and the number of artists involved. A larger space will require more artists being involved in order to spread the cost of operating the studios. Over an extended period of time there will be greater demands made on the studio administration to monitor both the financial commitments of the studio and the physical maintenance of the space. Maintenance responsibilities will involve addressing general wear and tear, electrics, plumbing, heating, keys, locks and security – all the usual stuff that comes with a building over time.

With less space to manage and maintain, smaller group studios will have lower overheads and will not be as exposed to financial risk should one or two individuals decide to leave the group. It will be easier to find a suitable replacement for the missing share of the operating costs.

Larger studio groups can experience a higher turnover of artists. This places a greater demand on the administrative resources of the studio to find suitable replacements for empty studios or to monitor sub letting arrangements. The administration must also monitor individual artist arrears in rent and utilities (Gas & ESB).

Studio Models

Good results are relatively easy to accommodate. It is when you have to resolve unexpected problems that the core structure and foundations of your studio group will come into focus and you will need to consider issues of power, responsibility, benefits and risks that are implicit within a studio group from the start.

Try to consider the early stages of the studio's development and any associated 'teething problems' as an opportunity to discover how the studio will work best, given the circumstances and what's available to you at that time. In Ireland the type of studio group structures in operation are as diverse and complex as the buildings they occupy. Generally they fall into five practical models or types of structure.

The responsibility of any studio group is to work out how you are going to operate the studio, the work that needs to be done regularly and who's going to do it? Rather than go into too much detail, I've summarised the basic outline of a potential studio structure with examples for reference.

Group Studios with Shared Responsibilities

Sharing equal responsibility with all members of a group can increase your immediate resources in terms of simplicity, budgets and people to work with. It may also mean that you are depending on each individual participant to contribute to the initial business of setting up and eventual responsibility for the workspace. For smaller groups, advantages can be found by creating simple systems to share the work involved in paying bills and keeping the space in order – for example by setting a fixed term for each member of the group to attend to the administration or offering reduced rent to a group member in exchange for work undertaken. Developing studios in a rural location using this model has its own rewards but can incur different pressures to its urban equivalent.

- Cork Artists Collective, Cork
  www.thecollective.ie

- New Art Studio, Dublin
  www.newartstudio.org

- Visual Arts Centre, Dublin
  www.visualartscentre.ie

- Stoney Batter Studio, Dublin
  www.stoneybatterstudio.com

- Belmont Mill Artists Studios, Co. Offaly
  www.belmontmill.com

Artist-led Group Studios with a Board of Management

This can be a way of developing a larger space for studios with a core group, who take responsibility for the legal and financial management of the space whilst offering studio space for rent to non-members of the group.

- Art Space Studios, Galway
  www.artspacegalway.com

- Backwater Artists Group, Cork
  www.backwaterartists.ie

- Flax Art Studios, Belfast
  www.flaxartstudios.org

Independent Artist-Led Initiatives

Independent artist-led initiatives that are managed by an individual or partnership can be a way of responding to an opportunity to develop a space quickly without having to wait for approval from a large group of diverse and individual stakeholders. In this situation, the individual or partners take complete responsibility for the studio and will offer studio space to rent to other artists under their particular terms of agreement.

- Broadstone Studios, Dublin
  www.broadstonestudios.com

- Common Place, Dublin
  www.commonplace.ie

- Pallas Studios, Dublin
  www.pallasstudios.org

Partnerships with Other Organisations

Another type of development for studio space involves finding an organisation locally that is willing to barter space for services from the group. This could be with a local authority, a local business, a health centre or a community group. In this situation an agreement to exchange services for studio space within a specific timeframe can be negotiated with a host organisation that is willing to avail of the artist's specialised skills and expertise. The group could offer the provision of services like workshops or classes, possibly organising an annual event or exhibition with specialised groups during the period of time the studio is housed by the host or partnership organisations.

- Contact Studios, Limerick
  E: doran.carl@gmail.com

- The Dock, Co. Leitrim
  www.thedock.ie

Specialist Group Studios

These are studios that are set up to provide resources or facilities for a specific art form. If your work requires access to particular equipment e.g. graphic and printing equipment, construction and fabrication equipment or expensive digital technology, then pooling your resources and sharing the equipment is a way to generate access to tools you may not be able to afford individually.

- Black Church Print Studio, Dublin
  www.print.ie

- Limerick Printmakers, Limerick
  www.limerickprintmakers.com

The factors that will affect the choice of structure / model you opt for are relative to the number of people involved, the resources you have available, the physical scale of the space and in particular the length of tenancy you can secure from a potential landlord. There is little point in creating an elaborate management structure if you can only secure the space for a limited period of time. Equally it would be unwise to invest a lot of time, money and energy into a space that you will have to vacate before you can get any realistic return from your investment.

In view of the limited availability of space within most urban environments in Ireland today and their associated prohibitive costs, working with smaller groups in the beginning can be a much simpler way of managing your project whilst establishing stability within the group. It is not necessary, and in many cases not possible, to know every detail of how you will operate the studios from the start – this is something that will evolve organically and is relative to the concerns of the group involved. However when renting space collectively it is essential that you establish from the start who is taking responsibility for the legal and financial obligations associated with any rental agreement or legal contracts.

Legal Identities

When working with a small group of artists, it may not be necessary to formulate a legal identity for the group unless entering into legal contracts. The group can simply agree the ground rules of how you will conduct business together. Having a formal legal structure is advantageous if you intend trying to source financial support for the studio in the future. A formal legal structure presents a clearly identifiable legal commitment to mange any potential funding offers in a responsible manner. This equally applies when signing lease agreements; a building owner or property agent will normally request either an individual to sign or a group with a legal identity that can be held accountable for the terms of the contract.

Demonstrating accountability to potential funding agencies and the measures that have been taken to limit legal liability should things go wrong, is an essential requirement of all funding applications. The reason you need to demonstrate accountability is to assure potential stakeholders that you have taken the appropriate steps to safeguard the studio as an organisation; that the activities of the studio are legal; and that all financial activities are regularly monitored and recorded.

Choosing a legal structure is not of itself difficult, but it is not always clear what is most appropriate for development, and trying to change later on can cause difficulties. The issue should be thought out carefully and discussed with a professional adviser.

Legal Structures

There is no standard organisational or legal form for non-profit groups in Ireland – there are different types of legal structure to suit different kinds of organisations and situations. A group needs a structure to work properly; it sets out basic rules and relationships for management.

Business Name

A group can trade under any name it likes, provided the name is registered with the Companies Office. Registering a name is not the same as having legal status. It should be kept in mind that the owners of the Business

61

Name are liable for any debts. Opening a bank account for the studio will require a certificate of the registered business name, if you intend trading in that name.

The studio business name can be registered as a partnership with all the studio partners named on the business name registration application. Registration can be made via the CRO website at a reduced fee for on-line applications.

www.cro.ie – Companies Registration Office, Dublin

Constitution

This is the simplest form of legal structure for a voluntary organisation. It does not require registration. A constitution sets out the rules of the group and includes:

- The name of the group
- The area of operation and activities
- Membership and voting rights
- Committees and officers
- Finance
- Decision making

Any constitution can be easily adapted to suit the needs of another group, club, society or association.

The disadvantage of a constitution is that the members do not have separate legal status from the group. It is not really suitable for an organisation that intends to enter into contracts, to own property or employ staff. All the members can be held responsible for the group's activities.

Other sources of information for draft constitution: Revenue Commissioners: www.revenue.ie – draft constitution, draft articles, memorandum and lots more Irish Charities Tax research: www.ictr.ie – for up to date information on charities regulation.

The information on legal structures was generously provided by: The Irish Fundraising Handbook, 6th edition (2007), available from Create.

Finding a Space

To find a space that is both manageable and affordable will take some time and effort. As well as checking out all the obvious sources, like commercial letting agents, local newspapers, notice boards and e-bulletins; make sure to let people know you are looking as word of mouth can produce surprising results. Finding the right space may seem elusive, but by remaining focused you will eventually discover several possibilities.

When viewing potential studio space, you will need to know from the start whether you can afford it and if there are any hidden costs that you are not aware of, plus other important issues relating to access and safety such as:

- The annual rent and what that includes – light, heat or insurance?
- Are rates included or is that an additional expense?
- What are the terms of the rental – can you get a lease or written contract?
- Is there any heating or ventilation?
- In an emergency is there a safe way to get out of the space?
- Do you have 24/7 access to the space or is this restricted?
- What condition is the building in?
- Are there any parking facilities available or access to local transport?
- Is there insurance cover for the public areas, car parks, stairwells, entrance and exits?
- What security measures are in place?
- Who are the other tenants of the building?

Look at as many different types of space as you can before deciding which space will work for you and never sign any agreements or contracts on first viewing. You will need to look at all the costs involved and weigh up the advantages or disadvantages of the different spaces relative to your particular needs.

Location

This obviously depends on where you choose to work, with different issues for studios in rural and urban locations. Circumstances tend to reverse for both; either you are in a rural environment which is much cheaper than its urban equivalent with lots of space available but limited access to resources or the latter where space is very limited and costly, but comes with extensive access to resources, facilities, critics, curators, galleries, institutions and other artists. You should think about the times when you use the studio. If you have other work commitments during the day and can only get to the studio in the evening, consider what it's like to go there at night and how safe it feels. If you need to get large work in or out of the space, is there adequate access? Perhaps you will require materials to be delivered or work to be collected by transporters; are there any parking facilities or public transport services close to the studio?

Leasing / Renting a Studio Space

When you find a space that is suitable and before you sign any contracts, remember you may have room to negotiate the terms of the lease or rental before you commit yourself. It is highly recommended that you get the terms of the rental written down and signed by both the owner/landlord and the appointed studio representative. You may then refer back to this signed agreement or contract if issues of conflict arise. If you do sign a contract on behalf of a group without formulating any type of legal structure for the studio group, then all responsibility for the terms of the contract agreement will rest with you personally. Some guidelines to consider before signing any contract are:

Read all contracts very carefully and do not sign anything before taking time to read the small print thoroughly.

If you are unsure about any particular details of the contract or if there's anything you don't quite understand, then ask to have it explained and clarified in writing, or seek advice at one of the suggested agencies above.

You can make revisions – if there are any unacceptable elements of the lease or contract, you have the right to ask for these to be eliminated before you sign.

If the space requires a lot of work before it is useable, for example if it's full of rubbish and it will take time to clean the space up, you could try to negotiate a rent-free period. In this case you are probably about to take on a space that the owner has had difficulty in renting to other businesses. This gives you the opportunity to either clean up the space or make changes to create a workable space, before you actually start paying rent.

If you improve the property, then don't hesitate in asking for a rent reduction in exchange for the improvements made by you to the landlords property, or indeed ask the owner to pay for any substantial improvements you have made to the space.

If you plan to make any substantial alterations to the space, it might be best to get the landlord's approval. It would be a shame to invest time and money into improvements only to discover that these changes present a problem for the owner.

Avoid any verbal agreements and if possible make sure everything you have agreed verbally is written down.

Know your rights:
www.irishstatutebook.ie/1980/en/act/pub/0010/index.html
Landlord and Tenant (Amendment) Act, 1980

Potential Costs Involved in Setting up a Studio

Setting up the studio will incur costs at each stage of the development. Marginally overestimating the initial costs may prove more beneficial than underestimating potential expenses, as it will allow some room for unforeseen costs that you had not anticipated. These can be broken down into three basic stages:

Setting up costs

This is when all the preliminary research takes place – travelling to view potential spaces, setting up meetings with the group or partners, appointments with agents, telephone calls, postage, internet research, stationary and the time spent communicating with your associates. Generally this takes the form of 'sweat equity', which refers to unpaid expenses and time invested in the research phase that is identified within

64

the overall budget as a real expense. It can be recorded as a credit or attributed to individuals later in lieu of rent. You should consider checking out your local Enterprise Board who may support this phase of research with a feasibility study grant.

www.enterpriseboards.ie
County and City Enterprise Boards.

Professional services

If you are able to secure a lease for the premises, there will be costs associated with that lease. You may require legal advice when negotiating the terms of the lease or to interpret particular details associated with legal contracts. If the space is bigger than 150m you may need the help of an architect to assist you with a design to get the best use out of the space, whilst ensuring designated fire safety exists from the building.

Construction and refurbishment costs

The space might require construction work to be undertaken. Even if you can do this yourself or you have friends who will help, you will still need to account for the material costs of building individual studio units within the space, as well as electrical and plumbing services. If equipment needs to be installed you will have to look at where this will be located, as this will occupy space that may or may not generate income for the studio.

Operating costs

Apart from the monthly or annual rent, there are additional costs associated with operating the space:

- Insurance; public liability, equipment, employees
- Building rtes
- Water rates
- Utilities – heating and lighting, electricity, gas
- Telephone, postage, internet / broadband
- Waste disposal
- Maintenance and repairs
- Cleaning
- Security – locks, keys, external lighting etc
- Provision for bad debts (5 – 7% approx. loss on unpaid rents)
- Management and administration
- Accountancy or book-keeping services
- Legal services
- Advertising, promotion and marketing.

Management and Administration

Once you have secured a space to develop as a studio, you now need to consider how you will manage the space. At its simplest, administration involves dealing with the day-to-day responsibilities of the space occupied by the studio group – controlling finances, creating a safe working environment, managing people, allocating space and making plans for the future in order to achieve the aims and ambitions of the studio. Managing the studio is about keeping it on track with your original vision for the space, defining a clear direction for what you want to achieve, whilst responding to various problems and opportunities along the way. Decisions need to be made and it's important to know how you will deal with these issues as they arise.

You may decide on a democratic model where everyone has an equal voice; or you may identify individuals within the group with particular skills and expertise to act on behalf of the other members. As a group it is important to define your goals and build trust and support for one another. The decision making process should be clear to everyone involved. For this, you need to agree the ground rules for making decisions – will it be made by a majority vote or perhaps by two thirds vote? For a larger group you may consider setting up a management team or steering committee with a clearly defined brief of their responsibilities.

Communication is an essential component to either of these choices. If delegating responsibility on behalf of the group to a number of individuals then you will need to arrange regular meetings where the delegates can report back to the group on issues arising so that everyone is included and one individual cannot act on behalf of the group without the agreement of those involved. Simply meeting as a group will not guarantee an outcome and it helps to set a few ground rules, decide what exactly the meeting is about, distribute an agenda, limit the agenda to four or five specific items and agree a timeframe of one or two hours maximum. Having a clear agenda will focus the group and help produce positive results.

Funding Applications

A lot of forward planning is required if you intend to make a funding application on behalf of the studio. You will need to plan for development in the following year, as well as provide a good record of how you have managed the studios resources in the current year. To do this you will need to prepare a mission statement identifying your aims and objectives, whilst recording all your expenditure and activities to produce a realistic analysis of estimated costs for future events or activities. This time consuming work is essential if you hope to secure any financial support for your studio. As a group you will have to decide how you will make these decisions and who will take responsibility for particular tasks.

Arts Council annual funding for studios is available by application, however applications from individuals or unincorporated bodies are not normally eligible. Equally, funding is normally only offered to organisations that operate on a not-for-profit basis. It is highly recommend that you contact the Arts Council in advance of your application for annual funding to seek advice.

You can find information on Arts Council funding on their website. www.artscouncil.ie

Administration

The administration of the studio focuses on implementing decisions made by your management team and dealing with the day-to-day demands of operating the space. For a small studio group or studios with limited resources both of these work areas will overlap and it's advisable to find a way to share the workload. Just leaving it up to the person who is good at these tasks is not necessarily the best solution, as there will be many demands on their time and the stability of the studio depends on it. General administrative tasks will include advertising vacant studios, showing people around, answering queries, communicating with the landlord and other tenants of the building, attend to repairs and maintenance, collecting rent and utility charges, dealing with the waste and rubbish, paying bills and keeping records of all the financial transactions and possibly organising group events and activities.

Studio Applications

It is important to have a system in place for processing studio requests and applications. Studios with a strict application procedure do so in order to ensure a level of quality, commitment and professional practice within the studio. A standard criterion for studio applications requires three basic items in order to ascertain the suitability of a potential studio member, these are:

- A letter of application, outlying the intended use of the studio
- A current CV, to outline the applicants professional history
- Documentation of their work, to indicate the quality of their practice.

Studio Contracts

Having studio contracts in place is of benefit to both the studio artist and the studio organisation. For a new member entering a studio complex, it clarifies the terms of agreement between the artist renting a studio and the organisation offering the space – for example the length of time they will have in the studio, the monthly or weekly rent, a record of any deposit paid and what is required to vacate the studio. For the organisation it provides an agreed set of terms under which it will offer a studio, how and when the rent is to be paid, what happens if arrears or money due exceeds the deposit held against the contract and specifies the minimum notice required if quitting the studio. Adequate notice allows time for the administration to find a replacement so that no loss of income will occur.

Although the term 'rent' is used in this instance for purposes of clarity, legally it is preferably to use the term 'fees' in studio contracts or licensee agreements. The term 'rent' can constitute tenants rights, which may create difficulties as the studio develops if new members are not involved with the core organisation.

Insurance

When dealing with members of the public or renting space to other artists, it is essential to protect the studio by purchasing Public Liability insurance on an annual basis. Technically the studio is your 'place of businesses. Accidents can happen and, should an incident occur in the studio, you are liable if an individual needs to sue for damages.

Public Liability insurance covers any awards or damages given to a member of the public because of an injury or damage to them or their property caused by you or your business. It also covers any related legal fees, costs and expenses, as well as costs for hospital expenses. Premiums will depend on the type of work you do and the level of exposure to hazardous chemicals or dangerous equipment. There are excellent offers available from a number of companies in Ireland that work specifically with the arts sector. These companies are familiar with the type of risk associated with studio groups. It's not as expensive as you may think, but essential should anything go wrong. Equally it is worth insuring your equipment, as often these resources are hard earned facilities and its best to protect your investments.

The personal safety of anyone entering the space and evidence of appropriate insurance policies are required by law. Emergency lighting and fire access routes should be clearly marked. Equally, corridor space and door exits need to be reasonably free of obstructions.

Practicalities

- Get a studio group bank account
- Draw up health and safety procedures
- Keep detailed records of all financial transactions
- Arrange for monthly Standing Orders to collect studio fees
- Pay rent promptly to your landlord
- Allocate a common area for artists to meet and talk
- Set up a large sink area for work purposes
- Introduce recycling facilities
- Keep the space in order
- Find space for shared tools; cleaning materials, mops, ladders, recycle bins,
- Enjoy the company of your fellow artists

By Jacinta Lynch
68

I'm Thinking of Getting a Studio

What is a Studio?

A studio can be defined as a room where an artist works. It can be as big as a warehouse or as small as a kitchen table. When a studio is highly structured it becomes an atelier or workshop; but this can also happen on the screen of a laptop computer, depending on what is being made. When assessing what kind of studio is required you first have to consider the practice or the type of work that might happen there. Big messy sculpture is difficult to successfully produce in a small apartment. Equally, it might seem futile for an artist to rent a warehouse space. Having said that, I know artists who do just this – sometimes there is an inverse size requirement to the size of the work made. The key point in understanding what studio is required is also figuring out what kind of space will be comfortable to work in. This is not always obvious. As your practice develops, your needs will change. Often, however, there is little choice available but it is worth considering some options before deciding what kind of studio to go for. There are exceptions to every rule and so bear with me while I attempt to cover the issues involved.

What Does the Studio Represent for Artists?

Ideally a studio is a place where art is made. Within the complexity of current art processes this can range from the place where the paint hits the canvas, blowtorch melts the metal or darkroom where prints are developed. It can also be the place where only the ideas happen, with the artwork realised elsewhere or fabricated by someone else. It can function as a small office set-up, where the administration and market dealings are confined to, i.e. not brought home. For most though, it is the place where work is produced, or at least somewhere to experiment with ideas and materials.

Very few artists are able to devote their energies full-time to their practice and often hold down a part-time job or two. Even artists who have reasonable sales need to do some part-time work elsewhere if only to provide a regular income, which is pretty impossible to depend on otherwise. As a result many view their studios as a kind of refuge from the outside world, and from distractions from others. The eureka moments can happen anywhere but the production or making tends to require a certain amount of space, both mental and physical. And even in these times of much hyped 'post-production' and socially engaged practice, I have been pleasantly surprised by the number of 'very' contemporary artists who still feel the need for a studio space. It is a busy world and finding a quiet place to think can be crucial.

What Can a Studio Comprise of?

There are a wide range of sizes and types of studios in operation. Unlike the industrial sector, artists rarely go it alone and rent a small industrial unit to work in. For many artists their income from art is irregular and not sizable enough to allow them to set up on their own. There are a few artists lucky enough to have the land and money to build their own studio but this is rare enough. Most studios are group or collective models where facilities and financial responsibilities can be shared. These often originate with a few friends, possibly after graduation from art college, who are all looking for a space to work in. There are several of these types of studios dotted around Dublin city and many have been quietly functioning away for many decades. With the ever changing property market however, many of these buildings are available to artists at low rents only while the owner/landlord waits for financing, development schemes or planning permission to use the building or site more lucratively. With Ireland being the most expensive property market in Europe however, this has become rarer. For this reason there are some great studio spaces outside of Dublin and several artists who have sold their Dublin homes and moved West have been able to build their own studios, which would be inconceivable in Dublin.

Urban regeneration can also have a significant effect on studios, in terms of both quality and quantity. When, for example, Temple Bar was being redeveloped as a 'cultural quarter' in the early 1990's, some of the existing studios were significantly renovated. However, other spaces were lost and some were nearly lost – artists using the spaces had to fight to retain rights to the building they were working in, as was the case with the studio building on Eustace Street. Tragically or typically, with many regeneration schemes, it is the artists who made a run-down area 'funky' and ripe for redevelopment who are often the first ones to be displaced to make way for apartments, restaurants and shops. Nevertheless, apart from that, landlords change significantly during times of regeneration, hopefully for the better. The speculative landowner, who let the place run down, thus making rents affordable to artists, does not generally provide essential basic services in their rental agreements. A property development or property management company, however, should be able to provide all the necessary services, albeit with a considerable increase in costs and red tape.

Publicly Funded Studios

The publicly funded studio complexes receive funding from the Arts Council or local authority, which contributes towards the running costs, thus lowering the rent for the artists. Public funding may have only been provided to cover capital costs however – for example, renovating an existing building for use as a studio. Additional income from public sources means that these types of studios are generally better equipped but not always necessarily cheaper to rent. The more established studios get more funding, thus helping sustain them further. Younger studios, while possibly more flexible to work with, run the risk of a short life span with inadequate, if any, public funding to sustain and encourage growth. The funding therefore determines how the studios operate and to what extent they can support their artists.

Artist-led Studios

Many artists opt for low cost, low red tape situations, as places are limited in the publicly funded or more established studios. Artist-led spaces may be easier to get into but they tend to be dictated by precarious financial circumstances. While this enables you to just move in and get going as quickly as possible, the downside is that you may be surrendering important rights in the process.

With any rental situation it is vital that a lease or rental agreement document exists. Despite the ease of word of mouth or casual arrangements, you need to know that your tenure is secure for a particular period of time and that the landlord is not going to 'skip' your studio once there is a better offer or if redevelopment opportunities arise. With most group or communal studios leases are the norm. It is the renewal of the lease that differs between places as some institutions have a limited time period for individual artists. This mainly happens with institutions that receive major Arts Council funding, as certain operational objectives have to be enacted, the main one being a three-year limit on each artist's studio, so as to allow others the opportunity to avail of the services offered. Again, this is not always the case as funding is different for every space (because they are all quite different) and at present it is not possible to expect compliance when there is not a level playing field. Funding and politics are closely connected in the studios sector as a result.

There are many different models in operation across the country. For the most part they all charge rent and even if they don't there can be hidden costs, like having to re-locate to a particular place to take up a studio award or residency opportunity. Equally, some private spaces can offer low cost rents but very little long-term security or even basic insurance. A typical scenario is when artists rent a building that is shortly to be redeveloped. The owner is happy to have someone occupy the space for security reasons rather than renting at full commercial value, which would be impossible anyway because of the state of disrepair. This can yield fantastic spaces that can range from fine Georgian houses to modern office spaces stuck in a real estate limbo. Again, the downside is that they are generally very short-term and often very cold in the winter.

Commercial Studios

Some group studios are commercial endeavours and therefore profit making businesses. There have been and continue to be some fairly unscrupulous studio managers/landlords who provide the minimum services and facilities, with no security, insurance or support, for the same going rate as other better managed places. With the booming property market in Ireland it is becoming more difficult to find low cost spaces and as a result there are opportunities for artists to be exploited, especially those who do not have much experience or knowledge of studio practices

The differences between well run spaces and others comes down to basic issues of security of lease, but also important are working environment concerns like insurance liability and health and safety. Unfortunately, however, the latter two elements are rarely thought of or dealt with in many studios as artists just want to get on with what they do. It is better than to look for a studio set-up that has decent management, at the very least keeping corridors clear, removing rubbish, checking fire extinguishers, providing doors to enclose spaces fully, etc. There are many health and safety regulations ignored in most studio complexes as the funds just do not exist to fit out these places properly. It would be wrong to be alarmist about these places being hazardous in any serious way but with the increasing regulation in this area it is something that needs to be reviewed seriously by the studio community as a whole.

What are the Different Types of Studios?

As I mentioned above, a studio can range from a large warehouse to a small desk. In fact there are some studio complexes like Cell in London that rent desk space rather than an enclosed room. This recent development acknowledges that not all artists need physical space to work in, just somewhere to focus and put the head down.

Communal studios offer many advantages to individual artists. Apart from the shared kitchen or canteen area, equipment and facilities can be bought by the group or simply shared. Examples of this include photographic darkrooms or printing presses. Some studios have developed into or were set up as medium specific spaces, like the Black Church Studios in Temple Bar, which mainly caters to print makers. Similarly, there are other complexes, which have mainly illustrators or animators, others that have metal fabricators and others that only contain painters. When like-minds congregate they obviously can share expertise and contacts also. Networking is too strong a word to use in this instance as it is generally quite casual and social rather than premeditated and aggressive. The beauty of a studio complex is also that you can shut the door and ignore all this if you need to.

Why Might You Want a Studio?

When deciding on getting a studio you need to consider firstly how much time you have to devote to the space or rather how much you need. As a break from the home environment it is sometimes great to remove the clutter of tools and supplies from the spare room or kitchen table. A studio can also be a great central storage area for artworks. Having said that Flax Studios in Belfast was burnt down a few years ago and some artists lost all their work. However, this also happened at MOMART in London, which is a professional authority on the handling of fine arts and antiquities!

Production requirements are different with every artist and sometimes commissions or projects arise that require a bigger space to work in. One temporary solution is facilities like the National Sculpture Factory in Cork, Leitrim or the Fire Station Artist's Studios in Dublin. These facilities offer temporary rental space within a large workshop area which is mainly used by artists working on large public sculpture projects, but also by artists working on individual large-scale projects that cannot fit in their regular studio space. The ongoing rental commitment to a studio complex can become quite a burden if income is not being regularly generated by the art or coming from elsewhere and so it is worth looking into such temporary spaces only if there is a specific project that needs working on.

What Kind of Studio Will Suit Your Practice?

Generally a reasonable sized room is what is on offer in most studios, anywhere from 10 square metres to 50 square metres. As discussed above, certain communal studios have specific facilities. These differ from place to place so some will have great computer equipment, some will have none at all, some will have a darkroom, printmaking equipment, power tools or cutting equipment, ventilation or extraction fans, kilns, etc. It all depends on the material and processes you are using so it is important to check beforehand to see what is available. Obviously there is a greater choice in a larger city but then there is also greater competition in getting a place in any complex.

Some studios also have gallery spaces. This can offer a chance to see and participate in a gallery programme but securing an exhibition space is more difficult and functions under a different range of curatorial parameters. For the most part it is rare that studio artists will automatically get to show in the studio gallery. Typically the gallery is separately managed and funded as is the case with Temple Bar Gallery or spaces in London like Chisenhale or Delfina. These three exhibition spaces started off as studio gallery spaces but over the years developed their programming or expanded their curatorial remit beyond their founders. A recent development in Dublin is the rental gallery with spaces like Monstertruck, La Catedral Back Loft or the Crow Gallery who all charge a rental fee for the use of their exhibition space. While this is the norm in countries like Australia, where the artist gets charged for the use of the gallery for an exhibition, it is not here. Non-private galleries receive public funding that requires them to give the exhibiting artist an honorarium but this is not the case with private spaces. Broadstone XL is a different and more diverse space which is modelled more as a research and development unit. The space hosts exhibitions but the large space is also used for theatrical rehearsals and other mixed uses.

One other type of studio is the residency. These are short-term awards in studio complexes that offer a space to work in a unique location like the Irish Museum of Modern Art, the Tyrone Guthrie Centre or the Fire Station Artist's Studios. These are competitive or open submission awards, and rental fees are generally well subsidised or even waived in some cases. The main expense can be in re-locating to somewhere else for a short period of time, from a few weeks to a few months, as bills will still have to be paid in your permanent place of residence. There are many residency opportunities outside of Ireland however these require additional travel and subsistence funding as well. Again, there are a few fantastic set ups like IASPIS in Stockholm but it is by invitation only.

When is the Right Time to Get a Studio?

When considering getting a studio you have to have the finances in place to pay the rental on an ongoing basis and have the time to utilise it appropriately. Some artists initially give themselves six months in a studio complex to see if they like it and if it is productive. As long as the studio has 24-hour 7-day access you can fit it in around your daily schedule. If you are a 9 to 5 working artist all the better, but this is rare. Having an upcoming exhibition is obviously a good incentive to get a studio but so is an objective of applying for one. Extracting yourself from the home environment can be the kick you need to formulate a solid body of work for a show or proposal. Again, it does take a certain kind of commitment to develop a routine where you are there, working or thinking, but being productive in some way.

By Alan Phelan

Undertaking Residencies

What is an Artist Residency?

The term 'artist residency' covers a broad spectrum of activity and opportunity for artists. There is no set format for a residency and it can take many forms and be based in a broad range of organisations. Residencies can last from as little as two weeks to as long as a year. Some are literally 'residential', offering artists both a living and working environment while others are less full-time, based around a studio space or simply a structure for engagement between the artist and host organisation. What all residencies have in common, however, is an invitation for an artist to engage with a particular environment and for them to undertake some element of their practice in this context. This invitation more often than not has a particular time frame placed upon it and a clear objective on behalf of the inviting organisation.

Who Offers Artist Residencies?

Many of the more renowned residency programmes are linked into galleries and museums, where a studio programme is run as part of a wider artistic programme. Examples of these are the Irish Museum of Modern Art, Kunstwerke and Smart Project Space in Amsterdam. These programmes usually offer a working and living space connected to the gallery and is generally offered by invitation or in partnership with a cultural agency. A few, such as IMMA, select from an open application process.

There are many organisations that are dedicated to providing artists' residencies. Internationally these include Kunstlerhaus Bethanien, Berlin, IASPIS in Stockholm, International Studio and Curatorial Programme, New York and Location One in New York, the latter being the current location for the Arts Council and Irish American Cultural Institute residency previously held at P.S.1 New York. In Ireland Cill Rialaig, the Tyrone Guthrie Centre and the Balilnglen Foundation are all organisations dedicated to artists' residencies. Many of the international residency opportunities are again offered by invitation, often in partnership with cultural organisations, and occasionally by selection from open applications. The creative potential of international exchange between artists is at the core of these organisations and participating artists are deliberately selected from a wide range of countries. Organisations such as Kunstlerhaus Bethanien, ISCP and IASPIS provide participants with a well-structured programme of talks, seminars and promotion through organised studio visits with curators and critics.

A number of organisations were established to provide access for artists to a very specific context or environment. There are many examples of residencies offering artists access to remote and dramatic landscapes, Cill Rialaig's position in a renovated famine village is one of the most notable examples of this. Similarly, Cove Park in Scotland invites artists to spend time in a nature reserve living in the log cabins originally used in the BBC's series 'Castaway'. For both organisations the remoteness and isolation available to artists provides the focus for the residency. Other organisations invite artists to engage with a conceptual rather than physical environment. For example Grizedale Arts' residencies invite artists to participate in Grizedale's particular curatorial focus of context specific projects staged in the public realm. They state clearly on their website that they are interested in artists 'who present new ways of thinking' and while the Lake District provides a unique environment for the residencies this is treated as one of many possible subjects for artists to address within Grizedale's conceptual framework rather than a focus.

Resource organisations such as the National Sculpture Factory in Cork and the DAS (Digital Art Studios) in Belfast offer medium-specific residencies which are focused around a particular approach to art making with technical support offered for artists to improve their skills.

Increasingly residencies happen outside the art world and are often used by the host organisation as an effective structure through which to introduce artists into their environment to provide an alternative view on their day-to-day operations. 'Non art world' residencies most usually take place in public institutions such as hospitals, schools, libraries and universities. This type of residency may include a working space but they are more likely to be structured around a series of organised workshops, defined projects or talks that ensure engagement between the artist and the constituency of the hosting organisation.

What Do Residencies Offer – Conceptually?

Most residencies have at their core a chance for artists expand their practice in some way. Increasingly organisations are moving away from a requirement for artists to complete a body of work for exhibition or presentation at the end of the residency, focusing instead on the research and development of work. IMMA's studio programme is an example of this and from the beginning a clear policy behind the programme has been the support of 'the working process rather than the finished product'.

Studio based residencies, whether in rural or urban environments, provide artists with time and space to concentrate on work and develop new ideas. More remote residencies combine this concentration on practice with the opportunity to be in an extreme environment that will directly inspire work.

Many of the larger international residency programmes are based in cities with vibrant and active art scenes. Consequently they combine an opportunity to spend time in the studio focusing on new work with a chance for artists to position themselves in a new art scene. A key element of these residencies is the networking opportunities, such as studio visits by critics and curators established by the host organisation which is emphasised, as central to the residency programme. The mix of artists included in international residency programmes also offers the opportunity for more informal, less structured networking opportunities between artists. Connections between artists established during residency programmes can be an extremely effective way for artists to place their work in an ongoing international dialogue.

Residency programmes offered by organisations such as Banff in Canada deliberately try to set up a creative environment where artists are encouraged to challenge and develop their thinking. Support is offered for artists to try new technologies and a multi-disciplinary environment encourages artists to approach their work from new positions. Similarly, residencies established in universities (for example those offered by the Ruskin Lab in Oxford and Kettle's Yard Gallery in Cambridge) allow artists access to specialist research that can directly influence their practice.

Grizedale Arts offers artists the opportunity to work closely with the Grizedale curators and support is given to make new work that may not be possible in other arts organisations. The Grizedale curators offer their expertise in fundraising as a resource for artists and help them secure funding for ambitious projects that may come out of research time spent in Grizedale. A deliberately flexible approach is taken in terms of time and some Grizedale residencies can last for several years as projects develop.

This artist-focused approach is also taken at the Tyrone Guthrie Centre where the artists dictate the terms of their residencies based on what is most beneficial to their practice at the time.

What Do Residencies Offer – Practically?

Most residencies would aim to offer artists enough support to allow them to take a break from their working commitments and concentrate fully on their work for a period of time. This support can range from the provision of a studio space to a more complete package of living space and a small stipend. Those programmes offering higher levels of support may ask the artist to guarantee a certain time commitment to the residency programme to ensure that the residency provides an effective break from exhibition and other working commitments.

Some organisations are in a position to provide access to a gallery space where artists can show their work. IMMA does not exhibit work made in the artists' studios as part of the main exhibition programme but it does provide access to the 'Process Room', a gallery in the main building where the studio artists can stage small project type exhibitions of work in progress. The possibility of an exhibition is usually very clearly stated in the terms of a residency programme and is rarely something that can be negotiated as an exception to the normal procedures.

Resource organisations such as the National Sculpture Factory, provide practical support for artists to develop their work technically and access to specialist facilities.

The amount of administrative support provided can vary depending on the organisation but at a minimum most would offer Internet access and limited use of the office facilities. Those organisations dedicated to artists residencies would provide the most structured and accessible administrative support.

Fees, other than stipends are unusual as most support provided is in kind rather than financial (studio living space, practical support). However residencies that place requirements upon artists other than developing their practice (for example residencies in non art world organisations) should normally provide a fee in the place of some of the other support outlined above.

What Might be Asked of You?

These can vary from a basic requirement of a certain time commitment on behalf of the artist to participation in public talks and workshops. Residencies that position artists in non art world organisations such as schools or hospitals would normally have a higher level of requirements placed upon the artists to ensure that their presence is noticed and of benefit to the constituency of the host organisation. Requirements placed upon artists should be clearly outlined by the host organisation at the start of the residency but if it is at all unclear it is important that the artist ensures there is a clear understanding of what may be expected before undertaking the residency. This is particularly important in a non art world organisation where unrealistic expectations can be placed upon the artist.

Possible Gains and Benefits

These can vary widely and really depend on the reason the artist has undertaken the residency in the first place. The most straightforward and perhaps the most important is a clear development in an artist's practice. This is not always as clear cut as a completed body of new work – many artists find the residency period goes very quickly and after a period of adjustment never quite find the time to make work but on return to their normal working environment are very inspired to make new work.

Wider gains and benefits can be an introduction to new international networks with other artists and curators. These connections are an invaluable means through which an artist can maintain an international profile for their work after returning to their home environment.

For many artists undertaking residencies in large cities, the chance to see a wide range of internationally significant art work at first hand is extremely beneficial and can have a direct impact on their practice.

Possible Drawbacks

Residencies can be very rigid and demand a total immersion in a new environment for a certain amount of time. For some artists this isolation from their normal working environment can be difficult for practical, personal and conceptual reasons. As artists' become more established in their careers other commitments (whether teaching, family or exhibition) make it harder and harder to dedicate a significant length of time to being in a new environment and residencies are no longer a useful means of support.

Expectations on behalf of both the artist and the host organisation can be too high and lead to disappointment. Residency programmes linked into galleries and museums can feel much removed from the day-to-day running of the organisation and artists hoping for access into the gallery's networks and level of operations can feel over-looked and secondary to the gallery's main focus. Similarly, artists' dropped into a non-art world environment such as a university can find it hard to establish the right connections to fully utilise the opportunities the residency offers. Without the right support an artist can be left on their own trying to make inroads into what can be a much closed environment.

On the other side host organisations can have an unrealistic perspective of the support that they are offering artists and what this can mean to an artist's practice. Sometimes the provision of a working space or access to a unique environment is not as beneficial as envisaged without additional conceptual and practical support such as engagement with the work, introduction to new networks or access to office facilities. Artists can be left feeling lonely and disconnected from basic day-to-day requirements such as Internet access. Non art world organisations inviting artists to interact with them can easily have an unrealistic expectation of the impact that an artist can have, and again a lack of understanding of the ways in which artists work can mean that the lack of necessary support reduces the ways in which the artist can effectively navigate the organisation and make their presence felt.

Summary

Undertaking residencies can be an extremely useful way for an artist to create time to focus on their practice, find inspiration for new work and connect with international networks. However, it is essential that the context of the residency is fully understood before embarking on what can be a major commitment – the environment, support offered, requirements and likely outcomes all need to be carefully considered. A residency should not be undertaken unless the artist is confident that the context being offered is one that will be of benefit to their practice both conceptually and practically, and ultimately be one that they enjoy and find rewarding.

By Sarah Glennie

The Financial Side

Budgeting and Financing

Introduction

This article will be of interest to self-employed artists. It aims to provide guidelines on how to manage and control the day-to-day finances associated with their work. What follows describes what a hypothetical artist, Karen, should do once she has finished at art college and has started exhibiting and selling her work. Karen should keep separate in her mind and in practice the finances associated with her personal life and the finances associated with her business of creating and selling art. In many cases, it is easy to determine whether an expense is 'personal' or 'business'. In other instances this is not straightforward, particularly where a payment – *e.g.* for electricity or travel – may be partly business and partly personal. A key aspect to identifying and quantifying this differentiation is to adopt a systematic approach to keeping records and to preparing and reviewing budgets.

Banks and Bank Accounts

Karen has had a bank account for several years. She should continue this account to deal with her personal finances. **However, she should open a separate account to keep track of her business transactions**. To avoid confusion, this account should have a slightly different name. For instance, 'Karen – Business Account'.

Banks are businesses established to make money for their owners / shareholders. They do this by borrowing and lending money and providing associated financial services. Banks **borrow** money (receive deposits) and pay the lenders (those from whom they borrow) a fee (interest). Banks also **lend** money and charge the borrowers a higher rate of interest. The difference in the two rates of interest reflects their profit.

Banks compete with each other, often quite aggressively, by offering different rates of interest and different types of service: just as supermarkets compete with each other by varying their prices. Like shops, in order to survive banks (money shops) need a continual supply of new customers. Karen should never feel intimidated or over-awed by the bank she deals with. She should regard it as she would any other shop. It is in the bank's best interests to help and facilitate Karen to the greatest possible extent. After all, it needs her business. If she is not satisfied with the service, she has the option to go elsewhere.

When setting up her business account, Karen should tell the bank staff about her work as an artist. She might give them a copy of her graduation certificate, exhibition catalogues and other information about what she is doing. As time goes by, she should keep the bank informed about how her business is progressing. This will help the bank to build up a profile of Karen. She will become more than just an account number. So, when Karen needs financial assistance – such as a loan to develop her business or a mortgage – the bank will be all the more ready to help her and, she hopes, offer preferential terms. Karen probably already has a good personal relationship with other providers of services she needs regularly – her doctor, hairdresser, shops etc. For precisely the same reasons she should seek to build up a personal relationship with her bank.

Having separate bank accounts will help Karen to keep the financial aspects of her life separate and distinct. **It is essential that Karen use her business bank account only for transactions that relate entirely or mainly to her business. Similarly, her personal bank account should be used only for transactions that relate entirely or mainly to her personal life**. Some financial transactions will relate to both parts of her life. Perhaps her studio is a room in her home. When she goes on holiday she takes the opportunity to visit studios and exhibitions in other countries. From time to time she uses her partner's car to deliver her works and pick up materials. It is usually best to use her business account to pay for items which relate to both parts of her life. Keeping clear records is key to maintaining clarity and avoiding confusion.

Financial Records

Inevitably, there will be a good deal of paper associated with financial transactions. The issue for Karen is either the volume of paper overwhelms her or she controls the paper!

Karen needs to keep all financial documentation systematically filed, for the following reasons:

To make sure that no business expense is overlooked.

At the end of each year, Karen will probably hand her financial records to an accountant, who will prepare an account to show how things are going, financially, and to prepare her tax return. The accountant will aim to maximize the level of Karen's business expenses and so keep her profit for tax purposes as low a figure as possible. It is the small expenses that many people, especially those self-employed, tend to overlook.

To keep the accountant's fees to a minimum.

Fees tend to reflect the time spent on a job. The more systematically Karen keeps the documentation, the less time the accountant will need to spend preparing her accounts.

To minimise the length of time she spends on accounts work.

Karen's business is creating art. She does not wish to spend more time than absolutely necessary on dealing with her finances. A systematic filing system reflects effective time management and will enable Karen to concentrate on the core part of her business.

A simple method of filing accounts records is to have five lever-arch files.

They should be labelled 'Bank', 'Credit Card', 'Payments', 'Receipts' and 'Tax' (*Note: the term 'receipt' has two meanings: it can refer to either a document or a sum of money. See section entitled 'Some Definitions'*).

The **BANK** file will hold bank statements and other paper-work from the bank. Karen should ask the bank to send her a statement at least once a month and she should ensure that she understands all the information on the statement – there is a surprising amount. If Karen is unsure about anything, she should ask the bank to explain. They will be glad to do so.

The **PAYMENTS** file will hold paper relating to all payments (other than credit card transactions) made in the course of Karen's business. She should make as many payments as possible by cheque or by electronic funds transfer from her account. Inevitably, some payments will be made by cash.

Every payment relating to goods or services purchased in connection with Karen's business as an artist, no matter for what, how made, or for how little, must be supported by a corresponding piece of paper.

This may be an invoice given by the supplier with the goods, a receipt, a checkout slip from a shop or simply a note scribbled by Karen, dated and saying what the payment was for. For instance, Karen may pick up stationery while she is in the local supermarket. She should keep the receipt, highlight the items purchased for business use and place it on the file. Karen should not forget to include bus, tram and train tickets, parking meter tickets, receipts for books and other art publications. If she travels in her partner's car on business, the date and kilometres travelled should be noted on the file. If the payment is for a domestic utility such as electricity, gas or telephone, Karen should place the associated bill on the file with all the others, leaving to her accountant the job of determining what proportion relates to business use. If the documentation relates to a cheque Karen has written, she should write the cheque number and date in the top right hand corner. Payments by laser card are debited to the bank account so should be documented the same way as payments by cheque. If cash is withdrawn, for whatever purpose, Karen should write a brief note saying for what purpose the cash was needed. If there is cash over, it should be re-lodged and entered on the Receipts side of the analysis book.

CREDIT CARD statements should be kept in a separate file. Karen should keep all the credit card purchase receipts and staple these to the back of the relevant statements.

The **RECEIPTS** file will hold paper relating to all money received (receipts) in the course of Karen's business. Most receipts probably will relate to works sold by Karen. She should give a sales invoice to each purchaser and place a copy on the Receipts file. When payment is received, the copy invoice should be 'marked off' with the date of the receipt. Karen may give occasional lectures or talks. Any documentation received with cheques in payment of fees should be filed.

The **TAX** file should hold all material received from the Revenue Commissioners / Inspector of Taxes. Also, if Karen has PAYE income from a part-time job, P45s, pay slips and P60s should be kept here.

From time to time, Karen will need financial advice on some aspect of her business, so she should engage an accountant. She should seek recommendations of suitable persons from her colleagues in the art world. Ideally, her accountant should have knowledge of and sympathy for the arts sector. As already mentioned, at the end of each year the accountant will prepare an account and file a tax return. This must be done, even if Karen has been granted artist's exemption from income tax. If the return is late, Karen will be liable for financial penalties.

Analysing Payments and Receipts

Note: The following is an outline of a simple receipts and payments analysis system, maintained manually. This outline is intended as a pointer to what needs to be done. It does not cover all aspects of the process. Those who wish to set up a system are strongly advised to seek advice from an accountant or accounting technician.

As her business develops, from time to time Karen will want to know how things are doing financially. Is she paying her way? Is she making a profit or a loss? She needs to make a profit to support herself financially. Many of her friends will be in employed positions and receive a regular pay cheque. Self-employed persons, such as Karen, earn a profit. In simplest terms, **a profit is total business expenses for any given period *minus* total business receipts** for the same period.

At the end of the year, the accountant will calculate Karen's profit. However, **during the year, Karen can obtain a fair idea of how her business is doing financially by analysing in a systematic way** the payments and receipts referred to previously. There are simple accounts software programs that will help her do this. Initially, however, Karen may find it more convenient to do so by hand. For this she will need a Receipts and Payments analysis book. Receipts (money in) are recorded on the left-hand page, payments (money out) for the same period on the right-hand page. Each page has the following columns:

Date of Transaction: When the money is received or payment is made.

Details: Names of those from whom money is received / to whom payments are made

Reference: A narrow column for a reference number. *e.g.* cheque number or bank statement reference

Total Column: The first cash column is generally used for the total value of the receipt or payment

Other Columns: The remaining cash columns are used to analyse the total amount under various headings appropriate to the business

A well-designed analysis book (also called a 'cash' book) will tend to have a greater number of columns on the right (for analysing payments) than on the left (for receipts). Karen should ensure that there are plenty of analysis columns provided for payments. An artist's Receipts and Payments analysis book might have the following financial columns.

At the bottom of each page, Karen should add up all the columns and check that the total of money columns... 2, 3, 4 ...equals the total of the first money column 1. She then should carry forward all the totals to the top of the next page. It is probably best for Karen to continue carrying forward the totals to succeeding pages until the end of her financial year (usually 31 December). This will enable her from time to time to compare her actual receipts and payments against her **budget** for the year (see section on budgets).

It is important to note that the transactions recorded in an analysis book such as that described above should relate to one bank account only. If there is a second bank account, then a second analysis book should be used. Other options for analysing payments and receipts are:

Use an EXCEL computer spreadsheet
Use accounting software.

When using manual analysis books, some categories of payment may have to share the same column. The use of spreadsheets and accounts software avoids this.

Working with Cash

Karen should aim as far as possible to make all payments by cheque, laser or credit card. It can be time consuming to have to deal with cash and record cash transactions properly. Inevitably, Karen will occasionally make minor cash purchases using her personal, non-business money. Whenever she does this, she should immediately refund herself with a business account cheque and place the documentation on the Payments file.

If her business involves selling items for cash, she will need to put in place additional procedures. These will ensure that details of cash received are fully recorded and that money is lodged regularly to her business account.

Karen should never use cash received from selling her work to buy items for her business. To do this can lead to confusion and distorts her financial records. It adds to the amount of work her accountant must do at the end of the year. If cash is needed, draw it from the bank account, not from cash receipts.

No matter what the nature of the business, the rule is 'Always lodge cash receipts to the bank *gross*, that is without using any of it for purchases'

Some Definitions:

- **Invoice:** A document giving a detailed description of goods or services bought or sold and their prices. Typically, an invoice will contain the names and addresses of the supplier and the customer, the tax or VAT number of the supplier, the date of the sale, a detailed description and price of the items sold and a total. Invoices are usually numbered.

A *purchase invoice* is a document received by a purchaser that provides evidence of goods or services bought. As previously stated, Karen's accounting records should contain a purchase invoice or other document supporting each payment / purchase by her.

A *sales invoice* is a document given by Karen to a person who buys her work.

Most shops and supermarkets give small automatically generated checkout slips when they sell goods. These often are, in effect, invoices as they usually contain all the essential data. Karen should place them on her Payments file. If she feels that a checkout slip is not adequate in the case of a purchase, she should request a more detailed document. For instance, checkout slips seldom record the name of the purchaser. It is important that Karen's business name appears on as many invoices as possible. Stores sometimes find requests for fully detailed invoices bothersome but they cannot reasonably refuse.

In everyday language, purchase invoices are often referred to as '*bills*'. Accountants prefer the more precise term, *invoice.*

– Receipt (1): A document stating how much cash has been received from a named person and the date it was received. When payment is made by cheque a receipt is not necessary, as the cheque is evidence of payment.

- Receipt (2): This term is also used by accountants to refer to money received in the course of business.

- Statement (of account): A summary list of invoices, taken from a supplier's accounting records. Usually statements contain only the date and total amount of each invoice. A statement is not adequate evidence of a purchase. If Karen receives a statement from a supplier but does not have the invoices listed on it, she should immediately ask for copies.

-Bank Statement: A document issued regularly by a bank detailing transactions on an account with its customer. Bank statements are highly important core accounting records and should be kept carefully in date order.

Budgets

So far we have:

- reviewed Karen's bank accounts and explained why she should develop a good relationship with her bank;
- emphasised the importance of having a system for filing the paperwork associated with her finances;
- described a simple system for recording and analysing receipts (money in) and payments (money out) during the year;

- looked at issues to be considered when working with cash;
- pointed to the necessity of engaging an accountant and making an annual tax return on time.

We now turn to the preparation of financial budgets.

A budget is a financial plan for the future. It could relate to next week, next month, the next six months. Karen will usually find that a budget for a year in advance will be appropriate.

Like any plan, a budget seldom ends up precisely as initially hoped. A budget may be revised at any time. Some items may have cost more than expected, some less. A project may not have taken place; some unforeseen activity may start six months into the year in question. It is essential to have a financial plan. A plan provides focus and direction and will help Karen to maintain control of finances and the business as a whole. It ensures that, as far as possible, no major financial occurrence is overlooked.

Until her business has been running for a year, it may be a little difficult to draw up a realistic budget. However, towards the end of the first year, Karen should be in good position to plan for the next.

When preparing a budget, the starting point is to list all the categories of payments and receipts that relate to the business. Then place an annualised figure against each category. (An 'annualised' amount is a figure that relates to a twelve month period). Karen will find that the analysis of receipts and payments for the current year (see section on analysing receipts and payments) will be a helpful guide. Most budget figures will be estimates. However, they will be based on Karen's personal experience of her business and her own future plans. Karen is the best placed person to prepare the budget. Budget figures should be realistic – that is, they should be a fair reflection of planned activities. It is unwise and foolish to insert figures merely because they serve to create the desired financial outcome.

The lines in a budget should be identical to those in the Receipts and Payments book A typical budget for an artist might be as follows:

Income (Receipts)	Expenditure (Payments)*
Work sold	Materials
Commission fees	Equipment
Lecture fees	Rent of studio*
Awards	Books and Magazines
Other income	Training courses attended
	Business Travel
	Car Expenses*

Income (Receipts)	Expenditure (Payments)*
	Light and Heat*
	Phone*
	Stationery
	Computer expenses
	Advertising
	Subscriptions to organisations
	Insurances*
	Accountant's fees
	Pension contribution
	Legal fees
Total Income for the year	**Total Expenditure for the year**

* These figures should be an estimate of the business proportion of any expenses that also relate to Karen's personal life.

(Note: Strictly speaking, there is a difference between the terms 'Receipts and Payments' and 'Income and Expenditure'. Karen's accountant will explain.)

For the business to be financially solvent, total estimated Expenditure must be greater than total estimated Income. This is because the budget refers only to Karen's business, not her personal life.

The difference between the two amounts is, broadly speaking, Profit. Karen needs to make a Profit to meet her personal, non-business expenses. A Profit is equivalent to the pay Karen would earn if she were in an employed position. Profit also is used to develop the business: *e.g.* to buy new equipment, extend a studio, mount a one-person exhibition.

The article on Costing and Pricing your Work provides detailed advice about how to ensure that Profit comes in at the right level.

Once Karen has established a budget, she can use it as a reference point during the year to confirm whether she is achieving the planned outcome. She does this by comparing actual expenditure to date, as shown by the analysis of payments and receipts (see relevant section) with the figures in the budget. If things are not going to plan, some change of plan may be necessary. It is usually easier to identify a solution to a financial problem if the difficulty is faced at an early stage. To defer remedial action is seldom a good idea. Financial control is a key to running a successful and profitable business.

Conclusion

In conclusion, we return to the opening paragraphs of this article. Karen should regard herself in two distinct roles.

Karen, the **individual**, who needs money to pay for her home, food, clothes, family, entertainment, holidays, and the like. She has to earn money to do this and has chosen to do so by running her own business.

Karen, the **business**, who needs to create a profit sufficient to support her personal life and also to provide cash with which to grow the business.

Karen should find that this article and Costing and Pricing Your Work will help her to understand the financial fundamentals of running her business. She now would be well advised to book time with an accountant or accounting technician who will give her more detailed advice about putting into practice the principles set out in these articles.

By David McConnel

Pensions for Artists

Introduction

Financial planning for the future is something that is not always at the forefront of our minds. The question that is more usual is how to finance life and art at the same time. For quite a few artists this means having PAYE and/or non-art related jobs to pay the bills, and dedicating whatever time is left to a practice. Even for artists who qualify for the Tax Exemption scheme, studies have shown that 81% of these earn under €10,000 per annum.

Outside of the exemption scheme, other sources of income from part-time and full-time employment cannot be claimed for and are therefore subject to standard levels of taxation. When this is combined with some thoughts towards future financial arrangements, it is a sobering thought that most artists are part of the more than one million Irish workers who have no pension arrangements. Many are reliant on the state pension to provide for them in retirement. At present there are five working people paying tax to every person claiming the state pension, however by 2050 it is expected that this will be just two working people to every one pensioner. The reason for this is that that our life expectancy is increasing but the number of babies being born each year is reducing. This is why artists need to take more a more proactive approach to their retirement planning.

PRSA

Personal Retirement Savings Accounts (PRSA) were introduced by the Government in 2003 as a pension product that is low-cost, flexible and fully portable. The government is aiming to increase pension coverage in Ireland.

Visual Artists Ireland has been in discussion with tax advisors on this matter. Taking into consideration, that artists may have a varied income, we wanted to explore how best to take advantage of the tax benefits on non-creative income, as well as put in place some financial planning for the future. As a result of these discussions, Ross Ingram of the Taxation Advice Bureau has provided some examples of why the PRSA is suitable for artists.

PRSA for Artists

Some examples why the PRSA is suitable for artists. . .

Flexible Plan

You decide how much you want to pay on a monthly, annually or once off lump sum basis. If you want to stop paying contributions for a time, you can simply halt them and restart at a time that suits you.

Tax-efficient

One of the great features of a pension is they are a very tax efficient way of saving for your retirement in different ways:

- Tax relief on your contributions
- Tax free growth on the value of your fund
- Tax-free cash at retirement

Subject to your age related limits, you will receive full PAYE and PRSI relief on the contributions that you make to a PRSA.

Portable Pension

A PRSA is individually owned so you can pay into it while you are self-employed, or bring it with you from job to job if your employment status changes.

Advice for Artists

Like most things financial, there are sets of conditions and also a range of variables that need to be taken into consideration when talking about one's own personal situation. For this reason, we have asked Ross to make himself available to members of Visual Artists Ireland to discuss planning for the future. To find out more Ross can be contacted on 01 6768633 or ross@tab.ie As with all of our support services, your feedback is very important. Therefore, please let us know how you get on (info@visualartists.ie) and we can then provide this back to Ross and The Taxation Advice Bureau so that they can improve their service to members.

Additional Information

Citizens Information
Information and advice on retirement savings accounts

The Pensions Board
www.pensionsboard.ie

Taxation Advice Bureau
independent financial and tax consultants
www.tab.ie

Tax and Self-Employment

While every effort is made to ensure the information in this article is accurate, Visual Artists Ireland and the author can accept no responsibility for loss or distress to any person acting or refraining from acting as a result of the material contained herein.

Self-Employment – The Advantages

Being self-employed means you are carrying on your own business rather than working for an employer. With this there are many advantages and disadvantages.

From a financial view point the primary advantage of being self-employed is that you are given greater flexibility in the expenses you can claim for tax purposes. Costs allowable under the PAYE system (where you are employed by another person or company) are very limited in comparison.

There are more tax planning opportunities available to the self-employed. For example, suppose you had intended carrying out repairs on your studio next year. You also plan to travel for 6 months and you know that you won't be earning much income. However, this year you're earning quite a lot and you know your income will be taxed at the higher tax rate. You could bring forward the planned renovation to the current year, as it will be tax deductible at the higher tax rate. Being able in part to control the timing of your expenses and income allows you to maximise the tax break.

As a self-employed artist you may qualify for the **Artists Tax Exemption**. The artists tax exemption is only available to the self-employed – so you must be registered as self-employed to avail of this tax break. You can be in employment part-time (earning PAYE income) while also being considered self-employed for your other work, which qualifies for the Artist Tax Exemption. Note that you only receive the Artists Tax Exemption on your self-employed income – that is your creative earnings. If you have a PAYE position that involves doing creative work that would otherwise qualify for artist exemption it will fail to do so on the grounds that it is a PAYE position. A PAYE salary is liable to income tax. Your self-employed creative work will qualify for the Artists Tax Exemption.

The Artists Tax Exemption is dealt with in more detail towards the end of this article.

Other advantages of working for yourself include:

- The flexibility it affords

- Greater control over your work/life balance

- Retaining responsibility for the direction of your career

- Increased potential for financial reward

- Added motivation

Self-Employment – The Challenges

One of the main challenges of being a self-employed artist is that your income can be sporadic, especially when starting out. You alone are responsible for the amount you can earn so motivation and a determination to succeed is key.

To be self-employed and run your art practice as a business you may need to broaden your range of business skills. You are responsible for every aspect of your work. For example, as self-employed individuals, artists have a duty under health and safety law to ensure that their working environment complies with health and safety legislation (you can read a text on Health and Safety for Artists on this website here). You will also need to learn about book-keeping and cash-flow management.

If you're not careful you may end up spending more time running your business than you are on doing the work that attracted you to self-employment in the first place.

Once you become self-employed you fall within the provisions of self-assessment for tax purposes. This means that you are personally responsible for ensuring that your tax affairs are kept up to date.

Keeping on top of your tax obligations requires discipline. Most self-assessed taxpayers pay their income tax in one lump sum each year, which requires effective budgeting so that the cost can be met on an annual basis.

So there are many additional stresses that come with working for yourself, another one being that as a self-employed individual you cannot receive holiday or sick pay from an employer.

Ultimately, being your own boss and making a successful business for yourself is hugely rewarding, and if you're willing to accept the additional risk and stress involved it is worth the extra effort.

Registering as Self-Employed

Once you become self-employed it will be necessary to register with Revenue for Income Tax. If one of the following applies;

1.   You are registered for PAYE Anytime

2.   You are registered for the Revenue Online Service (ROS)

3.   You are represented by a Tax Agent (accountant or tax advisor)

Then you must use the Revenue eRegistration Service to do so;

Online registration must be done via ROS, which you can register for here. Once you have ROS up and running you can set up your income tax registration and manage your tax affairs using the service.

If none of the above three scenarios apply to you then you can complete a paper form TR1, which is available on the Revenue website. Parts A & B need to be completed to register for Income Tax. This form is also used to register for VAT, PAYE (if you are an employer) and for RCT (Relevant Contracts Tax – It is used in the construction, forestry and meat processing industries and will not be relevant to most artists). Thus, much of the form will not be applicable when you first register for income tax.

It is advisable to register for income tax as soon as you begin trading, although the registration can be backdated. Normally you must file and pay your tax for each year by 31 October of the following year, but Revenue offer a "year's grace" for the first year of filing. For example, if you started trading in 2013 then you are not required to file your first tax return until 31 October 2015, at which point you must also file for the tax year 2014. So in this case you will need to register in time to file your first tax returns by 31 October 2015 (Note that the Revenue Commissioners currently offer an extension to the income tax deadline of approximately two weeks if the tax return is filed and paid online.

It is important to note that although the income tax registration can be backdated as is necessary, the Artist Tax Exemption application is not as flexible. The exemption must be applied for before the end of the current year if it is to apply from the 1st January of that year. So for example if you started trading in 2014 and needed the exemption in place for that year, then you will need to register for income tax as well as apply for Artist Tax Exemption by 31 December 2014.

Being Employed as well as Self-Employed

There are specific Tax/PRSI/USC implications if you are both in employment as well as being self-employed. Many individuals have a PAYE position (i.e. are in employment part-time – for example teaching or theatre work) in addition to their self-employed income. This can provide a good balance, which works well in practice. The PAYE employment provides a regular income as well as entitlements to social welfare benefits that might otherwise be foregone. You can also claim a PAYE tax credit for each year of employment, which is equal to 20% of your PAYE salary in the year, subject to a maximum credit of €1,650 (as per 2014 list of tax credits).

When earning income from both PAYE/employment and self-employment it is still necessary to register for income tax under the self-assessment system. The employer will deduct the necessary PAYE/PRSI/USC from the employment income and you will need to account for any additional tax due when filing your tax return.

The total income i.e. employment and self-employed income is declared to Revenue. The tax is calculated on the total income and the taxpayer receives a credit for the deductions that the employer has taken at source. Any taxable welfare payments received in the year should also be declared on your income tax return..

Being Unemployed as well as Self-Employed

As a self-employed taxpayer you may still be entitled to some form of unemployment benefit from the Department of Social Protection, and you do not need to de-register as self-employed in order to claim such benefits.

There are two separate unemployment benefits available, Jobseekers Benefit and Jobseekers Allowance.

Jobseekers Benefit is a set weekly payment, and is taxable when added to your other income in the year. Jobseekers Allowance is means tested and is non-taxable, regardless of how much other income you earn in the year.

In order to qualify for Jobseekers Benefit you must have worked as an employee (full time or part time) in the last 4 years, paying Class A PRSI on that income. A qualifying condition for the full rate is that you must be available for full time work.

Self-employed taxpayers pay Class S PRSI, which only covers you for certain social welfare payments. It does not **entitle** you for Jobseeker's Benefit. For this reason, and also for the fact that you may not be available for full time work as a self-employed individual, it is possible that you do not qualify for full Jobseekers Benefit.

If you do not qualify for Jobseekers Benefit, or if you only qualify for a reduced rate, you can ask to be assessed for Jobseekers Allowance, which may be more beneficial to your circumstances. Jobseekers Allowance also has the advantage that it is not taxable when added to any other income you might earn in the year.

In order to qualify for Jobseekers Allowance your means must be below a certain level to qualify. As well as assessing your existing household income, the Department of Social Protection will also ask for details on any assets, investments, savings...etc that you own.

The Citizen's Information Board has pooled all of its information for self-employed individuals on a microsite www.selfemployedsupports.ie, which is quite a useful resource.

The Department of Social Protection has also introduced a new service called Intreo, which will provide a single point of contact for all employment/unemployment and income supports. If you think you may be entitled to some form of unemployment benefit you should contact your local Intreo office.

Books and Records

Once you become self-employed it is necessary to maintain proper books and records to enable you to make your returns to Revenue. This is a requirement according to Revenue legislation, and becomes important if your business and tax affairs are ever selected for a Revenue audit.

Recording Income & Expenses

When invoicing clients the following information should be included:

- your name and address
- name and address of the customer
- date of issue of the invoice
- date of supply of the goods or services
- full description of the goods or services
- the quantity or volume of the goods supplied
- cost of the goods or services
- sequential invoice number

As well as keeping copies of all invoices issued and received you will need to record the details of all your sales and purchases. Details of how to record your financial information can be found in the 'Analysing Payments & Receipts' section of the article on 'Budgeting and Financing' by David McConnell.

Allowable Expenses

You can claim for any business expense that you have incurred in order to earn your profits. These expenses are normally referred to as revenue expenditure. Revenue expenditure can be seen as the day to day running costs of your business, and may include such items as:

- Art Materials
- Training Specific to your trade
- Telephone/internet
- Office/computer supplies
- Rent of business/studio space
- Professional/legal/accounting fees
- Agent commission
- Research – books, journals, subscriptions etc
- Visits to museums/galleries
- Postage/couriers
- Motor expenses
- Travel & subsistence

Disallowed Expenses

Any expense, not wholly and exclusively incurred for the purposes of your profession is not allowed. This would include any private or domestic expenditure. For example food & clothing (except protective clothing) cannot be claimed. Also, business entertainment expenditure – i.e. provision of accommodation, food, drink or any other form of hospitality to clients or buyers is specifically disallowed.

Mixed Expenses

Where expenditure relates to both business and private use, only that part which relates to your business will be allowed. Examples of such expenditure are rent, electricity, telephone charges etc., where a business is operated from home. These expenses will need to be apportioned to exclude the element of private use.

Revenue will accept estimates for business use. For example if someone works from home they would typically claim 1/3 of their light and heat bills as business expenditure.

Motor Expenses

You can claim a deduction for the running expenses of a motor vehicle used for business purposes. This includes a suitable portion of insurance, motor tax, NCT and general maintenance, as well as petrol and diesel. However if you have a regular place of work then journeys between here and home are normally treated as private and not business.

Capital Expenditure

Expenditure is regarded as 'capital' if it has been spent on acquiring or altering assets which are of lasting use in your business, for example, the purchase of a computer or other equipment. You cannot deduct the cost of this type of expenditure in arriving at your taxable profit. You can, however, claim capital allowances on expenditure incurred on items such as office equipment and business vehicles.

Capital Allowances are calculated at a rate of 12.5% (per year) of the net cost. The allowance is granted for 8 years until the full cost of the asset has been claimed. For example, if you purchase a computer for €1,600 in 2014 you can claim €200 (12.5% of 1600) of the cost as a tax-deductible expense each year from 2014 to 2021 inclusive. By claiming €200 each year for 8 years you are getting a deduction for the full €1,600 paid for the computer. Note that in the first year of purchase a full capital allowance is given regardless of when in the year the asset was purchased. As long as it was in use on the last day of your accounting year the full allowance is afforded at 12.5% for that year.

Keeping Books & Records

Under the self-assessment system you do not have to present your books and records to Revenue when filing your tax return. When you submit a return you must give details of your income and expenditure, but you do not provide any supporting documentation. However you must retain your books and records for 7 years as Revenue have the right to audit your return and request access to your accounting information at any time during this period. In the event of an audit Revenue will want to see sales invoices, purchase invoices/receipts bank statements and credit card statements.

Preparing Your Accounts

Once you have recorded your income and expenditure you will be in a position to prepare your accounts. This is simply a matter of transferring your totals from your sales and purchases books into an income and expenditure account. The result should look something like the example below. Once done, you are ready to input the figures onto your tax return.

MS. ARTIST

INCOME & EXPENDITURE ACCOUNT

YEAR ENDED 31st DECEMBER 2013

Income		€	€
	Non-PAYE Teaching	8,000	
	Art Sales	12,000	20,000
Expenditure			
	Materials	1,200	
	Research	300	
	Utilities	250	
	Commission	600	
	Telephone	1,200	
	Motor Expenses	600	
	Subsistence	800	4,950
Net Profit			**15,050**
Capital Allowance @ 12.5% (Computer Bought for €1,600)			200
Profit After Capital Allowances			**14,850**

Filing Your Return

The due date for filing your 2013 income tax return is 31 October 2014, with the availability of an approx. two week extension if return is filed and paid online via www.ros.ie. Further benefits of using ROS include quicker filing/processing times, more tailored and straightforward forms to complete, and access to your tax calculation before filing your return.

The tax return itself is filed on a 'Form 11', the paper version of which is available on the Revenue website. Revenue also provide a useful guide to completing the form which is updated annually.

Calculating your tax – Rates & Allowances

There are 2 concepts to understand in calculating your income tax. These are "Tax Bands" and "Tax Credits".

Tax Bands

There are two income tax rates. The standard rate is 20% and the higher rate is 41%. In 2013 & 2014, for a single person the first €32,800 of income is taxable at the lower rate and the balance is taxable at the higher rate. The tax band represents the amount that is taxable at the lower rate. This is also known as your "cut-off point".

For married people tax bands and tax credits can be transferred between spouses so they are best utilised for tax purposes.

Tax Credits

Tax credits are offset against the income tax payable. There is a standard personal tax credit of €1,650 for 2013 & 2014. A married couple would have a joint personal tax credit of €3,300 (€1,650 x 2) that can be divided between the spouses in the most tax efficient manner. Tax bands and credits are best illustrated by way of an example.

Income Tax Calculation for 2013 (assuming single person & ignoring Universal Social Charge/PRSI)

Taxable Profits (from trade)	€40,000
32,800 @ 20%	6,560
7,200 @ 41%	2,952
Total Tax	9,512
Less Tax Credit	(1,650)
Net Tax	**7,862**

Universal Social Charge (USC)

The Universal Social Charge came into effect on 1st January 2011, and it replaces the old income levy and health levy. It is payable on gross income, after relief for most capital allowances, but before pension contributions. It is also payable on artist exempt profits, but is not charged on social welfare payments.

All individuals pay the USC if their income exceeds €10,036 per annum. The rates and thresholds for self-employed individuals are as follows:

- 2% – on income up to €10,036 per annum
- 4% – on income between €10,037 and €16,016 per annum
- 7% – on income between €16,016 and €100,000 per annum
- 10% – on income over €100,000 per annum

Exemptions to USC

Those earning less than €10,036 per year are exempt from the USC.

All social welfare payments are exempt from the USC.

Self-employed individuals aged over 70, and those under 70 who hold a full medical card, pay a top rate of the USC of 7%. If someone over 70 earns more than €10,036 per annum then they are charged 2% on the first €10,036 as normal, 4% on the next €89,964, and 7% on the remaining balance above €100,000.

Penalties & Interest

Failure to file an income tax return on time will lead to a tax-geared penalty. Late filing within 2 months leads to a 5% penalty and after 2 months the penalty is 10%. Revenue can also charge interest on late payments of tax at a rate of approx. 8% per annum.

Preliminary Tax

The 31 October deadline is also the due date for preliminary tax (extended for electronic filing). Preliminary tax is a payment of tax, on account, for the current year. PAYE workers have their income taxed as they earn it so there would be a huge cashflow advantage to self-employed people if they didn't have to pay tax on earnings until 10 months after their year end.

To redress this, Revenue attempt to tax a self-employed person's income in the year they earn it by way of preliminary tax. So preliminary tax for 2014 is due by 31 October 2014 and it is fully refundable to the extent that it covers the final tax liability for the year. If preliminary tax does not cover the final liability for 2014 then the balance is payable by 31 October 2015 (extended for ROS filing).

In order to avoid a potential charge to interest (approx. 8% per annum) on any underpayment, Revenue offer two main methods to calculate preliminary tax;

1. To pay preliminary tax at 100% of the prior year's liability

– This is the most common method, and guarantees that, even if you underpay in preliminary tax, you will be considered to have met your preliminary tax obligation, and avoid any potential charge to interest. Many taxpayers prefer this method for the certainty it provides.

2. To pay preliminary tax at 90% of the actual current year liability

– This method is normally used if the taxpayer is confident that their tax liability for the current year will be a lot less than the tax liability of the prior year (for which they are filing). Option 1 would amount to an overpayment of preliminary tax, and would likely be an amount that they could ill afford (if their tax liability is due to decrease, then this is probably due to the fact that they have earned less in the year, meaning they cannot afford to be paying tax at the previous year's rate).

– The problem with option 2 is that you need to make the preliminary tax decision by 31 October in the year. With potentially two months still left in the year it can be difficult to make an accurate estimate of what your tax liability might be for the year.

It may be best to explain this in more detail by way of an example. Let's take an individual who has been trading for a number of years and their income tax liabilities have been calculated as follows:

Tax Year	Tax Liability
2012	1,500
2013	5,500
2014	3,500

The 2012 income tax is due for payment on 31 October 2013. This is also the due date for preliminary tax for 2013. For 2013's preliminary tax we can pay either 100% of the 2012 liability (€1,500) or 90% of the 2013 liability (€4,950). 100% of the 2012 liability is less so that is the minimum amount we should pay. The total paid at 31 October 2013 would be €3,000, being €1,500 for the 2012 liability (assuming no preliminary tax had been paid already for that year) and €1,500 towards 2012.

The balance of the 2013 income tax then falls due on 31 October 2014, which is also the due date for 2014's preliminary tax. The balance owed for 2013 is €4,000, being €5,500 less the €1,500 paid in October 2013. The preliminary tax for 2014 again can be 100% of the 2013 liability (€5,500) or 90% of the 2014 liability (€3,150). As 90% of the 2011 liability is less this is the amount we might want to pay. The total payable on 31st October 2014 will therefore be €7,150.

In practice you will not know the exact 2014 liability at the time of filing in October 2014, so a conservative estimate should be made at that point. For example some people might aim to cover 95% of the estimated liability instead of 90%, just to be safe.

When the final liability for 2014 is filed in October 2015, Revenue will look at the payments retrospectively to see if either 90% of the 2014 liability, or 100% of the 2013 liability, was covered by preliminary tax. If neither figure was met then the taxpayer faces a potential interest charge at approx. 8% per annum on the full underpayment.

Notice of Assessment

Once you have filed your income tax return Revenue will issue you with a notice of assessment. This will reflect the figures you have submitted on your "Form 11" and show Revenue's calculation of your Income Tax and PRSI/USC for the year under review, along with any balance of tax due or refundable.

PRSI and Social Insurance Benefits

Pay Related Social Insurance (PRSI)

PRSI payments go into the Social Insurance Fund which helps pay for Social Welfare benefits and pensions.

'Reckonable income' for the purposes of PRSI is profit after capital allowances but before reliefs and deductions. The current rate of PRSI is 4%, which is charged on all reckonable income, including artist exempt income.

Using the same example as before, but this time including USC & PRSI

Income Tax Calculation for 2013 (single person)

Taxable Profits (from trade)	**€40,000**
32,800 @ 20%	6,560
7,200 @ 41%	2,952
Total Tax	9,512
Less Tax Credit	(1,650)
Net Tax	**7,862**
PRSI: 40,000 @ 4%	1,600
USC: 10,036 @ 2%	201
5,980 @ 4%	239
23,984 @ 7%	1,679
Total USC:	2,119

Total Tax, PRSI & USC: 11,581

Minimum PRSI Payment

Anyone with self-employed income in excess of €5,000 must pay at least the minimum PRSI of €253. If 4% of their reckonable income is greater than €253 then they will be liable for the larger amount. In summary the PRSI liabilities are as follows:

Taxable income	PRSI payable
Less than €5,000	Nil
€5,000 – 6,325	€253
> €,6325	4% of reckonable income

Social insurance benefits

There are a wide range of benefits that are available to people who have paid social insurance. Entitlement to these benefits is dependent on a number of conditions other than the social insurance requirements. The payments that are available include:

- Jobseeker's Benefit
- Illness Benefit
- Maternity Benefit
- Adoptive Benefit
- Health and Safety Benefit
- Invalidity Pension
- Widow's/Widowers Contributory Pension
- Guardian's Payment (Contributory)
- State Pension (Contributory)
- State Pension (Transition)
- Bereavement Grant
- Treatment Benefit
- Occupational Injuries Benefit
- Carer's Benefit

It should be noted that some social welfare benefits are taxable and some are not. The USC is not chargeable on any social welfare payments.

Voluntary Contributions

If your income is below €5,000 you will not have to pay PRSI, and if this is the case you might want to consider making voluntary contributions. These allow you to remain insured through times when you are not earning, and maintain entitlement to some social welfare benefits. Voluntary contributions cover for long-term benefits, such as State Pension, but do not cover short-term benefits such as those for illness, unemployment, maternity, occupational injuries and dental and optical treatment.

There are some restrictions on how and when you can make voluntary contributions. Below is an extract from the Welfare website that explains these in more detail;

To become a voluntary contributor you must:

• *have paid at least 364 weeks [7 years] PRSI in either employment or self-employment*

and

• *apply within 12 months of the end of the year during which you last paid compulsory insurance or you were last awarded a credited contribution*

and

• *agree to pay voluntary contributions from the start of the contribution week that follows the week in which you leave compulsory insurance.*

The amount of contributions required to become a voluntary contributor on or after 6 April 2014 are as follows:

• *you must have previously paid 468 weeks [9 years] PRSI if becoming a voluntary contributor on or after 6 April 2014*

• *you must have previously paid 520 weeks [10 years] PRSI if becoming a voluntary contributor on or after 6 April 2015.*

Artists Tax Exemption

The Artists Tax Exemption Scheme allows earnings made by artists from the sale of original and creative works to be exempt from income tax. It applies to visual artists, sculptors, composers of music, and writers.

The scheme is governed by Section 195 of the Taxes Consolidation Act, 1997. In order to qualify the Revenue Commissioners must make a determination that the works are – a) original; and b) generally recognised as having cultural or artistic merit.

The exemption granted applies only to income derived from the sale of these creative and original works. The Act specifically lists these works as: a book or other writing, a play, a musical composition, a painting or other like picture and a sculpture.

More info on the Artists Tax Exemption Scheme is available on the Revenue website.

Note that the article makes reference to the High Income Individuals Restriction, which came into effect in 2007. At the time this restricted how much income that artists could claim as tax free. The €250,000 restriction (referred to in article) remained in effect from 2007 – 2009, and in 2010 it was restricted further, to €125,000 and €80,000 under certain circumstances. From 2011 onwards the High Income Individuals Restriction does not apply to the Artist Tax Exemption.

Instead, from 1st January 2011, there is a separate annual cap on Artist Exemption of €40,000. Any artist exempt profits above this threshold are taxed as normal.

Payments to Artists that are Exempt from Income Tax

The following payments are exempt from tax from when they are made to an artist whose has received an Artists Exemption:

- • Arts Council bursaries
- • Cnuas payments made under the Aosdana Scheme
- • Artists' Resale Right Royalties
- • Payments from the sale of works that are considered eligible under the Artists Exemption scheme

How to Apply

To apply for Artists Exemption, you should submit a claim form here to the Revenue Commissioners, together with samples of your work and any supporting documentation that you consider appropriate.

You will need the following samples and supporting documents for the following categories:

- Books or other writing – 1 published copy of the book
- Plays – a copy of the play, together with a production contract
- Musical compositions – CDs or cassettes
- Paintings or other similar pictures- 8/10 photographs or slides, invoices and your CV, if available
- Sculptures – 8/10 photographs or slides, invoices and your CV, if available.

Income Tax Requirements

You must return your Artist Exempt profit figure on your Form 11 income tax return. Note that the only relief available on qualifying artist exempt profits is that of income tax (20% / 41% rate).

PRSI and USC are both payable on all income, including your artist exempt profits. So for artist exempt profits under €40,000 (but above €5,000) the rates of deductions would be as follows:

First €10,036   6% (2% USC + 4% PRSI)

Next €5,980   8%   (4% USC + 4% PRSI)

Next €23,984   11%   (7% USC + 4% PRSI)

These charges are collected as normal through your Form 11 income tax return (and should be included in your preliminary tax calculations).

An example of how a calculation of income tax, PRSI and USC might look in 2013 for an artist with exempt profits of €90,000 is laid out below:

Total Artist Profits	€90,000
Artist Exempt Profits Restricted	(€40,000)
Taxable Portion of Profits	€50,000
Taxed: 32,8000 @ 20%	6,560
17,200 @ 41%	7,052
Total Tax	13,612
Less Tax Credit	(1,650)
Net Tax	**11,962**
PRSI: 90,000 @ 4%	**3,600**
USC: 10,036 @ 2%	201
5,980 @ 4%	239
73,984 @ 7%	5,179
Total USC:	**5,619**
Total Tax, PRSI & USC	**21,181**

Apportioning Artist Exempt Income.

Where you have multiple income streams and not all of them qualify for Artist Exemption then you will need to apportion your profit on a pro-rata basis to get the taxable profit and artist exempt figure.

From the income and expenditure example in the "Preparing Your Accounts" section of this article the tax-exempt artist income was €12,000 and the taxable teaching income was €8,000. Assuming the artist income qualifies for tax exemption we need to apportion the total profit to find the taxable profit for the year. We do this by taking the final profit figure and dividing it by the total income. The result is then multiplied by the total taxable income (in this example the teaching income). This gives us the taxable profit for the year as follows:

$$\frac{\textbf{Profit}}{\textbf{Total Income}} \quad \text{x} \quad \textbf{Taxable Income} = \textbf{Taxable Profit}$$

$$\frac{€14,850}{€20,000} \quad \text{x } €8,000 = €5940$$

The tax-exempt portion of the profit is €8,910, calculated as follows:

$$\frac{\textbf{Profit}}{} \quad \text{x} \quad \textbf{Tax-exempt Income} =$$

Total Income	Tax-exempt Profit
€14,850	
€20,000	x €12,000 = €8,910

The taxable profit and the tax-exempt profit will equal
the total profit i.e. €5,940 + €8,910 = €14,850

Awards and Grants

There is no uniform treatment for all grants. Most grants & awards are
likely to be regarded as taxable income although there are exceptions.
Where there is any doubt it is advisable to seek confirmation from the grant
provider, the Revenue Commissioners or a tax advisor/ accountant.

Some general points to note are:

If you have the Artist's Tax Exemption then the Arts Councils Bursary
Awards and Aosdána Cnuas payments will be exempt from income tax.
Bursary Awards and Aosdána Cnuas payments are provided by the Arts
Council in order to allow an artist to 'buy time' rather than for spend on a
defined project. They represent a direct personal income to the artist and
they have been officially approved by the Revenue Commissioners as
being eligible for exemption from income tax.

Project grants (ie. where you are awarded a grant to make a particular
project happen rather than the grant being given simply for your own
personal benefit) are different and technically they are subject to tax. But
remember that only your profits are subject to tax. For the most part a
project grant will be offset against the cost of undertaking the project so no
profit will arise to be taxed upon. However, there may be occasions where
a grant of €1,000 has been awarded for a project but you only spend €700
on carrying out the project. You should be aware that there are tax
consequences of having made a 'profit' of €300. Similarly if you pay
yourself a fee out of the grant then that will be subject to tax too.

So if the income from the award exceeds the actual costs incurred the
balance will be taxable. If the expenses to which the grant related exceed
the income the additional cost (or "losses") can be claimed against other
income in the period.

To ensure compliance you should check the conditions of receiving the
grant or award with the awarding body and if in doubt you should take
advice from a specialist in this area.

Income arising from a scholarship held by a person receiving full-time
instruction is exempt from tax.

Regardless of whether a grant or award is tax exempt or not the artist is
required to record receipt of all awards, grants, scholarships and bursaries
in their tax returns.

Capital and Revenue Grants

Just as there is capital and revenue expenditure there are capital and revenue grants.

A revenue grant is one that is provided to fund revenue expenditure. For example a grant provided for the purpose of funding a research trip would be a Revenue grant. The income from a Revenue grant is allocated in full to the year it is received and the expenditure to which it relates is directly offset against it.

A capital grant is a grant that is provided for the purpose of capital expenditure e.g. a grant to fund the furnishing of a studio. As the capital expenditure must be claimed at a rate of 12.5% over 8 years as explained earlier in this article, the capital grant is also amortised over the same period.

So let's assume you have received a grant of €10,000 towards the fit-out of a studio. The total cost of the fit-out came to €16,000. Each year for 8 years you need to record grant income of €1,250 and claim capital allowances of €2,000. This effectively means you are getting a tax deduction of €750 over 8 years which comes to a total of €6,000 being the difference between the actual cost to you and the grant income.

The safest way to deal with grants and awards is to assume that they are taxable until it can be shown that they are not.

Do You Need An Accountant?

An accountant is not a requirement. Revenue will accept returns direct from all members of the public. The main factors you would probably need to consider are:

- How comfortable you are preparing you own returns
- The complexity of your return
- The potential liability if the return is wrong
- The cost of engaging an accountant
- The time being taken up by preparing your own returns
- Are there any other parties that require accountant's confirmations?
- General awareness of other business issues.

If you are not sure about your return, but would like to prepare it yourself I would recommend that you contact an accountant with a view to looking over the return once you have prepared it, especially if it is your first tax return. An accountant should be able to quote a reasonable fee for simply reviewing a tax return.

If all of your income qualifies for Artist Exemption then your liability for an incorrect return will probably be relatively small. If for example you don't claim all your expenses correctly and consequently overstate your profit by €2,000 your additional liability will be a maximum of €280 (14% – 10% top rate USC plus 4% PRSI). This is less than what some accountants might charge for completion of accounts and income tax return for one year.

If your income is not artist exempt and you overstate profit by €2,000 then you might be paying as much as €1,100 (55% – 41% top rate tax, 10% top rate USC plus 4% PRSI) more than you should.

For people in all businesses, including artists, bookkeeping and preparing tax returns isn't a value adding activity. The time spent doing these tasks is always better employed in the studio. The cost of an accountant should be weighed against the time consumed by doing the work yourself.

There are 3rd parties other than Revenue that may require you to have an accountant from time to time. The most obvious example is your bankers. When looking for loans or mortgages, banks will frequently require an accountant's certification of your income. Typically they look to certify 3 year's accounts for mortgages. However this can be often done on an ad-hoc basis.

Finally, an advantage of having an accountant is that they will be aware of other issues that might arise, and with the constant changes to tax laws and exemptions in particular it may be useful to have someone at hand who is up to speed on these issues.

By Gaby Smyth & Company

Tax and Self-Employment – Northern Ireland

While every effort is made to ensure the information in this article is accurate, Visual Artists Ireland and the author can accept no responsibility for loss or distress to any person acting or refraining from acting as a result of the material contained herein.

What Does it Mean to be Self-Employed

Self-employment means that you work for yourself or in partnership with others. Being self-employed enables you to choose the type of work you wish to undertake and the amount of time you wish to spend working on it. You have a greater flexibility and control of your career, and you are entitled to claim tax relief on certain expenses that you would not be able to claim as an employee.

However, there are disadvantages to being self-employed. You cannot be sure of a regular income, you do not receive holiday pay or other employee benefits and you have to run and manage your own business. You also have to carefully manage your cash flow, and if you take on employees you are legally responsible for collecting their tax when calculating their salary.

Being Employed as well as Self-Employed

Whether you are an employee or self-employed should be determined by the person you work for.

However, it is not unusual for an artist to be both an employee and self-employed. You can be a self-employed artist but also supplement your income as an employee – for example teaching or administration.

Employees have their tax and National Insurance deducted at source (by their employer). If you are self-employed you will be responsible for paying any additional tax and National Insurance due.

Anyone who is in receipt of self-employed income is obliged to complete a Self-Assessment tax return. The information on this tax return will enable HM Revenue & Customs to calculate your tax and National Insurance liability (although you have the option of calculating your own tax liability – see section below entitled Tax Obligations).

If you are both employed and self-employed you are required to complete a tax return. Your employer will have deducted tax from your salary but this information must still be included on your tax return.

Registering as Self-Employed

You must register with HM Revenue & Customs as self-employed within the first three months of trading. Failure to do so may result in a £100 penalty.

You can register in writing or by calling HM Revenue & Customs on 0845 915 4515.

Your registration will cover Tax and Class 2 National Insurance Contributions.

National Insurance (NIC)

*Class 2 NIC: As a self-employed artist you are obliged to pay Class 2 NIC, levied at a flat rate of £2.40 per week (2010/2011).

Paying Class 2 NIC entitles you to claim state benefits such as Maternity Allowance and Incapacity Benefit; and it also counts towards your basic state pension.

Class 2 NIC is payable either monthly or quarterly by direct debit or by quarterly bill.

If you believe that your business profits (income less business expenses) are going to be less than the Small Earning Exemption (SSE), currently £5,075 you can apply for an exemption from paying Class 2 NIC. Before you do this you should consider the effect that not paying National Insurance would have on your future benefits entitlement. If you retire after 2010 you will need to have paid National Insurance for 30 years up to your date of retirement to qualify for a full state pension. If you claim a Small Earning Exemption in any year, this year will not count towards the 30 years you need to claim a full pension.

* **Class 4 NIC:** Class 4 contributions are paid by the self-employed in addition to Class 2 but they do not count towards any additional benefits.

108

Class 4 NIC is paid to HM Revenue & Customs at the same time as a self employed individual's Income Tax liability.

Class 4 NIC is calculated on taxable business profits at the following rates:

2010/2011

Profits up to £5,715	**0%**
Profits from £5,715 to £43,875	**8%**
Profits over £43,875	**1%**

Business Records

When becoming self-employed you should try to separate your business finances from your personal finances. The best way to do this is to have a separate business bank account into which all your income can be lodged and all expenses paid.

Your basic records will normally include:

- A record of all your sales, with copies of any invoices you've issued. Your invoices should normally include the following information.
- a unique and sequential identifying number– time of supply
  – date of issue (if different from time of supply)
  – name and address of your business
  – customer's name and address
  – your VAT registration number (if VAT registered)
  – a description sufficient to identify the supply
  – the quantity of the goods or services, with a unit price
  – excluding VAT
  – the rate of VAT per item (if VAT registered)
  – the amount of VAT (if VAT registered)
  – the rate of any cash discount
- A record of all your business purchases and expenses
- Invoices for all your business purchases and expenses, unless they're for very small amount.
- Details of any amounts you personally pay into or take from the business
- Copies of business bank statements

HM Revenue & Customs will expect you to retain your records for at least six years as they have the right to request to view these at any time.

You will find additional advice on Budgeting and Financing on the Developmental Tools section of our site here.

Tax Obligations

Submitting your Tax Return

The tax year runs from 6 April to 5 April each year.

Once you have registered as self-employed HM Revenue & Customs will issue you with a Self-Assessment tax return every April.

Please note that particular care should be taken when considering the payment of taxes in the first year of trading.

This tax return must include details of your total income earned in the year to 5 April, and it is due for submission by the following 31 October. However, if you or your agent files the tax return online, there is an extension for filing to 31 January of the following year.

For example: If self employed, you should have received a tax return from HM Revenue & Customs during April 2011. You are required to provide details of the total income that you have earned in the year to 5 April 2011 on this Form. You have until 31 October 2011 to submit a manual version of this Form to HM Revenue & Customs, however, this deadline is extended to the following 31 January 2012 if you opt to file your return electronically online.

Payment of Tax

Self Assessment Tax and Class 4 NIC payments are normally payable as follows:

A first payment on account is due on the 31 January in the tax year to which the self assessment relates. This payment is due up front – i.e. prior to the end of the tax year.

A second payment on account is due on the 31 July following the end of the tax year.

Any balance of tax due is payable by the following 31 January.

The Self Assessment filing and payment obligations can be summarised as such:

31/01/11	05/04/11	31/07/11	31/10/11	31/01/12
I	I	I	I	I
First payment on account	End of tax year. Tax return issued by HMRC	Second payment on account	Manual tax return submitted	Online tax return submitted
				I
				Any balance of tax is due to be paid

Tax Rates & Personal Allowances:

The Current tax rates are as follows:

2010/2011

First £37,400 over personal allowances	20%
£37,400 to £150,000	40%
Over £150,000	50%

You can earn an amount up to your personal allowances which will be tax exempt. The amount of your personal allowances will depend on your personal circumstances. The current basic personal allowance is £6,475. For those earning in excess of £100,000, this personal allowance reduces by £1 for every £2 of income in excess of £100,000. Details of the current personal allowances available can be found atwww.hmrc.gov.uk/incometax/

Example: Taxable business Profits £36,000 in the tax year to 5 April 2011

Profits	36,000
Less personal allowance	6,475
Taxable	29,525
Tax due (@ 20%)	5,905

Averaging of Artists Profits

Artists who have fluctuating profits may have a large tax bill one year and a small tax bill the next. The March 2001 budget introduced a provision to allow artists to average their profits in successive tax years. This can help with the business cash flow, and potentially reduce the overall tax bill (Note – averaging will only lower your tax bill if your top rate of tax is different in each of the two years, or if you have not used all of your personal allowances in one year).

The profits to be averaged must be from the disposal of artistic works rather than the provision of services. Artistic works include paintings and sculptures but does not include works of craft, such as furniture.

Example: – If your taxable business profits for two years were £40,000 and £24,000

Assessable Profits	Without Averaging	With Averaging
Year 1	£40,000	£32,000
Year 2	£24,000	£32,000

(40,000 + 24,000 = 64,000)/2) = 32,000

Statutory Benefits

Class 2 National Insurance contributions count towards Incapacity Benefit, Bereavement Benefits, Retirement Pension and Maternity Allowance. If you do not pay any Class 2 (or if you are an employee, Class 1 NIC) during a tax year your entitlement to the above benefits may be affected. Currently, to obtain the full state retirement pension a man must have 44 years in which he has paid National Insurance; a woman must have 39 years. If you do not have a full contribution record you are normally given the option to buy extra years to protect your state pension entitlement.

Business Expenses

There is no extensive list of business expenses that can be set against profits.

Some examples of allowable business expenses would be:

- Materials used by your business to make goods to sell – example, canvas, paper, paint, print / sculpture materials etc
- Agent's fees/commission
- Goods purchased for resale (eg. if you are selling other artists work)
- Wages and staff costs
- Rental of your business premises / studio
- Electricity for heat and light
- Legitimate business trips
- Business telephone calls
- Some professional fees, eg. accountants fees for the preparation of accounts. (Note – professional fees are tax deductible or not depending upon the underlying reason for which they are incurred. Some professional fees may not be tax deductible, eg. fees in relation to the acquisition of property / studio etc.)
- Other professional fees e.g. engineers, builders, fabricators, foundries you may employ / appoint if undertaking a commission or in the creation of work
- Motor expenses (excluding personal use)
- Capital items such as furniture and vans or studio equipment such as cameras, video projectors etc. (A business can obtain full tax relief on capital expenditure up to £100,000. Above this amount, a writing down allowance of 25% will apply)

Examples of expenses that may not be set against profits:

- Costs that you incur for a non-business purpose, such as your own personal expenses
- Capital costs, such as buying a business premises
- Business entertaining
- Lunches or other food purchased for personal use. The only exception to this would be the reasonable costs of meals taken in conjunction with overnight

accommodation (made necessary by a legitimate business trip).

Grants, Awards and Bursaries

Tax treatment of awards depends on the individual circumstances of each participant. However, it should be noted that, in general, awards are likely to be regarded as taxable income. If appropriate your budget for a project supported by a grant should take the tax liability of the grant into account. For example, there may be occasions were a grant of £1,000 has been awarded for a project but you only spend £400 on carrying out the project. You should be aware that there are tax consequences of having made a 'profit' of £600. You should check the conditions of receiving the grant with the awarding body and if in doubt you should take advice from a specialist in this area.

An unsolicited prize awarded as a mark of honour, distinction or public esteem in recognition of outstanding achievement is not normally chargeable to tax.

There is an exception to these basic rules; in 1978 The Arts Council and the Inland Revenue agreed on the tax treatment of bursaries paid by the Arts Council. One of the items that was agreed upon was to exempt awards known as Buying Time Awards. These are made not to assist with a specific projects but to maintain the recipient to enable him / her to take time off to develop his / her personal talents.

Artists should note that regardless of whether a grant or award is tax exempt or not the the artist is required to record receipt of all awards, grants, scholarships and bursaries in their tax returns.

Late Tax Returns and Unpaid Tax

Under self-assessment HM Revenue & Customs can impose penalties, interest and surcharges on a taxpayer who does not submit a tax return or is late in paying their tax.

Late tax returns

You will incur a penalty of £100 if your return is submitted after 31 October (the following 31 January if submitted online). A further £100 penalty will be levied if the return is over six months late.

Unpaid tax

Interest is charged on all income tax and NIC paid late. In addition, if tax for the previous year (due on 31 January) is unpaid by 28 February a surcharge of 5% of the unpaid tax is imposed. If the tax is still unpaid by 31 July a further 5% surcharge will be imposed.

Tax and National Insurance Payable, an Example.

The calculation below shows the tax and national insurance payable for a self-employed artist with profits of £30,000 in the year to 5 April 2011.

Tax	Profits	30,000.00
	Less personal allowance	6,475.00
	Taxable	23,525.00
	Tax due (@ 20%)	**4,705.00**
Class 2 NIC	**£2.40 @ 52 weeks**	**124.80**
Class 4 NIC	Profits	30,000.00
	Lower annual limit	5,715.00
	Taxable	24,285.00
	NIC due (@ 8%)	**1,942.80**
	Total Profits before Tax and NIC	30,000.00
	Less Tax	(4,705.00)
	Less Class 2 NIC	(124.80)
	Less Class 4 NIC	(1,942.80)
	Net of all Tax and NIC	**23,227.40**

By Flannigan Edmonds Bannon

VAT and Artists

While every effort is made to ensure the information in this article is accurate, Visual Artists Ireland and the author can accept no responsibility for loss or distress to any person acting or refraining from acting as a result of the material contained herein.

Introduction to VAT

It should be noted from the outset that this text is a simple guide to VAT general rules and administration. Where large sums are involved it is in the interest of the artist to seek specialist advice especially in respect of larger commissions and particularly if that commission is in another EU country.

There is a huge amount of Revenue and EU legislation on VAT, which makes it a very complicated subject, where large amounts are involved the artist should always seek specialist advice.

Background to VAT

Value Added Tax is a European Tax, and every member state of the European Union must have a system of VAT which is compatible with European legislation.

VAT was introduced to Ireland on 1st November 1972

The primary Irish legislation is the VAT Act 1972. The VAT act is amended every year in the Finance Act.

The VAT Act lays down all the basic rules of the tax.

The secondary legislation is made up of VAT regulations and orders. The regulations are provided for in the primary act and are signed by the Revenue Commissioners. They have full statutory effect.

The European legislation governing VAT is contained in the 6th EC VAT Directive of 1977. This sets out the fundamental principles of VAT and is an attempt to harmonise the laws of EU member states relating to turnover taxes.

The Directive outlines to Member states the principle to be adopted and each state implements these principles into its own national legislation. There are a number of other directives, which also relate to VAT.

VAT Registration

Requirement to Register

In Ireland you are subject to VAT if you are self employed or work on a freelance basis and have sales in excess of the following thresholds: The threshold for registration is €37,500 for services and €75,000 for goods. If the income from your business activity exceeds these limits within any 12-month period it is necessary for you to register for VAT.

Artists can be deemed to be selling goods or services, it depends on what type of work you are doing. If you sell works – for example a painting – this is considered a sale of goods, and the €75,000 income threshold will apply.

You may also provide some 'services' which include restorations or admission fees – for example if you charge a fee to your exhibitions. Performance artists are generally providing services. Writers are also deemed to be providing a service.

The table below shows a list of selected art related activities deemed to be either goods or services. You will find more information in the Applicable VAT rates section below.

Goods	Services
Selling a painting or sculpture	Facilitating workshops or art classes *
Selling catalogues of your work	Giving a talk or presentation*
Sales of prints	Giving a performance
Undertaking a private commission***	Sales of video / new media artwork

115

**

Undertaking a public commission
***

* This activity is considered a service, but is generally VAT exempt and not applicable to the threshold.

** This activity is considered a service in the creative context. A video retailer is selling goods, but a person who is commissioned to make a video or a piece of media art is providing a service. A person who creates a piece of media artwork and regulates where it can be shown is providing a service. A person who makes their own videos and sells the videos independently is selling goods.

***These activities can be considered either goods or services. It depends on what is being commissioned. Where there is any doubt in your mind you should contact your local Revenue VAT district and seek clarification.

Option to Register

If your turnover is below these limits you can opt to register for VAT should you wish to do so. The advantage of being VAT registered is that you can reclaim VAT on your business costs, however this means that you also have to charge VAT on your income.

If your customers are VAT registered and entitled to reclaim VAT charged to them on the service provided then this option can be favourable. Where your customers are not able to reclaim the VAT it results in the service or goods being more expensive for your customer, and may have a negative impact on your sales.

How to register – TR1

If one of the following applies;

- You are registered for PAYE Anytime

- You are registered for the Revenue Online Service (ROS)

- You are represented by a Tax Agent (accountant or tax advisor)

Then you must use the Revenue eRegistration Service (details here) to apply for a VAT registration. This must be done via ROS, which you can register for here. Once you have ROS up and running you can set up your VAT registration and manage your tax affairs using the service.

If none of the above three scenarios apply to you then you can complete a paper form TR1 – in the case of individuals or partnerships, or a TR2 – in the case of companies. The TR1 is available from the Revenue website here. It is necessary to provide Revenue with bank account details to register, as they will only issue VAT refunds electronically.

When you can De-register

If you decide to stop being a practising artist for whatever reason you should deregister for VAT. This can be done easily via ROS, or by cancelling your registration by arrangement with the local inspector of taxes. Note that if you deregister Revenue assess the VAT that you have reclaimed on goods and services sold to you, and if this has not resulted in a work being produced and sold by yourself, they can ask for this money back.

Similarly, a person whose turnover has fallen below the appropriate turnover threshold may have the registration cancelled.

A person ceasing to trade should cease all taxes via ROS, or notify the inspector of taxes of this fact, so that the VAT registration number can be cancelled without delay. This is important to note, otherwise return forms and demands for estimated VAT liabilities will continue to be issued automatically.

Artist Exemption doesn't apply to VAT.

In cases where Artist Tax Exemption has been granted it is important to note that this applies to income tax only. The exemption does not extend to VAT.

Selling your work outside of Ireland

Some artists might sell their work outside of Ireland. If these sales are made to another EU country then you may be required to register for VAT in that EU country, regardless of whether you are VAT registered in Ireland or not.

Distance Sales

A sale is considered a "distance sale" if the goods are dispatched or transported from Ireland to a customer in another EU Member State, who is not registered for VAT. As art is quite often sold to individuals for private use then this would normally be considered a distance sale.

If you are registered for VAT in Ireland then you must charge Irish VAT on all distance sales as normal. However if your distance sales to a specific EU Member State reach a certain threshold then you must register and account for VAT in that Member State, as opposed to Irish VAT. A list of the relevant thresholds can be found here. For example, the threshold for UK VAT registration is £70,000 Stg. This means if you make more than £70,000 worth of distance sales to the UK in a twelve month period then you must register for and apply UK VAT to all UK distance sales.

Sales to VAT registered traders in another EU country

These are known as "Intra-Community Supplies". If you are registered for VAT in Ireland then sales of artwork made to VAT registered traders in another EU country can be "zero rated" if the following conditions are satisfied;

- the customer is registered for VAT in that other EU Member State
- the customer's VAT registration number (including country prefix) is obtained and retained in the supplier's records
- this number, together with the supplier's VAT registration number, is quoted on the sales invoice
- the goods are dispatched or transported to that other Member State.

Note that this also applies to goods/materials moving in the opposite direction. If you are VAT registered in Ireland then you should not get charged non Irish VAT on goods purchased from other EU countries. If you provide your supplier with your Irish VAT number this should be enough to zero rate the VAT.

Intra-Community supplies are dealt with in more detail later in the article, and Revenue offer some guidance.

Selling from within another EU country

If you sell your work from a location in another EU Member State (for example an art gallery) then there is a chance you will need to register for VAT in that country, regardless of whether or not you are registered for VAT in Ireland. For VAT purposes you are considered to be making taxable supplies in that country, and in most cases you must register for and charge VAT in that EU country.

Since 1st December 2012 if you sell _any amount_ of goods within the UK you must register for and charge UK VAT at 20% on all UK sales. This means if you are selling your artwork from a UK location, you must register for and account for UK VAT on all such sales.

This abolishment of registration thresholds is common throughout the EU. If you are making sales from within another EU country then it is recommended that specialist tax advice is sought.

Note that in some cases an artist might sell their work directly from Ireland to a gallery in another EU country. As ownership is transferred to the gallery the responsibility of VAT in that EU country lies with them, and not the artist. Normal Intra-Community or Distance Sales rules (1 & 2 above) will apply to the selling of work to the gallery, which might avoid the artist having to register for VAT in the EU country to which the sale is being made.

Sales made outside of the EU

Any sales made to countries outside of the EU, whether dispatched from Ireland or sold from within the non-EU country, is outside the scope of

VAT. This means that there is no need to charge VAT, Irish or other, on any sales made to or taking place outside of the EU.

The article from here deals mainly with Irish VAT. For artists who sell their work outside of Ireland and within the EU it is recommended that specialist tax advice is sought.

General Rules:

Charging VAT on Sales

Once you are VAT registered it is necessary to charge VAT on your sales. The rate of VAT charged depends on the goods or service you provide. The applicable VAT rates are 0%, 13.5%, 9% and 23%. These rates are occasionally changed by Finance Acts.

Most artists will have to charge VAT at 13.5% on sale their work. For admissions to cinemas, theatres, certain musical performances, museums and art gallery exhibitions the applicable rate of VAT has been reduced to 9% since 1st January 2011. More details on the applicable VAT rates are included below.

Claiming VAT on Expenses

The VAT that is charged on your income must be paid over to the Revenue Commissioners. From the VAT payable on your sales you may deduct the VAT charged on most goods and services that are used for the purposes of your taxable business. No deduction may be made for the VAT on goods and services used for any other purpose e.g. personal use. The purchases must be in "the course or furtherance of business".

Restricted expenses: A situation may arise where a portion of the purchases may be for the purposes of your taxable business and the remaining portion for your private use.

Example: Electricity, telephone charges & heating expenses where the business is carried on from your private residence. It can also arise that inputs may be used for both taxable and non-taxable activities. In such cases, only the amount of VAT that is appropriate to the taxable business is deductible. In practice this normally works by apportioning a percentage of the bills to your business.

If you use your car (if it is a diesel engined car) or have a van for business use you can claim back the VAT charged on your diesel bills but you must note that you cannot claim VAT on petrol even if you use a petrol engine car to transport your works.

Non-deductible expenses: You may not deduct VAT on any of the following, even when the goods and services in question are required or used for the purposes of your taxable business:-

• You can't reclaim VAT charged to you on restaurant or hotel bills or other personal services, for you – the taxable person -, your agents or

119

employees, except to the extent, if any, that such provision constitutes a supply of services in respect of which he or she is accountable for VAT.

• expenditure incurred by you on food or drink, or accommodation or other entertainment services, where such expenditure forms all or part of the cost of providing an advertising service in respect of which tax is due and payable by you.

• entertainment expenses incurred by you – the taxable person – , your agents or employees

• the acquisition (including hiring) of passenger motor vehicles otherwise than as stock-in-trade (that is, for resale) or for hire in a vehicle hire business or for use giving driving instruction in a driving school business

• the purchase of petrol otherwise than as stock-in-trade

As a general rule, if registered persons are not entitled to a credit on the purchase of goods for use in their business, they are not liable for VAT on the sale of such goods.

Self Supplies

A "Self Supply" occurs when a taxable person uses goods or materials for a personal i.e. non-business use. If VAT has been reclaimed on the original purchase of the goods then it must be repaid to Revenue.

Example: if you produce a work but decide that instead of selling it that you will hold onto it for yourself or even make a gift of it to someone then you have to pay back to the Revenue any VAT that you have reclaimed on materials and other costs associated with making that work.

Administration

The information given on invoices and credit notes normally establishes the VAT liability of the supplier of goods or services and the entitlement of the customer to a deduction, where applicable, for the VAT charged. It is therefore vital that these documents are properly drawn up and carefully retained.

Requirements of a VAT invoice

A taxable person who supplies taxable goods or services to another taxable person is obliged to issue a VAT invoice showing the following particulars:

- the name and address of the trader issuing the invoice
- the trader's VAT registration number
- the name and address of the customer
- the date of issue of the invoice
- the date of supply of the goods or services
- a full description of the goods or services
- the quantity or volume of the goods supplied
- the consideration exclusive of VAT expressed in euro

- the rate (including zero rate*) and amount of VAT at each rate.

*Zero Rated intra-Community Supplies (more on this below):

Where you sell your works to the UK or install works in the UK (including Northern Ireland) or any other EU country special rules apply. These rules say that you must, in addition to the above, show the VAT registration number of the customer in the other EU Member State.

Where payment in full or by installments for goods or services supplied to a VAT-registered person is made before the completion of the supply, the person receiving payment must issue an invoice in the proper form not later than the 15th day of the month following that during which each such payment was received.

Filing a VAT Return

VAT returns must be filed every 2 months in the first year of registration. After the first year you can opt for a quarterly, bi-annual or annual return subject to turnover limits.

The VAT return for Jan/Feb is due on the 19th March. For March/April on 19th May etc.

The form to be completed is a VAT 3.

If your annual vatable income is less than €1,250,000 you only have to return VAT on sales when you have received the payment. This is known as the "Cash Receipts Basis".

If you fail to make a VAT return on time Revenue can charge interest on the late payment of tax. The rate is 0.0219% per day (approx. 8% p.a.)

Penalties & Interest

Penalties can be charged for not keeping proper books and records, failing to register, filing false returns etc. The maximum fine is €126,970 and 5 years imprisonment. This is only in extreme cases; the standard penalty is €1,520 and can normally be mitigated.

Revenue Powers

Revenue have the authority to examine your books and records to make sure that you have paid the correct amount of VAT. If they find that you have made a mistake then the authorised Revenue official may remove and retain the relevant papers and records.

In the unlikely event that they believe that you have defrauded the Revenue they can also search for records if they believe they have not been produced in full. S/he may also search for goods, but may not remove them. Revenue powers are extensive in this area and they do not need a search warrant.

121

Keeping Records

A VAT-registered trader must keep full and true records of all business transactions that affect or may affect his or her liability to VAT. The records must be kept up to date and must be sufficiently detailed to enable a trader to accurately calculate any liability or repayment and also to enable the inspector of taxes to check the calculations, if necessary.

A taxable person must retain all books, records and documents relevant to the business, including invoices, credit and debit notes, receipts, accounts, cash register tally rolls, vouchers, VIES and intrastat returns, stamped copies of customs entries and other import documents and bank statements. These business records must be preserved for six years from the date of the latest transaction to which they refer

Persons who carry on business, even though they may not be taxable persons, must for VAT purposes keep all invoices issued to them in connection with the business and copies of customs entries in respect of goods imported

VIES & Intrastat Returns

VIES returns – When an Irish VAT-registered trader makes zero rated supplies of goods to a trader in another EU Member State, summary details of those supplies must be returned to Revenue on a quarterly or monthly basis. This return, known as the VIES return, is to enable the authorities in each EU Member State to ensure that intra-Community transactions are properly recorded and accounted for.

INTRASTAT returns -Traders engaged in intra-Community trade are also obliged to make a periodic INTRASTAT return, for statistical purposes, where the value of goods acquired by them from other Member States exceeds €191,000 per annum or the value of goods supplied by them to other EU Member States exceeds €635,000 per annum.

Industry Specific Issues – The Margin Scheme

Special VAT schemes operate in relation to the sale by dealers / commercial galleries, auctioneers of second-hand movable goods, works of art, collectors items and antiques. The principal feature of the scheme is that dealers, galleries and auctioneers effectively pay VAT only on their margin in certain circumstances. The Margin Scheme is explained in more detail below.

Important Note to Artists

The Margin Scheme for calculating VAT is an optional scheme so galleries / auctioneers etc can chose to use it or not. Before agreeing to sell your work through a gallery it is very important that you have a formal agreement in place with the gallery as to how the VAT will be calculated. You need to know in advance exactly what the gallery is going to do and ensure that you are happy to trade on those terms.

If you are VAT registered you are liable for 13.5% VAT. It is important therefore that you price your work plus 13.5%.

Example 1: Where the gallery operates the Margin Scheme and the artist is to get 50% of the sales price.

If the work sells for €2000 the artist needs to state that they agree to 50% of the gross sales price and should issue the gallery with a VAT invoice on receipt of their fee. The invoice should then be for a total of €1000 which includes 13.5% VAT.

Example 2: Where the Margin Scheme isn't in place, the gallery will deduct 23% first and then give the artist 50% of the remaining 77%.

If they do this then the artist should invoice the gallery for their cut / income + VAT of 13.5%. This effectively costs the artist an additional 9.5% in VAT as they have 23% deducted from their income and can only recover 13.5% from the gallery.

Example 3: Where the artist is not VAT registered

The big loss to artists is where the artist is not VAT registered and the gallery doesn't operate the Margin Scheme. The Gallery can charge the full 23% and then pay the artist the after VAT share. Here the artist can't recharge any of the VAT and has to suffer the 23% deduction.

The Margin Scheme: How it Works

The margin scheme provides that VAT is payable on the sale of margin scheme goods by reference to the difference between the sale price and the purchase price of the goods. This is illustrated as follows:

Dealer's sale price of goods   €500

Less dealer's purchase price   €300

Dealer's Margin   €200

The dealer's margin is a tax-inclusive amount. For supplies liable at the standard rate, at present 23%, the VAT payable is:

€200 X 23 / 121   **€38.01**

The margin for the purposes of this scheme is the difference between the sale price and purchase price of the goods. This margin should not be reduced by deducting the cost of repairs, accessories, overheads, etc.

Where the sale price is less than the purchase price, the margin is regarded as being nil and there is no VAT due on the sale. It should be noted that in such cases the dealer is not entitled to a refund of VAT in respect of the loss nor can it be offset against profits from other transactions.

The general rule is that the rate applicable to a margin scheme supply is the rate applicable to a normal supply. However, there are some exceptions to this rule and these are itemised in Appendix I of the Margin Scheme leaflet issued by revenue.

In the case of those goods the standard 23% rate applies when they are sold under the margin scheme, even though a different rate applies when they are sold under normal VAT rules.

Applicable VAT Rates – Exempt, 0%, 13.5%, 9%, 23%

Exempt from VAT:

- Providing Art Classes
- Theatrical performances where no food or drink is made available.
- Payments in respect of droit de suite / Artists' Resale Right
- Where an activity is exempt, VAT cannot be reclaimed on the purchases relating to that activity. Example: If an artist purchases art materials to use in creating an art work the VAT can be reclaimed, but if they use the materials for an art class the VAT cannot be reclaimed.

0% VAT - Intra-community Supplies

Where you sell your works to the UK or install works in the UK (including Northern Ireland) or any other EU country special rules apply. You can zero rate the supply of goods to a customer in another EU Member State if:

- the customer is registered for VAT in that other EU Member State
- the customer's VAT registration number (including country prefix) is obtained and retained in the supplier's records
- this number, together with the supplier's VAT registration number, is quoted on the sales invoice
- the goods are dispatched or transported to that other EU Member State.

If these four conditions are not met the supplier is liable for VAT at the appropriate Irish rate. If the supplier is not able to satisfy the inspector of taxes that particular consignments of goods have been sold and delivered to a VAT-registered person in another Member State, the supplier becomes liable for the payment of Irish VAT on the transaction. Where any of the above four conditions are not satisfied the seller should charge Irish VAT. If the conditions for zero-rating are subsequently established the customer is entitled to recover the VAT paid from the supplier. The supplier can then make an adjustment in his/her VAT return for the period.

Unlike exempt supplies VAT can be reclaimed on expenses relating to 0% supplies.

13.5% VAT – Reduced Rate

- Intra-community acquisitions of art (in certain circumstances)

124

- Importation of Art -Works of Art -Sculpture (with a limit of 10 for sculpture casts copies, but this can be exceeded if Revenue agrees)
- Limited Editions (30 copies) – This relates to photographic prints taken by, printed by or under the supervision of an artist. They must be signed and numbered.
- An original lithograph, engraving or print produced directly from lithographic stones, plates or other engraved surfaces which are entirely executed by hand. There is no limit on the number produced.
- Commissioned Video work

9% VAT – Second Reduced Rate

This new reduced rate was introduced on 1st July 2011 in an effort to provide a boost to the tourism industry. It was introduced as a temporary measure, due to expire 31st December 2013, but it has since been extended indefinitely. The 9% rate applies to certain goods and services previously liable at the 13.5% rate, including:

- restaurant and catering services
- hotel and holiday accommodation
- admissions to cinemas, theatres, certain musical performances, museums and art gallery exhibitions
- fairgrounds or amusement park services
- the use of sporting facilities
- hairdressing services
- printed matter such as brochures, maps, programmes, leaflets, catalogues and newspapers.

23% VAT – Standard Rate

- Acting as an agent
- Framing
- Hiring of works of art
- Non-commissioned video production
- Acting and commercial work.
- Any work which is created for a commercial purpose rather than an artistic one is liable at 23% e.g. where a picture is created for the purpose of using in an advertisement.

By Gaby Smyth & Company

Gaby Smyth & Company is a chartered accountancy practice located in Ballsbridge, Dublin, which specialises in the music, theatre, film and visual arts. The firm offers taxation, audit and management accounting services. Gaby Smyth has delivered courses in taxation and accounting for Dublin Business School, the Institute of Bankers, AIB Corporate and Treasury, and Goodbody Stockbrokers. In addition, the firm has run courses specialising in accounting and tax in the arts for Music Network,

Blackchurch Print Studio, Fire Station Artists Studios, Visual Artists Ireland and various county and city councils throughout the country.

VAT and Artists – Northern Ireland

While every effort is made to ensure the information in this article is accurate, Visual Artists Ireland and the author can accept no responsibility for loss or distress to any person acting or refraining from acting as a result of the material contained herein.

Introduction to VAT

It should be noted from the outset that this text is a simple guide to VAT general rules and administration. Where large sums are involved it is in the interest of the artist to seek specialist advice especially in respect of larger commissions and particularly if that commission is in another EU country.

VAT can be very complicated and where large amounts are involved the artist should definitely get specialist advice.

VAT is a sales tax levied throughout Europe.

The form and method of compliance is left to each individual EC country but EC law takes precedence if there are any inconsistencies with national law.

VAT was introduced in the UK on 1 April 1973.

VAT: Registration and Deregistration

You can register for VAT by completing and posting a Form VAT1 to HM Revenue & Customs. Alternatively, the Form VAT1 can now be completed and submitted online. This form (hard copy and online version) is available on the HM Revenue & Customs website in pdf format.

Registration for VAT is compulsory in certain situations, but is also available on a voluntary basis subject to specific criteria. The rules for both are summarised below.

Compulsory Registration

You are required to register for VAT if you are self employed or work on a freelance basis and receive turnover from taxable supplies in excess of the VAT registration threshold.

Taxable supplies would include transactions such as the sale of your artwork.

However, you may be in receipt of income from sources such as the facilitating of art classes. This income is exempt from VAT and is therefore not a taxable supply. See section below on VAT rates for further details.

126

The current VAT threshold is £75,000, so you are therefore required to register for VAT if:

- the turnover from your taxable supplies (for example, sales of artwork) in the past 12 months or less has exceeded £75,000

  or

- the turnover from your taxable supplies in the next 30 days alone is expected to exceed £75,000.

Voluntary Registration

If the value of your taxable supplies is below the £75,000 threshold, you may still want to register for VAT on a voluntary basis.

Voluntary VAT registration may be attractive as you can reclaim the VAT that you have incurred on your business costs.

However, registration means that you will also have to charge VAT on your sales.

Registration may be favourable if your customers / buyers are VAT registered and entitled to reclaim the VAT that you have charged to them on a sale.

Registration may not be favourable where your customers are not entitled to reclaim the VAT that you have charged to them on the sale. Your product / artwork become more expensive to the customer, which may affect sales.

For example: If you are VAT registered and sell a piece of artwork for £100, you will be required to charge VAT on the sale to your customer. The rate of VAT is likely to be 20%, so the VAT inclusive price that you will charge your customer is £120.00.

If your customer is VAT registered, and the purchase was for a business purpose, they will be able to reclaim the £20.00 VAT that you charged to them from HM Revenue & Customs. The net cost of the artwork to this type of customer is therefore £100.

However, if your customer is not VAT registered (or the customer is VAT registered but the purchase is not for a business purpose), they will have no way of reclaiming the VAT charged to them by you. The net cost to this customer is therefore £120.00.

Cancellation of Registration

You will be no longer required to be registered for VAT if your turnover excluding VAT over the next twelve months will be £68,000 or less. You can, however, remain registered if you wish so long as you continue to trade.

If you deregister, HM Revenue & Customs can look at the VAT that you have reclaimed on goods and services sold to you and if this has not resulted in a sale of a work they can ask for this money back. However, this should not be an issue provided the VAT in question does not amount to more than £1,000.

You can apply to have your registration cancelled by completing a Form VAT7 (available on the HM Revenue & Customs website).

General Rules

Charging VAT on Sales: Once you are VAT registered it is necessary to charge VAT on your sales.

For example, if you are VAT registered and sell a piece of artwork for £100, you will be required to charge VAT on the sale to your customer. The rate of VAT in most cases is likely to be 20%, so the VAT inclusive price that you will charge your customer is £120.00.

There may be some instances were the VAT rate is not 20%. See section entitled VAT rates for more information.

Claiming VAT on Expenses: The VAT that you charge on your sales (output tax) must be paid over to HM Revenue & Customs.

From the VAT that you charge on your sales you may deduct the VAT that you have paid on any goods and services (art materials / equipment etc) that are used for the purposes of your taxable business (input tax).

No deduction may be made for the VAT on purchases used for any other purpose e.g. for personal use. The purchases must be in the course of business.

*****Restricted expenses:** A situation may arise where a portion of your purchases may be for the purposes of your taxable business and the remaining portion for your private use – for example electricity, telephone charges and heating expenses if your business / studio is carried on from your private residence.

It can also arise that inputs may be used for both taxable and non-taxable activities.

In such cases, only the amount of VAT that is appropriate to the taxable business is deductible. In practice this normally works by apportioning a percentage of the bills to your business.

For example: Consider the situation where a VAT registered artist purchases materials costing £100 plus VAT of £20.00. If the artist is to use half of the materials on producing artwork that is to be sold, and the other half on producing artwork that is to be kept or used for some other purpose, only £10.00 of the VAT paid on the purchase of the materials may be reclaimed from HM Revenue & Customs (being £20.00/2).

***** Non-deductible Expenses:** Broadly, you may not deduct VAT on any of the following, even when the goods and services in question are required or used for the purposes of your taxable business:

- business entertainment, for example restaurant or hotel bills
- the acquisition of motor cars (unless used in specified businesses such as taxi firms etc. There is some scope for reclaiming back a portion of VAT on vehicle leasing charges)
- fuel where scale charges are not accounted for under agreement with HM Revenue & Customs

As a general rule, if registered persons are not entitled to a credit on the purchase of goods for use in their business, they are not liable to charge VAT on the sale of such goods.

* **Business fuel bills:** If your business vehicle fuel bills include fuel for private use, an adjustment must be made in respect of the non-business proportion.

For privately owned cars, this adjustment is made by way of the fuel scale charge. More information concerning the fuel scale charge, and motor expenses in general, can be found on HM Revenue & Customs website.

Self Supplies

"Self Supply" occurs when you – a taxable person – use goods or materials for a personal i.e. non-business use.

If VAT has been reclaimed on the original purchase of the goods then it must be repaid to HM Revenue & Customs.

For example: If you produce a work but decide that instead of selling it that you will hold onto it for yourself or even make a gift of it to someone then you have to pay back to HM Revenue & Customs any VAT that you have reclaimed on materials and other costs associated with making that work.

Administration

If you are a VAT registered artist you must supply tax invoices in respect of taxable supplies, keep a VAT account showing your calculations of the VAT liability for each tax period, and make returns to HM Revenue & Customs showing the VAT payable or repayable.

Requirements of a VAT invoice

A taxable person who supplies taxable goods or services to another taxable person is obliged to issue a VAT invoice showing the following particulars:

- The invoice number
- The date of issue of the invoice
- Your name, address, and VAT registration number
- Your customers name and address
- A description of the goods and services supplied, and for each type of goods, the quantity, rate of VAT and VAT exclusive amount payable

- The total amount payable excluding VAT
- The rate of cash discount offered
- Total VAT chargeable

Where you sell your works to any other EU country special rules apply. These rules say that you must, in addition to the above, show the VAT registration number of the customer in the other EU Member State.

Filing a VAT Return

At regular intervals (usually quarterly) registered persons must submit a return to HM Revenue & Customs, showing the input tax and output tax for the period covered by the return. Any excess of output tax over input tax is payable to HM Revenue & Customs, whilst any excess of input tax over output tax in repayable by HM Revenue & Customs.

For example: In a VAT quarter, if you have charged your customers VAT of £100 (output tax), and incurred VAT on your own purchases of £75 (input tax), you will be due to pay the difference (£25) over to HM Revenue & Customs.

Alternatively, if you have charged your customers VAT of £75 (output tax), and incurred VAT on your own purchases of £100 (input tax), you will receive a VAT refund from HM Revenue & Customs of the difference (£25).

The return is made on a Form VAT100 and must be submitted within one month of the end of the tax period (usually a quarter) to which it relates. VAT returns can also now be submitted via the internet. See HM Revenue & Customs website for details.

Interest, penalties and surcharge

HM Revenue & Customs can impose a wide variety of penalties for non-compliance with the VAT regulations.

In extreme cases of non-compliance, HM Revenue & Customs have the right to take criminal proceedings which could lead to a fine or imprisonment, or both.

The most common forms of penalty imposed by HM Revenue & Customs are interest on the late payment of VAT, and a surcharge penalty for the late submission of VAT returns.

HM Revenue & Customs have extensive powers to make sure that you have paid the correct amount of VAT, including the right of entry, without a warrant, to premises used in conjunction with the carrying on of a business.

Keeping Records

A VAT-registered artist must keep full and true records of all business transactions that affect or may affect his or her liability to VAT. The records must be kept up to date and must be sufficiently detailed to enable you to accurately calculate any liability or repayment and also to enable HM Revenue & Customs to check the calculations, if necessary.

You must retain all books, records and documents relevant to the business for six years from the date of the latest transaction to which they refer

Persons who carry on business, even though they may not be VAT registered, must for VAT purposes keep all invoices issued to them in connection with the business and copies of customs entries in respect of goods imported.

EU Trading

All VAT registered artists who have supplied goods to another EU member state (for example, selling an artwork to someone in France), or acquired goods from another EU member state (for example, purchasing materials from a person in Germany) must complete the relevant EU sections of their VAT return.

Additionally, all VAT registered businesses that make supplies to other VAT registered businesses in the EU must provide details of the transactions on the EC Sales List. The EC Sales List is to be submitted to HM Revenue & Customs each quarter.

If the value of the EU sales exceeds a legally set threshold, currently £250,000, businesses must also provide more detailed information to HM Revenue & Customs in Supplementary Declarations.

The Margin Scheme

Special VAT schemes operate in relation to the sale by dealers/commercial galleries of second-hand movable goods, works of art, collector's items and antiques.

The principal feature of the scheme is that dealers, galleries and auctioneers effectively only pay VAT to HM Revenue & Customs on their profit margin.

The Margin Scheme for calculating VAT is an optional scheme, so galleries/auctioneers etc can chose to use it or not.

Before agreeing to sell your work through a gallery it is very important that you have a formal agreement in place with the gallery as to how the VAT will be calculated.

You need to know in advance exactly what the gallery is going to do and ensure that you are happy to trade on those terms.

VAT Rates – Exempt, 0%, 20%

VAT is chargeable at 20%, unless detailed as either exempt or zero rated below:

Exempt from VAT

Providing Art Classes-

Where an activity is exempt, VAT cannot be reclaimed on the purchases relating to that activity. Example: If an artist purchases art materials to use in creating an artwork the VAT can be reclaimed, but if they use the materials for an art class the VAT cannot be reclaimed.

0% VAT - Intra-community Supplies

Where you sell your works to any other EU country special rules apply. You can zero-rate the supply of goods to a customer in another EU Member State if:

- the customer is registered for VAT in that other EU Member State
- the customer's VAT registration number (including country prefix) is obtained and retained in the supplier's records
- this number, together with the supplier 's VAT registration number, is quoted on the sales invoice
- the goods are dispatched or transported to that other EU Member State.

If these four conditions are not met the supplier should charge VAT. If the supplier is not able to satisfy HM Revenue & Customs that particular consignments of goods have been sold and delivered to a VAT-registered person in another Member State, the supplier becomes liable for the payment of VAT on the transaction. If the conditions for zero-rating are subsequently established the customer is entitled to recover the VAT paid from the supplier. The supplier can then make an adjustment in his/her VAT return for the period.

Unlike exempt supplies VAT can be reclaimed on expenses relating to 0% supplies.

By Flannigan Edmonds Bannon

The Pricing and Sales Conundrum

The Science and Art of Pricing and Costing Your Work

Introduction

Costing and Pricing are two separate but inter-related processes. Many artists focus on finding the right "price" for their work but this can't be done in the absence of knowing how much it costs to make. This text is intended to help you establish how much it costs you to make your work (the science bit) with a view to assisting you price it (the art bit). Realistic costing will help you find the right market and more importantly help you work out whether you can make a living as an artist.

Costing

Costing is not complicated – yet many artists when asked can't say for sure how much they spend on making their work. Why does it appear so complicated? The answer to that lies in the fact that there are three separate costing processes that need to be undertaken.

- Costing your practice
- Costing your time
- Costing your project

Costing Your Practice

Each individual piece or project undertaken by an artist must be seen in the context of the artist's practice. For the purposes of this paper I am assuming that you are a self employed practitioner with overheads, a place to work and expenses that need to be paid regardless of whether you make a piece or not. For many artists these costs will include: rent (or mortgage); heating, lighting, broadband access, insurance, materials etc. These costs are your overheads and are general to the business of being an artist and will also be somewhat specific to the type of practice you run. The first stage in costing is to quantify as accurately as possible how much you are spending on maintaining a practice as an artist. Do you know how much you spent on electricity last year?

You must then add to your overheads the amount of money you spend on personal expenses e.g. salary, holidays, your personal rent or mortgage (or the portion of it that applies to your personal time as distinct from your work time), your social life etc.

Once you have undertaken this exercise you have a clear idea of how much it costs to practice as an artist in advance of making your work. These two exercises also give you essential information to establish the second costing exercise – your time.

Costing Your Time

There are no fixed rates for working as an artist. Some artists benchmark their working time against VEC rates of pay for teaching staff. Others establish a random figure in relation to the duration of the piece of work or the price they think they can charge for a finished piece. Neither of these ways is useful unless it relates to the actual cost of your time. For example, if I am a digital artist whose overheads are a laptop, broadband connection and electricity my expenses will be considerably less than those of an artist who needs a large workshop space in which to make three dimensional work. The cost of my time must have a relationship with the overheads required to make the work

The way to calculate the cost of your time is as follows:

- Itemise the annual overheads of your practice
- Itemise your personal expenses
- Itemise the number of *actual* days you are available to work

€150 per working day is the minimum fee I must earn in order to break even. Remember: This **break even figure** of €150 per day is the minimum I must earn in order to maintain my practice and lifestyle. Once I start making work (i.e. incurring expenditure) my expenses will increase and my income must also increase.

Use the following spreadsheet as a guide to assist you in quantifying your professional and personal expenditure and establishing your own break even figure.

Costing Your Project

So far we have calculated the costs of maintaining a practice and a personal life. These costs will be incurred before and as well as any costs involved in taking on a particular project. The third costing exercise is related to the specific project(s) you undertake on an annual basis. Each individual project you undertake should be budgeted separately. This gives you accurate information on the exact costs of individual types of work and will give you a financial description of the project. You will have to undertake a budgeting exercise for most commissioning processes and it is an important way of not getting unwelcome surprises mid way through a project.

A basic budget for a project should include the following items (this is a generic list and should be modified to suit the individual circumstances of every artist).

It is essential to cost in every single element of making a piece. If for example you have access to materials in kind then you should put this in as an expense and as an income figure. The rule of thumb is that any and every cost associated with the piece should be represented in your budget.

Your fee can be based on a range of circumstances.

For example, if you know that it will take you 25 days to complete a project and you have established that your daily break even figure is €150 then your fee could be €3750.

If you know that you will have covered your break even figure for the year from other work then you have the flexibility to charge a lower or higher fee.

If you know what the budget for the project is you can adjust your budgeting to ensure that you are paid the amount you need to break even while also paying for your costs.

If you have established that you are operating at a loss then you have to consider a number of questions including:

Do I increase the number of days I am available to work?

Do I reduce my overheads?

Do I take on revenue generating work in addition to the days I work at my practice in order to increase income?

Can I afford to practice as an artist?

It's essential to know how much it costs you to practice as an artist, operating in the dark is not an option.

Pricing Your Work

A basic cost based approach to pricing is one way to go.

- You have established your practice costs
- You have established your breakeven point
- You have established your project costs

Why not add them all together, add a contingency figure of 10%, a profit margin of another 10%, add 100% for commission to a gallery or agent and voila! There's your price. However useful that formula is for making widgets, it doesn't take into account the very issues that make art unique and special. How do you measure quality? How do you measure value? How do you know what people will pay to collect your work? This is where the tricky issue of pricing really comes into play.

Unfortunately there really is no formula for working out how to price your work – that's why it's more of an art than a science. There are factors that you need to take into consideration though (apart from your break even figure) and they include:

- Originality
- Quality
- Uniqueness

- Costs incurred
- Your break even point
- Your reputation
- Your objective in making the work
- Whether you work in one offs or multiples

You also need to research your market and this will depend very much on your area of practice. It is important to maintain price integrity – i.e. a buyer should not purchase a piece and find out a month later that your prices have gone down or, they could have bought your work elsewhere at a cheaper price. Obviously your reputation as an artist is going to be a key factor in how much you can charge for your work. The gap between your break even figure and the price of your work depends on all of the factors outlined above and can only be tried and tested based on market factors.

Costing and Pricing Other Activities

You may also have a number of different areas of work e.g. teaching, running workshops, creating work in your studio for sale, working to commission etc…each of these activities may incur differing costs and may attract different prices. See Payment Guidelines for Visual Artists.

Relating each activity to the "market" in which you are operating is an important factor to bear in mind. If 10% of your available working time (e.g. 20 days on the basis of our previous exercise) is teaching which attracts a fixed rate of less than €150 per day then the remaining 180 days may need to attract a higher figure which will be reflected in the pricing of your work.

Another way of viewing this is – Can I afford to take on additional activities that offer a set rate below what I know I need to earn? Or must my additional work be paid at a higher rate than my daily break even figure? The fact that standard rates do not apply means that as an artist, you must be appraised of the costs of running your practice in order to make informed choices about the mix of paid work you undertake. Unfortunately there's no simple formula for this but once you get started doing an exercise like the above it does become easier.

Conclusion

By now I hope you will have recognised that you cannot price in the absence of knowing how much it costs to be in practice and make your work. The costing piece is relatively easy and can be practiced over time. The pricing piece is more difficult and can only be learned through trial and error aligned with a good degree of networking and market research. The major mistakes many artists make are under-pricing their time and work and these are generally related to not having undertaken a costing exercise. A costing exercise is as important for an artist who wants to sell commercially as it is for an artist whose work is not commercial. Each is part of a "market" and each has a break even figure which must be met if the bills are to be paid. The costing exercise gives you the bottom line from which to work upwards. The price of your work may bear no relationship to how much it costs to make but it should never cost you money to make your work.

By Annette Clancy

Making Sales: Video and New Media Artworks

Introduction – Resisting Easy Commodification?

The sale of artworks represents an important income stream for any artist. Comparatively speaking, video is now firmly established within the market, and now has a familiar place within public and private collections. In a recent report commissioned by The Contemporary Art Society, Sheila McGregor has suggested that 25% of local authority and university collections have acquired video and film works, which is good news indeed. Whilst it is true that, these days, video is much more established as a 'saleable' art form, this is not entirely the case with larger-scale video installations, particularly where hardware forms part of the work.

With technology-reliant works, however, potential income through sales is often de-emphasised in favour of income through residencies or commissions. In part, this is due to a general perception that much new media work is not particularly 'saleable.' Add to this, the predominantly 'non-materialist' ethos that has attended the establishment of new media practices, and the lack of gallery representation forthcoming for new media artists.

For artists who work with new media, the 'sales' question remains problematic, from philosophical and practical points of view. There is residual resistance to the market, and to the Commodification of artworks that it precipitates. New media artists are, as Francis McKee has suggested, often 'heavily invested in an "anti-materialist/anti-object" sentiment.' Often there is no 'object', so what is there actually to sell?

Increasingly, new media artists are invited to undertake commissions to create specific new works, for private, public or corporate collectors. This is one variant on selling, and subject to a different emphasis insofar as a commissioner is agreeing to pay you for your skill and labour, and negotiations will be conducted to agree terms. Another variant, which may gain greater popularity into the future, is licensing, particularly in relation to new media works. A license is a document that sets the terms of use for a piece of work that is agreed between the author or rights holder (*the licensee*) and intended user (*the licensor*).

In a practical vein, for the new media artist engaging in sales or commissions, or licensing their work, onus is placed upon them to administrate and facilitate agreements from their studio. For those artists prepared to do so, little information or guidance for conceptualising and preparing video or new media works for sale, and for negotiating or presenting details of sale, exists.

What follows is a series of questions and steps to help you:

- Conceptualise your video or new media works as 'saleable'
- Negotiate with interested parties in relation to sales of your work, or new commissions for specific works
- Prepare details of sale for your work

Dialogue with the Purchaser / Commissioner

Museums, galleries and private collectors are now beginning to consider purchasing or commissioning new media works. Institutions such as the Hugh Lane Gallery and IMMA in Dublin have been commissioning new media artworks, and Aberdeen City Art Gallery in Scotland have in recent years acquired two works that run from hard drives. Whether a collector expresses a general interest in your work, or makes more specific enquiries about acquiring or commissioning a new video or new media work from you, it is extremely important to establish a dialogue, and to ascertain such facts as:

Are they interested in a specific work that would lead to a sale?

Might they be interested in commissioning a new work from you based on what they have seen elsewhere?

In what context has the interested party seen your work, or the specific work in which they are interested?

Have they seen the work installed, or have they seen it in slides or reproduction?

Was it at your studio, as part of an exhibition, or installed as a commission?

It is important to establish these facts, as they will influence the buyer/commissioner's expectations of the work, and what they actually think the work 'is'. Those facts should hopefully prompt you towards various considerations, namely:

I am not sure that I could 'sell' that particular work as I installed it for that show, for practical reasons, and also for reasons to do with my intentions for it.

What the purchaser/commissioner saw was not the final version of the work that I displayed.

I have installed it in three separate venues, and each time, I have shown it differently. On one occasion, I added a few more elements, which I took out the next time. I am not sure which version I prefer, or which I would consider the definitive version. It could change again?

What Does the Work Constitute: A Checklist

When faced with a potential sale or commission, a frequent question is; 'Just how definitive about what the work 'is' should I be? I don't necessarily work in a 'definitive' way.' Below is a checklist of aspects for you to consider:

- What is the history of the work?
- Was it made/produced for an exhibition or for a commission?
- Has it been shown more than once?
- Has it been 'live'? For how long?
- Did you modify it from show to show?

What are the key elements of the work?

- The projected image? The monitor image? Why?
- A particular kind of space?
- The software? Why?
- The hardware? Why?
- A particular URL, or a flow of data?
- Objects?
- A particular functionality?
- Interactivity? User manipulation?

Which physical parts are 'specific,' and which are more 'generic' or 'variable'?

Do I care what kind of monitor the work is shown on, or how the monitor is configured? Do I require that the work is shown on a certain type of monitor, or do I require that it be shown on a certain model?

Do I care about hardware, or playback equipment? For instance, do I care whether CRT or LCD projectors are used?

What about additional items, like unicol stands, keyboards, furniture, or speakers?

Other factors

Does the work purposefully have a limited life span?

Could someone else install it?

'Self-Contained' Versus 'Live' or 'Networked' Pieces

A growing conundrum for new media artists is '*If I make 'live' works, should I 'sell' them? Should I only sell self-contained works?*' There are obvious ways in which a 'self-contained' new media work is considered more saleable than one that requires a constant network connection, and because of which the content of the work would likely continuously evolve or update. In part, this is informed by our perception that goods for sale or 'commodities' be 'fixed,' 'defined', and 'knowable'. Likewise, it is often suggested that video artworks that simply comprise the 'projected image' are much more saleable than video works that are multiple channel works, or those that require specific monitors or playback equipment as a sculptural element of the work. There is also conceivably a difference between 'live' works that reside solely on the web and those that have been installed in galleries, or between those that rely on 'live' information pulled off the web and those that function with pre-selected or archived data. A key issue is life span. It is important to ask yourself: Does a limited life-span limit the work as 'saleable'?

If your work has a limited life span, then it can still be sold, so long as you make the purchaser fully aware of this as an eventuality. Then they will be making an informed choice.

You might be happy to develop a simulation of a 'network-dependent' work in the future. However, this is a specialised kind of commitment to make to an artwork, one that needs to be carefully weighed against several factors.

You could make the work available in a large edition.

It may be that you consider licensing the work rather than selling it.

A related matter: Is it important to check whether the content of your work raises copyright issues?

This is a key question that arises with some new media and video works, particularly those that rely or reside on the Internet. Copyright issues may have implications for the purchaser's ability to display or loan the work for instance. It is important to clarify these issues, and be able to correctly inform and re-assure your potential purchaser. Own It is a free Intellectual Property on-line resource centre. Although it is a service targeted at London-based artists, it offers services, fact sheets, workshops, and advice that might be helpful.

See also a text prepared by Linda Scales on Copyright and Intellectual Property

Editioning: Benefits and Considerations

In an article, entitled *Editions or Series: Artists Be Clear (2004)*, Art Law solicitor, Henry Lydiate, outlines prints, photographs and cast sculptures as the most common examples of works that are editioned. These are examples where there is an original source, be it a screen, plate, transparency that is used to create multiple originals.

The concept of editions transfers to video and digital media insofar as they are reproducible and duplicable. It is also a way of maximising the potential sale return from a single work, or mitigating the sale of a work with limited lifespan at a lower cost. If artists are selling work that is live and has a limited life span, they often sell work of that nature inexpensively and in large editions.

With video works, editioning is a well-established principle. Those that comprise a DVD or tape, and can be shown very flexibly, can be issued in a variety of editions, such as 3, 5, 7, or even 15. It is important to retain an 'artists proof' or 'artists master' in these cases. So that a work would exist as an edition of 2 + artist's master. Video installations, that are multiple channels, or which comprise hardware, computer programs etc. are often sold as unique, or possibly as a limited edition of 2 or 3.

For further information about issues related to the editioning of work, read Henry Lydiate, Editions or Series: Artists Be Clear, 2004 available on the Artquest website

A related matter: Is it permissible to develop 'saleable' counterparts or versions of works?

Some artists do 'transcribe' or 'iterate' works and these present plausible options with new media works in particular. Sometimes, but rarely, an artist will consider this option in order to achieve a work that takes a more saleable or collectable form. Such instances are based on dialogue and the desire of artist and curator for a particular work to have some form of representation in a particular collection. It is important for you to consider whether these constitute additional works, or the same work.

For example:

I have produced an off-line, gallery version of a network dependent piece. I am going to produce an editioned CD-Rom as well.

I have produced a reduced version of my video installation, which can be shown more flexibly.

I have produced a suite of photographs comprising still images from a video work.

I have produced a suite of digital prints, using some of the visual material that my project generated.

More recently, the issue of re-versioning works has extended towards software. If you have developed a piece of software for a commission, can you then use that same software to make other works, subsequent to the commissioned work?

Do I need to give the purchaser a later version of the work? Can I sell later versions of the work to other interested parties?

I was commissioned to make a new work for a buyer, and would like to use the software that I developed for that work to make others.

In a sense, some new media works have a 'generational' aspect built into them, as part of the medium's capacity – for instance with re-versioning a work comprising Software (i.e. I/O/D's *Webstalker*).

However, the issue of re-using software incurs all kinds of considerations that relate to terms of agreement, to the covering of production costs, and they require clear communication from the outset with the potential purchaser, or commissioner.

Delivery

So, how do you decide what to hand over?

Do I need to hand over hard drive and hardware? What if I only want to hand over the hard drive?

Even if the work requires specific monitors, do I need to supply them? Or can I expect the purchaser to acquire them?

This varies from artist to artist, from purchaser to purchaser, and from work to work. Some collections /collectors will request specific formats. It will of course have some bearing on the price that you charge, and it is generally something that artists get a feel for with experience.

Some will give one Sub-master, and expect the purchaser to make their own display copies. Other artists supply one Sub-master + one display copy. Some hand over software only, or hard drives with no back ups. You may prefer to supply some items of hardware, and not others.

In essence, however, it is most important to know what you will literally 'hand over' to the purchaser, and be able to inform and reassure them that this constitutes 'the work.'

What about certificates, or instructions?

Will I be expected to supply a certificate? Is this something I have to do?

What about installation instructions?

Or in the instance of video, how to make exhibition copies?

It is useful to make these a part or feature of the 'saleable' work rather than an adjunct. It is important to note whether completion of payment by the purchaser will be dependent on the supply of such items.

Detailing the Sale: A Template

So, what do you need to convey to the potential buyer, or commissioner? Below is a possible template for specifying a work for sale:

Title: (is this a working title?)

Images: (possibly still images, screen grabs, or of the work as installed)

Dimensions / physical description:

Exhibition history /installation history:

Statement about the work: (which includes description of what you consider the work to be, (i.e. interactive or performed process, or a narrative) and reference to any possible subsequent works that may construe it as part of a series.)

The work will consist of the following items: (list the components that you are supplying as the work – include no. of DVD's or tapes supplied, or hard drive etc. Also, include any certification that you supply with the work.)

The work will further require the following item/s: (any other items necessary to the work's display, but which you are not delivering as part of the sale. If you have preferences about playback equipment for instance, state them here.)

The installation of the work: (describe how the work is to be installed, and outline features of the work's display that directly contribute to its meaning)

Copyright issues?

Availability & price: (state whether the work is available as a unique work, or part of an edition, and prices. You might want to give a purchaser the option to chose between acquiring a unique version (for a higher price), and an edition (for a lower price), in which case, cite both.)

Details of Sale: A Sample

Still Night, 2005 Projected video installation
Dimensions variable
4 projected images looped and synced
No sound, Total running time: 35mins

Statement about work:

Still Night is a work that combines four screens installed facing on to each other, which create 'a room within a room' in the gallery. The footage is back projected. It consists of four screens of night falling, filmed in different contexts – city, suburb, countryside, and at sea. As night 'falls', the screen is filled with an abstract image of sky, illuminated with shifting and distinct colour shifts to the point where 'night' seems arbitrarily to have been achieved. As 'night' is achieved, the footage is then reversed. Rather than the onset of 'dawn,' the viewer witnesses the 'undoing' of night.

Exhibition History

Spacex Gallery, Exeter, 25-04-2005 to 25-06-2005

The work will consist of the following items:
4 x Digibeta Master tapes
4 x DVD display copies
4x Pioneer 7300 DVD players
Certificate of authenticity
Installation instructions

The work will additionally require the following:

1x Cambridge Media Sync starter unit

143

The installation of the work:

It is intended that the work will create an environment, into which the viewer walks. Therefore, the work must always be projected, and cannot be shown on plasma screens or monitors. The work is of variable dimensions, and the exhibited size of the projected images would be dependent on the size of the exhibition space/ screens available. The work will be supplied with detailed installation instructions from the artist.

Availability:

Still Night can be acquired as a unique work, or as part of an edition of 7. The artist will retain an artist's copy.

Price for unique work: €XXXXX
Price for editioned work: €XXXX

Remember to note VAT costs where applicable.

The cost of this work can be adjusted if the gallery does not require, or already has appropriate DVD players.

Put it in Writing

When closing a sale, it is very important that you formalize the transaction in writing, in either a Bill of Sale or a Contract of Sale. Sales agreements do not have to take written form to be legally binding. However, it is considered good practice to generate some form of sales documentation which records your negotiations. This kind of paperwork can fulfil a number of purposes:

It constitutes proof of sale, and provides a record for your accounts. In Ireland there is added impetus in respect of the Artists Tax Exemption, whereby artists' income from the sales of work is exempt from income tax. Bills or Contracts of Sale are essential support documentation for artists, when they submit exemption claims to the Revenue Commissioner.

It also provides both artist and buyer with a clear and concrete expression, in writing, of their respective rights, and their obligations to each other and to the artwork.

Many artists prefer to conduct or record negotiations in the form of a letter rather than a 'contract,' particularly where they are responsible for drafting or producing any paperwork. If you are generating just such a letter, it should outline what you consider to have been agreed between yourself and the other party, and its content should satisfy what you both take the terms and conditions of sale to be. Print up TWO copies, and sign both. The purchaser/commissioner should also sign both, and then you should each retain a copy.

Bill of Sale

In 1977, Henry Lydiate offered a template for a Bill of Sale, which still holds well today: 'A Bill of sale operates more like a receipt. It is an agreement specific to an artwork, or set of works (i.e. a suite of prints). It should note the date and place of sale, describe the work, refer to the parties, and specify the price and terms of payment.'

Lydiate gives the following list of items for inclusion in a Bill of Sale:

- Artists Name:
- Date:
- Place of Sale:
- Title of Work:
- Description of Work:
- Sold to: [name/ address] * Price:
- Terms of Payment:
- Note: copyright remains in the Artist.
- Signed: Buyer Artist

Contract of Sale

A Contract of Sale includes a more elaborated document, which features *conditions* of sale – these can include a range of issues from maintenance of the work to loaning, and any and all issues the artist or purchaser might want to clarify.

Alternatively, a license agreement may on some occasions be more appropriate or useful in relation to new media works or commissions, where the installation may be for a specified period of time (i.e. one year, two years, five years etc.) An example would be Susan Collins' *Tate in Space*, which Tate has licensed for five years.

Artists Resale Rights

Artists Resale Rights was introduced in Ireland in June 2006 (and February 2006 in the UK). Artists Resale Rights is a new Intellectual Property right for creators of artworks from within the EEA and it applies for the duration that an artwork is in copyright. It entitles the creators of artworks to claim a royalty in the event of re-sale within certain terms and conditions. In Ireland, the Irish Visual Artists Rights Organisation (IVARO) collects and distributes the royalties on behalf of its entitled members. In the UK the Design and Artists Copyright Society (DACS) collects the royalties.

By Tina Fiske

Protecting Yourself

Contracts

Introduction

If you were to stop to consider how often you entered into a contract, you might be surprised. Much everyday activity involves the making of contracts: purchases of all kinds, from concert tickets to mobile phones; borrowing a video from the video shop; opening a bank account; obtaining a TV licence; engaging a plumber.

In their professional lives, artists enter into many contracts: they sell their works; they are commissioned to produce works; they exhibit in galleries; they give permission to reproduce their works for various purposes. All of these activities involve entering into contracts. In fact, virtually all professional dealings of the artist will involve the question of contract. And when something goes wrong in those dealings, and the artist seeks advice, the first issue that must be addressed is; "Was there a valid contract?"

What is a Contract?

A contract is a legally enforceable agreement between two or more people. But when is an agreement legally enforceable? The basic rules of contract give us the essential elements of an enforceable contract. They are these:

- Offer
- Acceptance
- Consideration
- Intention to create legal relations
- Capacity to contract, and
- Terms that are legal and capable of performance

Offer: An offer is a clear and unambiguous statement of the terms on which one party will enter into a contract, if the other party accepts.

Example: An art dealer offers to buy an unfinished painting from an artist for €2,000, if he likes it when it is completed. This is not a valid offer. It is conditional and could not be enforced by the artist.

Acceptance: Acceptance is a final and unequivocal expression of agreement to the terms of the offer.

Example: An artist offers to sell a painting for €10,000. The potential buyer agrees the price and sends a letter with a cheque for €2,000, promising to pay the balance in four further monthly instalments of €2,000. This acceptance is not valid and does not create an enforceable agreement. It does not match the offer.

Consideration: The law does not recognise a bare promise. For a contract to be enforceable, there must be "consideration". This is the payment of money, or performance of an act, which is either to the benefit, or the detriment of one of the parties.

Example: A hotel chain seeks permission from an artist to reproduce one of the artist's works in an advertisement, and instead of payment, offers free accommodation for a week in one of its hotels. The free accommodation is the consideration.

Intention to Create Legal Relations: There is no contract unless the parties intend to be legally bound.

Example: An artist receives an email saying, "What is your best price for the work entitled XXXX?" The artist sends an email in reply saying " My best price for XXXX would be €25,000". A few days later, the artist receives an offer of €30,000 for the work from another party, and sells it. The first party sues, claiming that there was an agreement to sell the work for €25,000. Was there an intention to be legally bound? A court will look at the circumstances to try and establish the intention of the parties, but without further information it appears unlikely that there was an intention to be legally bound. The artist was simply stating the price at which he or she would sell, if selling. There was no firm agreement to sell.

Capacity to contract: In order for a contract to be valid, the parties must have the capacity to enter into a contract. Minors (under 18 years) and persons of unsound mind have a restricted capacity. A company is confined to acting within the boundaries of its constitution.

The terms must be legal and capable of performance: The law will not uphold an agreement to commit a crime, or other legal wrong.

Example: An agreement to steal the Caravaggio from the National Gallery for an international crime syndicate. You guessed. Not enforceable.

Must a Contract be in Writing? With some exceptions (e.g. a contract for the sale of land), contracts may be verbal. Artists' professional contracts can all be entered into verbally, provided the essential elements of a contract are present. However, there is a fundamental problem with all verbal agreements: it is often very difficult to say precisely what (if anything) was agreed. Without written evidence of the terms of a contract, legal action is usually fraught with uncertainty.

How Much Needs to be Written Down?

In every contractual situation, there should be good written evidence of the following: the names and addresses of the parties to the agreement; the date of the agreement; the subject matter of the agreement; the consideration for the transaction; and the terms of the agreement that are important to the parties and that they might later want to enforce.

Implied Terms

Whether or not there is a written agreement, a court may (and often must) try to interpret the intention of the parties, in order to give effect to a valid contract. The court will look at all the circumstances and enforce terms that it considers were implied in the dealings between the parties.

Example: A museum buys an important sculpture directly from the artist. The only written document consists of a letter confirming the price. Prior to payment, the artist arranges delivery of the work to the museum. When it arrives and is removed from the packing case, it is clear that owing to some incident en route, the work is seriously damaged. Who suffers this loss? Is it the gallery, or the artist?

If the artist were to sue for payment, it seems likely that unless there was some evidence available to suggest that the gallery was responsible for carriage, or for insurance of the work in transit, a court would find that it was an implied term of the agreement that the price would be paid on delivery of the work in good condition.

By statute, some terms are automatically implied into certain types of contract. For example, legislation relating to the sale of goods provides that goods must be fit for the purpose intended and be free from hidden defects.

When Things go Wrong?

The law recognises that sometimes things occur that are beyond the power of the parties to anticipate or control. For example:

Frustration: A contract may be discharged if, after its formation, events occur that make its performance impossible.

Example: An artist agrees to sell a work. The purchaser pays a deposit and arranges to collect the work and pay the balance the following week. However, in the intervening period, the work is destroyed by an accidental fire in the artist's studio.

Mistake: A court may set aside a contract that was entered into on the basis of a genuine mistake.

Example: An artist agrees a sale with a purchaser. There is a genuine misunderstanding however, as to which work was the subject of the agreement.

Breach of Contract: The principal way in which "things go wrong" is that there is a real or perceived breach of one or more of the terms of the contract by one of the parties. The law says that a breach of contract occurs when a party, without lawful excuse, fails or refuses to perform, or performs defectively, or incapacitates himself or herself from performing the contract.

A breach may entitle the injured party to claim damages, or specific performance of the contract. Specific performance is a court decree ordering a party to perform his or her duties under the contract. A breach

148

may also give the injured party the right to cancel the contract. An action must be taken within six years of the breach, or two years if the claim includes a claim for personal injury.

Example: An artist is commissioned to produce a sculpture by a Local Authority. After a formal contract has been signed and work on the piece has commenced, the Arts Officer of the Local Authority seeks to re-negotiate the terms, due to cutbacks in the Local Authority budget. The artist is entitled to insist that the original terms are observed. Failing that, he or she may sue for specific performance, or damages for breach in lieu.

An issue, which is often overlooked until things go astray, is whether or not the other party to the contract is a "mark" for damages. If the party with whom you enter into a contract is a person with no assets, or a limited company without assets, then it may pointless to engage in legal action, because it will be impossible to recover either damages or legal costs. This fact sometimes protects impecunious artists from being sued, but it can also be the cause of significant loss to an artist who has invested time and expense in a project in anticipation of payment. This is an issue that should be considered at the beginning of any project. There may be ways of containing the risk.

A Contract for the Sale of an Artwork

A contract for the sale of an existing piece is rarely in writing. The transaction is usually conducted verbally, with a price being agreed and paid to the artist, in return for handing over the piece to the purchaser.

There may be special circumstances that dictate the need to reflect the terms of the agreement in writing. For example:

- The price is to be paid in installments, and the artist will retain title to the work until payment has been made in full.
- The artist wishes to have the right to borrow the piece for exhibition purposes.
- In the event of damage to the work, the artist wishes to have the right to repair it (subject to payment for this work).

However, even if there are no special circumstances, there is still a case to be made for always confirming the sale in writing. In the first place, a letter or note can act as a written record of the date of the sale, the amount paid, and the name and address of the purchaser. This record can occasionally prove valuable long after the sale. Secondly, it gives the artist an opportunity to ensure that the purchaser understands that the copyright in the work does not pass with the original piece, and that the artist's permission is needed for any reproduction of the work. Purchasers are often unaware of this fact.

A Contract to Commission a Work

Artworks are frequently commissioned by organisations such as local authorities and banks, for permanent public display. The commissioner will often present the artist with a contract, drafted by its own solicitor. This raises a question for the artist. Does he or she go to the expense of engaging a solicitor to evaluate the contract, and to negotiate whatever changes might be advisable?

It is clearly preferable to have advice on the contract. Moreover, it is often easier for the artist to secure the removal of unfavourable terms – without feeling that the whole contract is being endangered – with the assistance of a solicitor. The larger the commission, and the more valuable it is to the artist, the more important it is for the artist to have legal representation.

Sometimes the artist has the opportunity to produce the draft contract. Must he or she engage a solicitor in that event? Again, it is preferable to instruct a solicitor, ideally a solicitor with experience of arts-related contracts. However, if the artist simply cannot afford legal representation, or if the commission is not sufficiently valuable to justify legal fees, then it is certainly better that the artist drafts a document of some kind rather than rely on a verbal agreement.

A contract to commission a work is usually preceded by a period during which an artist is selected to produce the work. Sometimes this is by competition, sometimes by straightforward invitation. This pre-contract period can involve a substantial amount of work on the part of the artist in producing detailed proposals; drawings; maquettes; meetings with the commissioner, making site visits, and so forth, depending on the circumstances. It is very important, from the artist's perspective, that:

- It should be clear at any given point in time whether or not the artist has actually been selected, or is still just one of a number of artists under consideration.

- It should be clear whether or not preparatory pre-contract work and expenses will be remunerated by the commissioner.

- There should be no significant delay between selection of the artist, and the production of a formal contract. The artist cannot consider the commission to have been awarded until a contract is signed.

An Exhibition Contract

The period leading up to an exhibition may be an exciting time for an artist, but it can also be beset with practical problems. A satisfactory agreement between artist and gallery (or other exhibition host) put together at planning stage should provide a framework which will keep last minute problems to a minimum.

It would be unusual for this type of agreement to be drafted by a solicitor. The gallery will probably have a standard set of terms, which will be tailored to suit the individual circumstances. These typically will be incorporated in a letter rather than a formal contract, and the artist will be asked to confirm acceptance of the terms.

Below is a checklist of matters to be addressed, in setting out the terms of exhibiting

- Confirmation that the Gallery agrees to mount the exhibition
- The duration and dates of the exhibition.
- The number of works to be exhibited, with a description in so far as possible, including dimensions, media, framing, and any other relevant details. These can be set out in a schedule to the letter or agreement.
- The date for delivery of the works to the exhibition venue.
- The party responsible for transit arrangements, and insurance while in transit.
- Responsibility for hanging, and any special requirements of the artist.
- Times and terms of access to the gallery for the artist, while the exhibition is being prepared.
- The terms of sale of the works, or other remuneration for the artist, with date of payment by the gallery.
- Gallery commission
- Exhibition Payment Right – EPR (if applicable).
- Workshop/lecture fee (if applicable).
- Arrangements for opening reception, including publicity.
- Arrangements relating to exhibition catalogue, including permission of the artist for reproduction of artworks in the catalogue.
- Insurance of works by the Gallery for the duration of the exhibition.
- Security and invigilation arrangements.
- Procedure in case of damage to work.
- Responsibility for delivery of sold works to purchasers; and for dismantling of unsold works; return of unsold works to the artist; responsibility for carriage and insurance in transit.
- A procedure for handling any dispute, ideally by mediation.

When presented with a set of standard terms by a Gallery, the artist may find that not all pertinent matters are covered, or that they are not covered to the artist's satisfaction. Any issues arising should be settled by negotiation as early as possible and confirmed in supplementary correspondence, so that a proper paper-trail exists reflecting all matters that have been agreed.

151

It is essential that there is clarity about the party to bear the costs associated with matters such as framing; carriage; marketing and PR; catalogue; insurance.

A Licence to Reproduce an Artwork

This type of licence is a permission incorporated in a contract. The contents of reproduction licences vary widely, depending on the circumstances. The length can vary from two paragraphs to twenty pages. A licence may grant such a wide range of uses that the residual copyright vested in the artist is not capable of further exploitation. At the other end of the spectrum, a licence can be tightly drawn so as to grant a very limited range of uses, for a short period of time. Neither is right, or wrong – it is entirely a matter of agreement between the parties. What is important however from the perspective of the artist, is that the nature, extent and duration of the uses authorised by the licence be understood, and agreed.

Creative Commons Licences

Creative Commons Licences are occasionally used by artists. Creative Commons is a web-based corporation which promotes the use of simple forms of licence under which artists and others may make their works available free of charge, but subject to some very basic terms and conditions.

Their standard licences allow the creator of the work to specify that:

- The work may be used without limit, provided authorship is attributed;
- The work may be used without limit, provided that the uses are non-commercial;
- The work may be used without limit provided it remains unaltered;
- The work may be used without limit, provided all uses occur under a similar Creative Commons Licence.

A Creative Commons Licence is best seen as a way of securing some respect for work that an artist has already decided to make freely available on the Internet.

A CC attribution non-commercial Licence was held to be legally enforceable in a Dutch court, in March 2006.

Checklist of issues to be covered in a licence to reproduce an original work of art

A licence to reproduce an original work of art, granted by the artist, should deal with the following issues:

- The names and addresses of the artist, and licensee.
- The subject-matter of the licence (the artwork).
- The nature of the licence, i.e. whether *exclusive* (only the licensee can exercise the rights); *sole* (the artist and

the licensee can exercise the rights) or *non-exclusive* (the artists and other third parties licensed by the artist can exercise the rights)

- The specific uses of the work that are licensed, including where appropriate the size of reproduction, the number of reproductions, the media in which the reproduction is authorised, and so forth.
- Proofs to be authorised by the artist before printing, if appropriate.
- Cropping or other manipulation to occur only with the consent of the artist, if appropriate.
- Clarification that copyright ownership remains with the artist.
- Clarification that any additional uses will require an additional permission, and fee.
- Original material to be returned to the artist, if appropriate.
- Licensee to observe the moral rights of the artist.
- The purposes for which the reproductions may be used.
- Whether or not the licensee can grant sub-licenses to others.
- The duration of the licence.
- The territory in which the licence can be exercised.
- The fee/royalty payable by the licensee, and when payable.
- A provision permitting termination for non-payment or other material breach of the agreement.
- A procedure for dealing with disputes.

Do you need help licensing your work?

The Irish Visual Artists Rights Organisation (IVARO) can help you manage your copyright and deal with licence requests. IVARO acts as an intermediate between artists and copyright users to negotiate licenses, which allow for the reproduction of artists' work. IVARO ensures appropriate payment, terms and conditions for artists. Copyright users can count on standardised fees and a reliable and professional licensing service. IVARO belongs to an international network of sister societies in 21 countries, and can represent you worldwide. See www.ivaro.ie for more information.

By Linda Scales

Linda Scales is a solicitor and a copyright specialist. She advises a number of publicly-funded arts bodies and institutions. She also lectures in media law topics in the School of Art History and Cultural Policy at UCD. She is the author of a number of articles on arts-related legal issues, including the Guidelines for Board Members of Arts Boards, published by the Arts Council in 2006. Linda is a co-founder and board member of the Copyright

Association of Ireland, and former board member of the Irish Visual Artists Rights Organisation.

Copyright and the Visual Artist

What is copyright?

Copyright is a branch of the law of intellectual property. It is the legal right for the creator of an original work to exploit the work and to prevent others from doing so without permission.

The copyright owner has the exclusive right to make copies of the work, to make the work available to the public and may sell or licence these rights to third parties.

The law governing copyright in Ireland is contained in the Copyright and Related Rights Act, 2000.

What Works Qualify for Copyright Protection?

Copyright protects a wide range of works: original literary, dramatic, musical and artistic works; sound recordings; film; broadcasts; the typography of the published edition; databases and computer software.

In the case of the artistic work, effectively all forms and media are capable of protection, irrespective of artistic merit, as long as they are original. Some artworks are a combination of different protected forms. An installation, for example, may incorporate both artistic work and film, or artistic and literary works or film and music.

"Original"

There is no fixed definition of "original", but a work will normally pass the test if it is the result of a reasonable degree of "labour and skill or judgment" and if it is not merely copied from another source.

The amount of "labour and skill or judgment" required is modest. For example, technical drawings of simple parts for a loom, including a rivet, a screw and a stud, have been held to qualify as original works (1). Some things however are just too rudimentary. In a case involving rock band Adam and the Ants, three stripes of greasepaint applied to the face of a member of the band were held not to be a painting, and moreover to fail the originality test (2).

Mere copying is not always easy to assess in the context of an artistic work. In the Bridgeman Art Library case, in 1998, a US court decided that photographs of paintings were not original, as they were mere copies of the paintings (3). This case has not been followed in the UK, where it is generally believed that photography of painting is a skilled task and meets the requirements of originality, even though the purpose of the photographer is to produce a faithful copy.

Ideas and Principles

Note that ideas and principles underlying a work are not protected. While Christo would be entitled to prevent someone from reproducing his wrapped chairs, he could not prevent another artist from making *other* wrapped works. The idea of wrapping objects is not capable of protection. It is only the unique expression of the idea that is protected.

Derivative Works

It is possible for a derivative work to enjoy protection. By employing sufficient labour and skill or judgment in transforming an existing work into something new, a fresh copyright can be obtained in the new work. It is necessary however to obtain the permission of the creator of the original piece, unless it is out of copyright. Sean Hillen's *Irelantis Suite* provides some excellent examples of derivative work. Many of the collages in the suite use postcards by John Hinde to create surprising new pieces, undoubtedly qualifying for protection – as long as they do not infringe the copyright of Hinde!

(1) British Northrup Limited v. Texteam Blackburn Limited 1974 RPC 57
(2) Merchandising Corporation of America v. Harpbond Inc., 1983 FSR 32
(3) Bridgeman Art Library Ltd v. Corel Corp. 25 F. Supp 421, 1998

Copyright. Frequently Asked Questions

Does a work need to be registered in order to enjoy protection?

No. Copyright arises spontaneously on the creation of a work. There are no registration requirements.

Can you have more than one copyright in the same work?

Yes. It is not the case that for each protected work, there is just one copyright. It may be true of an original painting, but in a recorded song, for example, there is a copyright in the music, another in the lyric and a third in the sound recording itself. In a film, there is a multiplicity of copyrights, all normally vested in different persons, at least at the point of creation. They are usually brought together by the producer and sold to the distributor of the film.

For how long does copyright protection last?

Copyright protection in literary, dramatic, musical and artistic works lasts for the life of the creator and 70 years thereafter. For sound recordings, film, and broadcasts the term of protection is 50 years from the year of creation.

Who owns the copyright?

The first owner of the copyright in a work is the creator of the work, unless the work is created by an employee in the course of his or her employment, in which case the copyright belongs to the employer.

Misunderstandings as to ownership can arise when a work is commissioned. Commissioners often assume that because they paid for the work, they own the copyright. This is not the case. The copyright remains with the artist, unless it is assigned to the commissioner in a written agreement. However, case law in this area is developing the idea that by virtue of the *contract* between the parties, the commissioner will have at very least the right to use the work for the purpose for which it was commissioned, and may have a much wider set of rights. It is therefore prudent to spell out the position concerning ownership in a written agreement when the terms of the commission are being settled.

Another common misunderstanding concerning ownership involves making the distinction between the ownership of the piece of work, and the copyright in the work. Artwork is unlike other works, in that the primary act of exploitation is not usually publishing or recording, but sale of the original piece. It is not generally understood that when a work is sold, while the original piece passes to the purchaser, the copyright does not. Many infringements of the copyright in artworks arise innocently, because the purchaser of the work is unaware of this fact.

What does copyright ownership imply?

The copyright owner is legally entitled to prevent any third party from:

Making any reproduction of the work (i.e., any form of copying, including copying by electronic means)

Making the work available to the public, by any means (including all forms of publishing, posting on the internet, rental and lending, but excluding exhibition of the work)

Making an adaptation of the work (such as a translation).

These rights are often called the "economic rights" of the creator. In addition, all creators of copyright material enjoy "moral rights".

What are Moral Rights?

Moral rights were introduced in Ireland by the Copyright and Related Rights Act 2000. Long part of European law systems, the theory underlying them is that the creation of a work is a unique expression of the personality of the creator, who should continue to enjoy a certain nexus or connection with the work, even after the economic rights in the work have been transferred to a third party.

There are four types of moral right:

- The right of paternity – the right to be identified as the author of the work
- The right of integrity – the right to object to distortion, mutilation, or other derogatory modification of the work in a manner prejudicial to the reputation of the author
- The right of false attribution – the right *not* to have a work falsely attributed to you
- The right for a person, who commissions a photograph or film for private or domestic use, *not* to have the work made public.

These rights may not be assigned by the author or creator to any third party, although they can be waived in writing. They last for the copyright period and can pass under the Will of the artist. They do not apply to the works of an artist who died prior to the commencement of the Copyright and Related Rights Act 2000, viz., 1st January 2001.

What are the exceptions to copyright protection?

The law permits some uses of protected works without permission of the copyright owner. The most relevant exceptions, for an artist, are the following:

Insubstantial uses: For an infringement to occur, there must be a "substantial taking" of the work. Insubstantial uses are therefore indirectly exempt. Of course this begs the question as to what is meant by "substantial". Unfortunately every case must be judged on its merits, and so it is not always easy to determine precisely how much of a protected work can be used without permission. There are however some guidelines: "substantial" can be evaluated qualitatively as well as quantitatively; and uses can be evaluated cumulatively, so that "little and often" can amount to infringement. To say on the safe side of this issue, the amount of the work used should be insignificant.

Quotations and extracts: A related issue, the use of "quotations or extracts" from a published work is permitted, provided the use does not prejudice the interests of the copyright owner, and is accompanied by an acknowledgement. Again however there is the question of how extensive a "quotation or extract" may be, and there are no clear guidelines on this.

Fair dealing: Under certain conditions, it is permissible to use a work for one of the following three purposes:

- Research or private study
- Criticism or review
- Reporting current events

Incidental use: A use that is "incidental" is permitted. This would arise, for example, if RTE were to broadcast an interview with the Chairman of AIB Bank from the foyer of AIB Bankcentre, and in doing so, captured a work by Robert Ballagh hanging on the wall of the foyer. The use of the work in those circumstances would be regarded as incidental.

There are a small number of copyright exceptions peculiar to works of art. These are the following:

Public works: A building, a sculpture, a model for a building and a work of artistic craftsmanship, when situated in public or in a place open to the public, may be reproduced in two dimensions; photographed; filmed or broadcast, without infringing the copyright. In addition, those reproductions can be made available to the public (including by sale) without permission. Thus, you may take a photograph of the Spire in O'Connell Street, create a postcard from it, and sell the postcard. You may not however create miniature replicas of it for sale without infringing the copyright.

Advertising artistic work: A work may be reproduced in order to advertise its sale. It is this exemption that enables auction houses to publish glossy sales catalogues of art works.

Subsequent works: Where an artist has sold the copyright in a work, it is not an infringement to make a similar work, as long as the main design of the original piece is not replicated.

Can Copyright be Sold? Copyright is a property right which – like other property rights – may be the subject of various types of transaction. It may be sold outright (by an "assignment", which must be in writing), or licensed in whole or in part. Licences are often for a short term and cover only certain uses of the work. For example, you might grant a licence to a hotel chain for the use of a work in a newspaper advertising campaign, for a period of two years. While an assignment must be in writing, a licence can be verbal, although it is unwise to give any permission for the use of a work without some written evidence of the agreement.

Remedies and Penalties for Infringement. Copyright infringement has both civil and criminal dimensions. On the civil side, breach of copyright is actionable at the suit of the copyright owner and a range of remedies are available, the most common of which are injunctions and damages. On the criminal side, certain acts in relation to the copyright work are characterised in copyright legislation as offences, for which penalties are prescribed. These offences include, not only the making of counterfeit works but also dealing in infringing works – by, for example, importing them, selling or renting them. Criminal penalties extend to fines of up to €127,000 and/or terms of imprisonment of up to 5 years.

The Theory Applied: The Creator's Perspective It is useful to look at the practical application of the copyright rules from two standpoints: that of the creator of the copyright work, and that of the user of the work.

The Creator's Perspective: From the standpoint of the creator of a work, these questions are relevant:

- Am I sure that my work qualifies for copyright protection?
- Is there anything I can do to protect my copyright?
- What do I do if my rights are infringed?

1. Is the work protected? As already mentioned, there is a threshold requirement of originality for copyright in artistic works. The determining factor is whether or not sufficient labour and skill or judgment has been expended. Some art forms will be more problematic than others in this respect. Take the object trouvée or found object. This might be just an arrangement of shells or tree roots or pebbles. Does this exhibit labour and skill or judgment? Some famous works have consisted of everyday objects simply taken out of context. Duchamp, for example, exhibited a bottle rack as a sculpture. Joseph Kosuth mounted a photocopy of a dictionary definition of the word "art". The labour and skill in these works is minimal. It is impossible to say how they would be viewed by a court.

These types of work represent the exception rather then the rule. The work of most artists will be carefully planned and painstakingly executed, and will easily meet the originality requirement.

2. What can the creator do to protect his or her copyright? Because copyright ownership does not depend on registration or other formality, artists tend to feel that there is little they can do to guard against infringement. This is not the case. Consider the following possibilities:

* Use a copyright notice and/or the copyright symbol ©

There is no reason why a work of art should not carry a discrete copyright notice, such as: "The copyright in this work remains the property of the artist, even after sale. It may not be reproduced without the permission of the artist". The copyright symbol can also be used as a warning that the work is protected. It is normally used in this format: ©Robert Ballagh, 1988.

* Keep records of your works

A day may come when, in order to pursue an infringement, you will need to provide evidence that you created a work, and the date on which you did so. Theoretically at least, a way of doing this is to post a copy of the work to yourself by registered post, keeping the Post Office receipt and leaving the envelope unopened when you receive it. It is not certain however that anyone has ever succeeded in using this as a form of proof of ownership of copyright!

It will certainly however be of assistance in an action for infringement if you can provide good documentary or photographic records of your work. If you are concerned about proof, these records can be placed with a reliable third party for safekeeping, the date being recorded by the third party, who should be willing to testify to receipt of the material. Another way of putting the matter beyond doubt is to register the works with the US Copyright Office. This can be done online, at modest cost. It will not give you any additional protection for the works, but will act as proof positive of your claim to ownership at the date of registration.

* Reflect all agreements in writing.

This is possibly the single most important step that an artist can take in order to safeguard his or her copyright. Many cases of infringement fail because an artist agreed verbally to permit certain uses of a work, but did not adequately articulate the terms of the agreement and did not commit them to writing. If you agree that a work may be used, for example, in an advertisement, the agreement should be confirmed in a letter, in which there is set out at the very least a description of the work, the fee to be paid, the medium in which the advertisement will appear, the duration of the permission (or number of reproductions), the territory in which the permission will operate, and any other conditions of concern to you as artist, such as the quality or type of reproduction. Of course you may instruct a solicitor to draft a Licence Agreement, but in most cases a simple letter from the artist to the Licensee will suffice.

When a work is commissioned, it is imperative that the terms be set out in writing. Normally a commission is a lucrative and important engagement for an artist and it is worth asking a solicitor to draft an agreement or to approve an agreement furnished by the commissioner. A key issue in most commissions is the ownership of the copyright. The commissioner tends to assume that the ownership of the copyright will pass with the work. The artist on the other hand often wishes to retain the copyright, and grant only a licence, but is fearful of disappointing the commissioner. It has to be said that most commissions are offered on the understanding that the copyright will pass with the work. The artist should clarify the position at the outset, and the fee should be measured accordingly.

* Join a collective rights management society

Collective management bodies represent different types of author, collecting royalties for the exploitation of the copyright in their works. They normally also offer copyright information, advice and support in relation to infringements. In the visual arts sphere, the Irish Visual Artists' Rights Organisation (IVARO) was formed in 2005. Its establishment has been welcomed by Irish artists and it is gradually building the copyright-related services it offers to its members.

3. What action can I take if my copyright is infringed? It is important that you act immediately. Delay can be construed by the law as acquiescence.

You may instruct a solicitor. However that may not be necessary, at least initially. You can approach the infringer and complain about the infringement, pointing out that you are the copyright owner in the work, demanding cessation of the infringement and seeking compensation. The complaint can initially be a verbal one, but if so, it should be followed with a letter. You should make it clear that if the response is not satisfactory, the matter will be put in the hands of your solicitor.

IVARO aims to provide support for its members in relation to infringements. It will offer an opinion on whether the act complained of appears to be a legal infringement. It may also help to draft an initial letter of complaint, and assist the member in finding appropriate legal representation.

160

The Theory Applied: The User's Perspective If you wish to use all, or a material part of a protected work, it is likely that the permission of the copyright owner will be needed. In this context "use" means *reproduce* by any means, including electronically; *make available* to third parties by any means, including electronically and in the on-line environment, and *adapt* the work, for example, by translation.

Artists often use other protected works. Sometimes these are other visual works, but they may be literary or musical works, or other types of protected material, such as computer software.

There are some simple questions that can be asked, to help establish whether a work can be used without permission.

1. Is the work a protected work? See the section of this text captioned "What works qualify for copyright protection?" Note that permission is needed for reproduction of a *copy*, as well as the original.

2. Is the work still within the copyright term? See the section of this texts captioned "For how long does copyright protection last?" If the copyright term has expired, the work may be used freely without permission. Note however that if you are relying on a photograph of the work, or a copy published in a book or periodical, then although the original work may be out of copyright, the photographer and the publisher may have rights that may require clearance.

3. Is the proposed use covered by one of the exceptions to copyright? See the section in this text captioned "What are the exceptions to copyright protection?"

If the answer to the first two questions is "yes", and to the third question is "no", then the licence or permission of the copyright owner is needed in order to avoid a breach of copyright.

How to obtain permission. It is necessary to find the copyright owner or his or her agent or representative, and secure either an assignment of the copyright, or a licence to use the work for the intended purpose. You will normally be required to pay a fee.

It is not always possible to find the copyright owner in order to obtain permission. Increasingly however the development of collecting societies, which represent artists and other types of author, makes this easier. In Ireland, music composers are represented by IMRO (Irish Music Rights Organisation) andMCPS (Mechanical Copyright Protection Society). PPI (Phonographic Performance Ireland) represents recorded artists and performers. In the literary field, ICLA (the Irish Copyright Licensing Agency) represents authors and publishers. NLI (Newspaper Licensing Ireland) represents newspaper proprietors. And, of course, IVARO represents visual artists.

These collecting societies act as a starting point for the purpose of obtaining permission. Some societies will process the application for permission and the grant of a licence. Others will simply pass on the request to the author, if he or she is a member of the society. The system of

161

collecting societies is not however complete in Ireland and in some instances it is still necessary to find and negotiate directly with the author.

It is important to ensure that when a licence or permission is obtained it is sufficient to cover all of the proposed uses of the work. While a permission may be verbal, it is unwise to rely on a verbal exchange. Ensure that the permission is secured in writing, and that the terms are clear.

The Artist's Resale Right: An EU Directive A European Union Directive on the Artist's Resale Right, or Droit de Suite, was due to be implemented in all EU member states by 1st January 2006. The Irish Government was late in implementing the Directive. On 13th June 2006, when the hearing of legal proceedings taken by Robert Ballagh against the State for failure to implement the right was imminent, the Minister for Enterprise, Trade and Employment hastily produced a set of Regulations – entitled the European Communities (Artist's Resale Right) Regulations 2006.

The Regulations provide the right in a very bare form. They are intended to be a temporary measure only. The Government proposes to produce more detailed substantive copyright legislation on the topic at a later stage.

The Regulations provide living artists with an unwaivable right to a royalty on the resale of their original works of art. The right applies to re-sales in which an art market professional is involved. It does not apply to private sales. The royalty is payable by the seller. It does not apply to sales for less than Eur3,000.

The royalty is calculated as follows:

%	Description	Value
4%	**for the portion of the sales price up to**	**€50,000**
3%	**for the portion of the sales price from**	**€50,001 to €200,000**
1%	**for the portion of the sales price from**	**€200,001 to €350,000**
0.5%	**or the portion of the sales price from**	**€350,001 to €500,000**
1	**or the portion of the sales price from**	**€500,000**

There is a "cap" or maximum royalty of €12,500.

Artists may collect their own royalties directly from auction houses and dealers. Many have elected however to mandate IVARO to collect on their behalf. IVARO has reciprocal rights agreements with similar societies in other countries that enable it to collect resale royalties due to its members from re-sales in those countries.

Copyright Harmonisation: Copyright under International and European Instruments

In the current global environment, in which material can be disseminated world-wide at the click of a mouse, it has become very difficult to contain counterfeiting of creative works. The standardisation of laws and inter-state co-operation on enforcement are increasingly necessary to support the rights of creators.

As a result of a wide-ranging programme of harmonisation initiated by the European Commission some 15 years ago, copyright rules are largely similar in all EU Member States. Citizens of all EU countries enjoy the same rights in each member state as nationals of that country.

Internationally, the Berne Union, to which all EU Member States and most of the developed world belongs, has succeeded in reaching a remarkable level of agreement on standard copyright rules. As in the EU, there are conditions of reciprocity of protection for citizens of all member states of the Union.

Additionally, member states of the World Trade Organisation adhere to the TRIPs Agreement of 1994, which lays down minimum standards of intellectual property protection and enforcement rules, including appropriate remedies for infringement.

In the last decade, copyright law in Ireland has been the subject of dramatic change, primarily as a result of these European and international initiatives. The result has been to considerably enhance the position of Irish artists in relation to rights in their works.

By Linda Scales

Handling Disputes

Introduction

No one likes confrontation. Occasionally however an artist will have to manage a professional dispute. It may happen, for example, that you have been awarded a commission, and the commissioner decides to pull out of the agreement. You may come across an unauthorised copy of your work on an Internet site. The purchaser of a work may be very slow in paying for it, and appears to be avoiding you. In situations such as these, you will want to vindicate your rights. In other circumstances you may be accused of being in the wrong, and you may need to defend your position.

While it is impossible to avoid all prospect of becoming involved in a dispute, it is possible to minimise the chances of a dispute occurring. It is also possible, with proper handling, to prevent a disagreement from escalating into something more serious, and to contain the damage resulting from a dispute.

Avoiding Disputes

The following steps will help to avoid the possibility of disagreement:

* Be clear about your position in all dealings concerning your work. Articulate your expectations fully. Do not avoid issues you feel may be sensitive – they are the very ones which will cause problems later. For

example, the ownership of the rights in a work is an issue that is often inadequately dealt with in commissioning agreements – will the commissioner own all rights, or merely have a licence to use the work for specific purposes? The artist may want to insist on retaining the copyright, but may be afraid of upsetting the commissioner by stating this requirement. The resulting agreement may lack clarity on this point, almost certainly leading to difficulty afterwards.

* Reflect all agreements in writing. There are two good reasons for doing this. The first is to provide proof of the agreement. Many disputes involving artists turn on one word against another, because there was no witness to the verbal agreement. In these circumstances it is impossible to estimate the likely outcome of the dispute. The second reason is that writing down the elements of an agreement forces both parties to address their minds to the essential points of agreement. This reduces the possibility of misunderstanding. It is not necessary to have a solicitor draft an agreement in every case. A simple letter from one party to the other, undisputed at the time, is always vastly superior to a verbal agreement.

* Be realistic in what you expect from an agreement, and in what you can deliver. Do not, for example, under-price your work and regret it afterwards. Do not commit to a very tight time-schedule in order to please a gallery or a purchaser. Either the work will suffer, or you will fail to deliver.

* Envisage the possibility of a dispute. Inform yourself about protecting the rights in your work. Keep proper records. Make and seek payments promptly and in a businesslike manner. Good professional standards will help protect you against unnecessary conflict.

Damage Limitation

As soon as you perceive that you are embroiled in a disagreement, taking the following steps may help to prevent it from escalating into a full-blown dispute and may contain the damage that can be caused:

Accept that a difficulty exists and act quickly. The sooner the problem is addressed, the less likely it is to escalate. The first person to seek a method of resolving the dispute often has an advantage.

Decide whether or not you need the immediate advice of a solicitor or whether you will first attempt to deal with the problem yourself. If you are the party making the complaint, then there is little to be lost in writing a letter to the other party, setting out the problem and indicating that you will seek appropriate redress. The language used need not be formal or confrontational. The letter can be used to state the problem simply and to indicate that unless it can be resolved satisfactorily; further action will have to be taken. A sample letter can be found at the end of this text. Depending on the response, it may be possible to negotiate a satisfactory outcome without the help of a solicitor. The outcome need not involve an admission of liability, nor even payment of money. If it suits both parties, it can

164

consist of the purchase of a work, or the return of a work, or some other "payment in kind".

One word of warning however. If you are setting out terms of settlement of a dispute in writing, unless they are final terms accepted by both parties and you are simply confirming them, then any correspondence should be headed "without prejudice". This prevents the other party from using this correspondence against you in any subsequent legal action.

If you are accused of some wrongdoing, and especially if the penalty or remedy may be substantial, it is wisest to consult a solicitor at an early stage. If however you are quite sure that the matter is a minor one, and you are willing to acknowledge your responsibility, then do so as quickly as possible. Often an apology and a promise to refrain from repeating the offending act is all that is required.

Consulting a Solicitor

When you decide to consult a solicitor, these pointers may be helpful:

If you do not know a solicitor, do some investigating to find one with appropriate knowledge and experience. A large firm will usually have the expertise, but may also be more expensive, and unwilling to take on a small case. If you have to choose a firm without knowing whether or not it has the relevant expertise, then telephone, explain the nature of your problem and ask if this an area of law they practice. If you are happy with the response, then make an appointment.

At the first meeting, bring with you a written summary of the facts of the dispute, which you can leave with the solicitor. Bring, in addition, all relevant documents and correspondence, and an extra copy, if possible, for the solicitor. This will save time.

Be clear at the end of the meeting exactly what the solicitor proposes to do on your behalf. Be clear also about the charges. Solicitors are obliged to write to you setting out the basis on which they calculate their fees. For cases that are charged on a time basis, the rate of charge will probably fall in the range €200-300 per hour, plus VAT at 21%, and direct expenses (outlay).

If for any reason you feel unhappy with the advice you have received, or unsure that the solicitor is the right person to represent you, then simply write or phone and say that you have decided not to pursue the matter, at least for the present, and ask for a bill for the services rendered. Then start again! It is better to lose a little time, and the cost of a consultation, than to struggle on in a professional relationship in which you feel uncomfortable.

Legal Procedures for Resolving Disputes: Litigation

In June 2006, Robert Ballagh was successful in a High Court action against the Irish State for losses he incurred because the State was late in implementing the European Directive on the Artists' Resale Right. He was awarded damages, plus the costs of the action. His case was something of an exception. Not many cases involving artists come before the courts. This is primarily because unless the case is absolutely cast-iron (and if it is, it should not come to court at all), the artist cannot risk having to pay the legal costs. The party who loses an action must normally pay not only his or her own costs, but the costs of the successful party as well.

Before embarking on any form of litigation, your solicitor will attempt to resolve the dispute by engaging in correspondence and discussions with the other party or, more usually, with his or her solicitor. In the event that negotiations are not successful, before initiating formal proceedings, your solicitor will advise you of the chances of success in the action, and the costs you will incur in the event that you lose in court. The size of the costs will depend on the nature of the case, and the court in which the action is taken. Needless to say, no decision to litigate should be taken without this information.

The court in which your action will be taken will usually depend on the size of the claim, and of course, the smaller the claim and the lower the court, the more modest should be the legal costs.

The lowest court for civil claims is the District Court. It hears claims valued at up to €6,348,69 (the equivalent of £5,000). The Circuit Court hears claims valued at up to €38,092.14 (the equivalent of £30,000). Larger claims, and certain specific types of case are heard by the High Court. The Supreme Court is principally a court of appeal from the High Court on questions of law.

Other Forms of Dispute Resolution

It is not always necessary to go to court in order to bring a dispute to a conclusion. There are other possibilities:

1) ADR (or Alternative Dispute Resolution) is growing in popularity, as an alternative to litigation. There are two types of ADR: mediation and arbitration.

Mediation

In mediation, both parties agree to use a trained mediator to help solve the dispute. One of the advantages is that the parties themselves become involved in devising the solution. The lead-in time is short and the process itself is normally completed within a day. Mediation is a great deal less expensive than litigation. It is also confidential. Decisions made in mediation are not legally binding, unless the parties agree to make them so. It is said however that 80% of mediations are successful, in that both parties accept the decision reached, and act upon it.

Arbitration

Arbitration occurs when both parties agree to appoint a suitably qualified arbitrator to determine a dispute. Arbitration is more formal than mediation. The Arbitration Acts 1954-1998 govern the process. The

166

decision of the arbitrator is binding. Many contracts contain an arbitration clause obliging the parties to submit to arbitration in the event of dispute. In contrast to court litigation which occurs in public, arbitration is conducted in private. If the parties agree, the arbitrator can make his or her decision on the basis of documentary evidence, without the need for an oral hearing. Arbitration is also less costly than court litigation, but usually more costly than mediation.

It is not necessary to be represented by a solicitor in either process, although representation is a distinct advantage in the case of arbitration. A number of solicitors firms are enthusiastic about ADR. You can identify these through an internet search.

2) It is also possible that your dispute will come within the remit of one of the several organisations and agencies that process different types of complaint, mainly by consumers. These include Ombudsmen (such as the Financial Ombudsman) and Regulators (such as ComReg). Some trade and professional associations, such as the Law Society of Ireland, and the Advertising Standards Association, maintain codes of practice which they enforce against their members. Commissioners, such as the Information Commissioner, and the Data Protection Commissioner also handle complaints concerning infringements of rights to information, and data protection, respectively. The Labour Relations Commission offers a range of services relating to disputes in the workplace, including mediation.

Information concerning these organisations and agencies can be obtained from the Citizens Information Board

Sample Letter of Complaint

Dear Mr/Ms _____

I am an artist and the author of the work entitled "_____". It has come to my attention that you have posted a copy of the work on your website: www.xxxxx.com. As this use of the work was not authorised by me, it constitutes an infringement of my copyright.

In order to avoid formal legal action, you should let me hear from you by return, confirming that you will remove the work from the site, and will compensate me for the infringement. In relation to the latter, please let me know for how long the work has been exhibited on the site, and I will measure a reasonable fee.

Yours faithfully,

_____

Artist

By Linda Scales

Health and Safety in the Studio

An Introduction to Health & Safety Issues

Most artists are aware that some of the materials that they use and processes that they undertake can carry health and safety risks. What many artists may not be aware of is that they, as self-employed individuals, have a duty under health and safety law to ensure that their working environment complies with health and safety legislation.

For most artists their workplace is the studio; be it a purpose built facility, rented space or an extension to their home. The nature of artistic practice is such that artists use a very eclectic mix of materials in their day-to day work. They also undertake a wide range of physical activities and processes in producing work. Both materials used and production activities can be detrimental to an artist's health and safety, quality of life and career.

Apart from it being the law, it is in the interest of artists to protect their own health and safety as well as ensuring that studios and work environments are safe for visitors, family or clients. This text aims to provide a brief introduction to the law and requirements to have a safe and healthy workplace. It will cover the importance of the 'Safety Statement' and in particular 'Hazard Identification and Risk Assessment'.

The Health and Safety Authority (HSA) has a large number of publications and guides, which provide information and advice on the various hazards associated with different occupations. However, there are no guidelines which cover artists studio-work specifically, so it is up to you to assess your studio, work methods and materials; identify the risks associated in each case and implement measures to reduce or eliminate them.

The Legislation

If you are self-employed – as most artists are – you are legally bound to provide a safe working environment as set out in the Safety, Health and Welfare at Work Act 2005. You will find this as well as other health and safety legislative documents on the HSA website. Failure to provide a safe working environment can result in civil cases taken by visitors or employees (if you employ others to work with you in your studio) or criminal cases taken by the HSA.

The Act is the primary piece of health and safety legislation. This sets out your basic health and safety responsibilities. There are a number of . secondary pieces of legislation which essentially expand on these basic responsibilities. For instance, The Act (Primary) requires you to provide a safe place of work while the General Applications (Secondary) expands on what a safe place of work is.

The Safety Statement

The legislation demands that you as a self-employed individual manage health and safety in your work place. A 'Safety Statement' outlines how you will do this. The Statement should include a commitment to comply with all relevant Health and Safety Legislation and should identify the hazards and assess the risks of all activities undertaken in your workplace. It should also detail the protective and preventive measures taken to secure the safety, health and welfare of the people who work at or visit your workplace. The safety statement should be clearly displayed in your studio and brought to the attention of staff (if any) at least once a year, and whenever it is revised.

Risk Assessment

A risk assessment identifies the hazards in your workplace and evaluates the risks posed by these hazards. In order to fully comprehend the language of the legislation and to be able to draw up a risk assessment, it is helpful to understand the common terms used throughout – hazard, harm and risk.

- A Hazard can be defined as anything that has the potential to cause physical injury or damage to health, the environment or to property.
- Harm is the adverse effect on an individual that may result from exposure to a hazard
- A Risk is a measure of the probability of harm being caused and the severity of that harm.

Carrying Out a Risk Assessment

The Health and Safety Authority provides a systematic guide to carrying out a risk assessment.

Analyse your studio or workplace. This may involve listing all the activities carried out in your studio, drawing up a diagram of your space and mapping the location of equipment such as computers, sinks, radiators, shelving, kilns etc

Identify the hazards associated with your work activities. For example, electrical hazards associated with untrunked cables which may cause tripping or falling, chemical hazards associated with toxic materials, hazards that are associated with stone work – dust inhalation for example. Textile dyes are particularly hazardous to skin and photochemicals used by photographers are associated with skin and respiratory diseases. Some hazards may not seem so obvious such as unsecured shelving, the glare from PC monitors, for example, but even the chair that you sit on, if incorrectly adjusted, can cause back injury.

Rate the risk level associated with each hazard. To do this you need to evaluate the likelihood that injury might occur and the extent or severity of the injury. This assessment of risk is a question of judgement – you yourself must form an opinion. If you are unsure of the risk associated with a particular piece of equipment or chemical; it is up to you to find out by contacting the manufacturer or reading the label or safety manual.

Evaluate the 'controls' that you may already have in place to make hazards less hazardous. Controls are essentially precautions that you put in place to eliminate or reduce the risks. A control may take the form of signage near a leaking sink that warns of a slippery surface, warning labels on chemicals, Personal Protective Equipment (PPE) such as goggles and dust masks for working with stone or when printmaking for example.

Hierarchy of Controls

Once you have carried out a Risk Assessment of your studio or workplace you must then decide what efforts you will take to ensure that the risks you have identified are reduced or eliminated. The Health and Safety Legislation sets out a five-step hierarchy of controls on how to deal with or control risks. It is called a hierarchy because the most effective control is placed at the top. You should implement these controls in priority order starting at the top and working down the list.

- Eliminate: If you can eliminate the hazard altogether you should do so. So for example, avoid using a particular type of toxic chemical altogether or avoid carrying heavy loads yourself.
- Substitute: Can you substitute the materials or equipment for ones that are less hazardous? For example, can you use an alternative brand of paint – one that is less toxic or can you substitute that faulty heater for one that works a bit better.
- Engineering: Can you install Fire Extinguishers in your workplace? Ensure that the electrical installation in your studio is certified and maintained by a competent person.
- Administrative: Clearly display signage warning of hazards associated with materials such as chemicals and toxic paints or signage warning visitors of poor floor conditions or obstructions.
- Personal Protective Equipment (PPE): PPE is any safety clothing or equipment worn to protect against hazards. You should use goggles to protect against dust or debris for example.

Summary of Responsibilities

To summarise, you must display a Safety Statement in your workplace or studio. The Safety Statement must be accompanied by a Risk Assessment. This must include risks for all people including visitors. For every hazard identified, controls or preventions must be put in place to ensure the risk of harm is eliminated or reduced. Finally, your Statement and Risk

Assessment must be revised annually to ensure any new hazards are identified and controls implemented.

Chemical Hazards

Now we will look at some of the most common workplace hazards. The main categories of hazards to be mindful of are: biological, chemical, physical, human behaviour, and fire and explosion.

Chemical agents are considered hazardous not only because of what they contain but also because of the way in which they are used in the studio. Some hazardous chemical agents include:

Substances brought into the workplace and handled, stored and used in your work processes. These may include solvents, cleaning agents, paints, glues, and resin.

Substances generated by your work activity – fumes from welding, soldering, dust, solvent vapours from painting etc

Substances or mixtures produced by your work process – residues and waste for example.

The effects of exposure to chemical hazards can range from eye irritation to poisoning to chronic lung disease. Information on chemical agents can usually be found on packaging labels, information provided by the supplier and of course the Internet. The HSA data sheets will advise on how to prevent or eliminate risks associated with chemicals.

Biological Hazards

Biological hazards are usually invisible so the risks they pose are not always appreciated. They include bacteria, viruses, fungi (yeasts and moulds) and parasites. The essential difference between biological agents and other hazardous substances is their ability to reproduce. Exposure to biological agents can occur whenever people are in contact with the materials such as natural or organic materials like soil, clay, and plant materials (hay, straw, cotton etc); substances of animal origin (wool, hair, etc); food; organic dust (eg. flour, paper, dust) and waste or wastewater.

Some of the occupations at risk from biological hazards that artists may cross over into include working in areas with air conditioning systems and high humidity (eg. textile industry, print industry and paper production). This can cause allergies and respiratory disorders due to moulds and yeasts. Also, working in archives, museums and libraries can cause allergies and respiratory disorders.

Physical Hazards

Activities involving manual handling and trips and falls are probably the most common cause of workplace accidents. The common risks are associated with manual handling involve the load being too heavy, bad posture when lifting and environment factors such as uneven floors.

171

Visual Display Units

Though working at a computer may not seem particularly hazardous to your health there are health and safely issues associated with the use of computers and the workstation (desk, chair, lighting,) at which a person works. Anyone that works at a computer workstation for one continuous hour or more, as part of their everyday work should be aware of the hazards associated – eye strain, back injury, repetitive strain.

Fire

Probably the hazard that most people are aware of and that which is a hazard in every workplace. Common causes of fire include electrical faults, cooking, smoking and flammable liquids. Obviously, the best control to prevent fire is to isolate the three factors that cause fire – heat, fuel and oxygen. Thus, your studio should be kept neat and tidy to limit potential fuel sources. Ensure sockets are not overloaded and that electrical equipment is in good condition. A smoke detector and fire extinguisher should be installed in your studio.

By Niamh Looney

The Trinity of The Artist, The Gallery, & The Curator

Artist / Gallery Relationships – When trust proves itself to be misplaced...

Introduction

The business arrangements between artist and gallery have traditionally been based around honour; a handshake of mutual trust and respect. This system has worked to the benefit of both parties, apparently saving artists from mountains of contractual administration and legal paperwork, and allowing them to progress with their creative work, safe in the knowledge that the gallery/artist relationship is healthy and working to the benefit of all.

However, Visual Artists Ireland has seen an increase in this practice being taken advantage of by a small number of places that fail to follow sound business practices that they see as unnecessary within a sector based upon trust.

Cases of non-payment and works being mislaid are a constant complaint to Visual Artists Ireland's offices. We receive regular telephone calls and emails from artists in similar situations. On most occasions the artist contacting us will know of fellow gallery artists who have been treated in the same way, but this does not solve the sense of helplessness that can set in when a relationship of trust goes sour.

Of course, we must add very strongly that this is not with every gallery. In fact, if we look at the gallery sector as a whole, it is a small number of galleries and individuals that are acting in this way. For some, it comes from a negative economy or from a change in personal circumstances, but it has to be said that in a lot of cases it is comes from way before the downturn and may be seen as an indication of bad management and a lack of understanding of the art market place and how to work with artists.

Our concern in Visual Artists Ireland about this growing situation has led to a series of discussions with artists and galleries to understand the reality. The following is a brief summary of our findings.

The first points that we must understand are that there are many people in the commercial and not for profit sector today that are working hard to promote the work of visual artists in a professional and caring manner. There are also others who have set up art sales as either a hobby or as an idea that came to them in a sudden moment of clarity but without any research or knowledge of what is required for such a business. The symptoms are common: a lack of payment, not returning telephone calls, accusation and counter-accusation, works missing or damaged, or unable to return work to artists upon request. As we deal with this situation on such a regular basis, we have a set of guidelines that we offer to artists. Part of these we now offer here.

Prevention

The idea of showing and selling with a gallery appears to be the ideal thing; bringing with it that sense of achievement and pride that the public are going to get a chance to see and perhaps buy. Indeed, first conversations open up new ideas and provide support in terms of exploration and realization of different projects. This looks like it is going to be a long-term relationship between two equal parties; and let's add that in most cases it is... Therefore, our first piece of advice is

Stop, think, and do some research.

Who is the gallery that has approached you, or that you have chosen to give work to? A very simple step that is often ignored is the investigation of who else is being shown by that gallery. As the Irish art world is a relatively small group of people who are all very well interconnected, it is a simple task to look at the other artists and find one or two to approach and ask for their impression and experience of working with the gallery. Does the gallery achieve sales? What are the terms that the gallery offers to artists? What is the experience of other artists working with the gallery in terms of support, payments, and exhibition opportunities?

There may be a sense of urgency in terms of agreeing to give work to a gallery, but instead of an instant yes, we recommend offering the qualified yes, and then taking time to do the above research. We advise artists to make sure that they understand what they are looking for when they are providing work to be shown and/or sold, and with full knowledge then decide if the gallery team are people with which they would like to work.

What are the terms of your contract?

Our first question to artists contacting us is to ask if they have a contract, a letter of understanding, or anything in writing. Unfortunately, for the most part, there is rarely anything in place. However, it is easy for artists to remedy this situation and when an agreement has been reached with the gallery, any terms and conditions should be documented back to the gallery in written form. We also strongly recommend that all work handed over to the gallery is accompanied by a letter of consignment, including photo documentation of the work. In this letter, the artist should outline the work and the condition in which it is being provided, the period of the consignment, reproduction conditions, and clearly state that ownership of the works being consigned does not pass to the gallerist or buyer until the artist has received full payment. Artists may also like to include other aspects such as representing the work in media statements, insurance, etc. Both parties should sign the document before works are handed over.

174

Amongst other things, this will provide documented proof of ownership and the work's condition at the time of consignment. There may be moments when the person authorized by a gallery is not available to sign such a document, or there may be reluctance to sign. By having nobody available to sign, it opens the potential that the document will never be signed. We suggest very strongly that reluctance should be a sign of problems ahead.

Keep updated on where your unsold work is

Taking a small lesson from stock taking in the commercial world, it is wise to check with a gallery on a regular basis (every 6 or 12 months depending on your understanding of a gallery's turnover and based on your level of trust) about the status of the work they are holding on your behalf. When work is delivered send two copies of a signed inventory that is based on what has been consigned and not reported as sold and request that they provide a signed copy back by return. If they don't do this, or refuse to do it, then perhaps it is time to consider asking them to return all artwork to you within a reasonable length of time (e.g. two weeks).

Building and managing the relationship.

This is where the confidence in a relationship comes into play. Building a working relationship involves open and clear communications. We find that if, for good solid reasons, the gallery may experience cash flow problems, the relationship will allow an artist to have continued confidence in the business partnership and will allow for solid negotiations to take place.

In some of the cases that we see, we find that once good relations become sour when communications either stop, or in extreme cases become abusive. Visual Artists Ireland always recommends trying to work through issues when there has been a good relationship. We offer to mediate and to build a mutually agreed plan for working out problems that have appeared. But when the relationship has soured and turned into an abusive and accusation filled battle, we find that for the most part the only area of recourse is through what can become, in a severe case, a prolonged legal-based battle.

But, what happens if this all goes wrong?

Let's start with the premise that most galleries want to pay their artists, maintain their good reputations, and to keep everybody happy. We keep this as a given when starting to look at cases. Therefore, our first recommendation is:

Communicate

Making contact with a gallery to look at the status of work, or looking for payment needs to be kept on a business basis. If started with a telephone call, we always recommend a follow up at all times with a confirmation email or letter. The ideal situation is to receive payment in full, but we also recommend looking to setting up a schedule of payments from the gallery.

The above is when working in a clear professional environment. Unfortunately this is not always the case, and as has been experienced by many artists, deadlines for payments are consistently missed, and dates and times are ignored, leaving artists both out of pocket and without work.

Document

What to do next is more complex and we usually deal with it on a case-by-case basis. Our first question is always to ask what documentation an artist has. The first task that we set an artist is to outline a chronology of the relationship, showing works provided, and copying emails and letters that have been exchanged. This is usually an exhaustive task, but in this documentation lie the future solutions. Ideally, a contract or letter of consignment is in place. Ireland places a lot of emphasis on verbal contracts especially in cases where there is evidence of other parties being subjected to the same treatment.

Identify

Once this chronology and gathering of communications is in place, the next task is to identify if there is a deliberate deception in place. If so, this becomes a serious case that is potentially understood to be fraud; the obtaining of work under false pretences. This becomes a matter for a police investigation through the Special Branch. This is the extreme, but from recommendations from the Harcourt Street Gardaí anti-racketeering office, taking the above documentation to a local special branch officer may result in a criminal investigation.

More likely, there is no fraud, but it will be a matter of mismanagement. In this case, the first point of reference is to find out what is the status of the work involved. If an artist has been told that it has been sold, or the work is not available for return to the artist, the next step is for the artist to raise an invoice for the full amount due to them, clearly indicating terms and conditions for payment.

As this is a commercial transaction, it is worth noting that as and from the 1st January 2012, the late payment interest rate is 8% per annum (that is based on the ECB rate of 1% plus the margin of 7%). That rate equates to a daily rate of 0.022%. Penalty interest due for late payments should be calculated on a daily basis. (http://www.djei.ie/enterprise/smes/latepay.htm)

If a gallery is paid either in full or has agreed to be paid through instalments, but the artist has not been paid, the artist should contact the gallery requiring payment or to have the work returned immediately under the terms of their letters of consignment and the terms and conditions of their invoices. It will be a business decision between the gallery and the artist on how to deal with unpaid for work. However, going back to the original idea of the letter of consignment, the work has been offered to the

176

gallery as the artist's agent. This means that there is no transfer of ownership until the item has been paid for in full. Some artists will know to whom the work has been sold. Not many galleries relish their reputations been sullied by the knowledge that an artist or their agent may appear at a client's door looking for the return of their work. This of course should be managed in a clear and legal manner.

The final destination, when all other avenues fail, is the legal route. Depending on individual situations, it may be possible to turn the matter over to an official debt collector, or the matter may require taking specific legal advice and end up in courts.

For the most part, artists are reluctant to go that final step, and we recommend it only after an artist has taken advice based on all of the evidence gathered as outlined above. But, it must be said, that the initial steps that we have outlined in terms of prevention may go a long way to avoid this.

If we are to see ourselves as professionals in our field, then the first step is to ensure that we protect ourselves at all stages of our careers.

Our message is: **Think** before you say yes to any relationship; **Document** all aspects of the relationship and agreements; **Communicate** openly, clearly and in a businesslike manner – always confirming in writing or by email any decisions made; **Be consistent** and open with communications; and **Act** in a clear and professional manner at all times.

Finally, remember, you're not alone in this and if you need any further advice Visual Artists Ireland is available for confidential chats and advice.

By Noel Kelly

Artists and Curators

Introduction

In recent years the definition of the role of the curator has undergone a dramatic change, and continues still to be refined and challenged. With this change there is also the associated re-definition of the relationship between the artist and curator. This implies a direct impact on the relationship between artist and audience. In this text we will look at some broad definitions of curator, and look at the benefits of the relationship between artist and curator.

What is a Curator?

The term curator comes from the traditional museum background. The role of curator/keeper was once seen as *"One who manages or oversees, as the administrative director of a museum collection or a library"** derived from the Latin curator, overseer, from curates, past participle of curare, to take care of.

To quote from FÁS on the key aspects of the curatorial role, '*To arrange an exhibition, curators choose which objects to display and organise the loan of exhibits from other collections if they need to. They also organise the transportation, insurance and storage of objects. Curators make sure that objects are displayed in a clear and attractive way. They also co-ordinate, and in many cases, write and compile exhibition catalogues and the texts that accompany exhibits. Large museums or galleries often employ education officers to involve schools or promote tourism. Curators may liaise with them to produce slides, work sheets and demonstrations.*'

Today we see curator in a much broader context. The presence of the 'curator' within visual arts both in Ireland and more expansively in the International context has increased dramatically in the last 10 years. The roles, the functions, the positions, and the influence that they exert has changed both their own careers and also has created a new form of relationship between the general audience, the artist and art institution. Art critic and curator, Michael Brenson best reflects these changes in an interesting observation. He posits the following as potential key characteristics of contemporary curators: '*aesthetician, diplomat, economist, critic, historian, politician, audience developer, and promoter.*'
**

Also, the independent curator is often the generator of projects that are interrelated to other projects originated by that same curator. They may be working without a clear programming policy or strategy in institutional terms but are also capable of interfacing with authorities and organisations in the development and realisation of projects.

Curatorial Practice

The goal of curatorial practice is the best representation of contemporary visual art to an identified audience. In this there is a mutual symbiotic relationship between the artist, the curator and the audience. Through policy and research, institutions, biennials, and independent projects start with a concept of what is to be proposed by any programme of exhibitions and supporting events. It is fundamental that such research is an on-going requirement for curators. They may specialise in specific areas, and some may follow a number of artists, updating themselves on progress in specific practices.

To some artists, curators may offer advice on direction, and become a confidante to whom the artist may turn when in need of advice, support and even challenges to particular ideas or directions. This allows them to consciously reflect current artistic practice, theory, presentation and care in preparation for future exhibitions, whilst they at the same time deliver on the expectations of the target audience.

For biennials, interested parties may include government ministries, national institutions, local authorities as well as international event organisers. At the more local and/or independent level the curator may be working with an artistic director, or artist lead initiatives of a few people.

178

From this we can see that different forms of presentation will have their own criteria for selection, be it political, thematic, social, financial, or historical.

The Artist / Curator Relationship

It is important for artists to have their work seen by curators. Outside of the given potential for public presentation of the artist's work, there is also a valuable opportunity to engage in a critical discussion of their practice. Against the background of presentation, distribution and contextualization, the curator can offer direction based within a 'world view'.

This form of discussion includes looking at the artists oeuvre in term of 'aboutness' with consideration given to the conceptual and practical layers. The artist's own feelings about their work provide a starting point. From this deeper investigations into placement form a persuasive argument. It is not necessarily the case that the discussions and interpretations constitute an 'absolute' right, but may contribute towards a convincing, enlightening, and informative stance from which the artist may progress. At times these discussions also open up the potentiality that the artist's work, when viewed with the eyes of the potential audience, may be open to more or different interpretation.

This form of 'critique' is a useful platform for further development of practice, and may lead the curator to introduce the artist to other avenues of thought, and on a more practical level to specialists both within and outside the arts with a view to furthering knowledge and opening opportunities of experimentation.

Developing Exhibitions and Projects

The development of exhibitions is also a critical aspect of the artist/curator relationship. The many forms of exhibition have the ability to present, challenge, provoke, and, at times, even prompt actions. This is an active facilitation and offers more than just guidance. The curator becomes an editor of what will be displayed, and how it will be shown to its best advantage within the context of the work and the theme to be portrayed. The decisiveness of this moment can become key in the success of the representation of the artist's work to the wider audience, and may provide opportunity of assessment or extension of awareness of the ways the audience understand the artist's works, and through that the world around them.

The curator also provides an overview of all of the factors that must be taken into consideration when planning. Looking at contingencies, understanding the potential for underlying power plays, and knowledge of practicalities; the curator becomes a key decision maker and facilitator who leads and mediates across agencies responsible for the delivery of the project. Whether commissioning of new work or exhibition of existing work the curator is the central point around which contractors, technicians, and other cultural workers collaboratively gather to achieve their goal of presentation.

The curator also becomes a key voice in the presentation of the work to press and media. The preparation of media material is formed from a background of placement as well as the provision of the most basic details of what, when and where. Through networks of contacts with critics, journalists and fellow directors and curators, the curator can raise the profile of artists and provide opportunities for further presentation and development.

The curator may also agree with the artist on a strategy of documentation. Catalogues, monographs, or placement within a wider critical publication provide the artist with the means to place their work within a larger context. At the same time such publications become important research documents. It is crucial that the curator ensures that the publication is undertaken with a specific reason that stands on merit. Through the discussion the curator may dissuade the artist from entering into a publication cycle. As it is a costly and time consuming exercise it may be found that the financial aspect of the project could be better placed elsewhere, and publications deferred until a more important juncture in the artist's practice. From experience curators will be able to identify the reasons for publication and to offer advice on circulation and targeted marketing.

Conclusion

We have now seen the curator and confidante, advisor and facilitator. We have also seen the curator constantly researching and providing opportunities both in and out of established consensus. Curators may choose to work with artists and audiences in a provocative and courageous manner. But there are pitfalls along the way. More and more we see evidence of heavy handed curatorial practice. Although denied, this form of practice places key importance on high level concept and the artist becomes subservient. This has led to the cult of the 'super star' curator and has caused much misunderstanding and distrust. It is therefore important that both artist and curator develop a common language and open dialogue. The artist and curator must communicate both openly and frankly, taking criticism and suggestions seriously. Through this, both gain the opportunity to identify demands, advantages, and opportunities.

The job of being a curator is privileged and not merely an assigned right. Therefore power games and posturing have no place within any professional definition of the role. It is also a position of trust. This trust is built upon experience and requires both artist and curator to work together, rather than in opposition. At times the artist may not be present during an exhibition and the levels of professional confidence displayed by a curator then becomes the comfort zone upon which the artist can rely when releasing their work for exhibition.

180

The mobility and reach of curators provides them with the potential for great influence. But, as time passes curators need to re-assess their positions. Areas of interest need to be addressed in terms of intellectual worth and value. Moving with trends, or purposely taking a stance against establish fashions may be equally difficult. Therefore the curator must be able to express and defend responses and opinions while at the same time recognizing personal preconceived notions. Heading down a focused path may have a short term advantage, however working with a forward view provides more open and sympathetic opportunities for the curator and artists that they choose to work with.

*Museum/Art Gallery
Curator Career Details – Career Directions
**Art Journal, Vol. 57, 1998

By Noel Kelly

Artists, Commercial Galleries & the International Art Market

The contents of this text reflect the views of the author and do not necessarily reflect the official views or policy of all commercial galleries.

Introduction

This text seeks to be an introduction to how commercial galleries work, how they differ from museums or other public spaces, how they exist in the wider international art market and their relationships with artists.

Who is Behind Commercial Galleries?

Most commercial galleries are the brainchild of one or two people, and are founded for the most part by people who are interested in contemporary art or have a background in the visual arts from college or university. Most galleries are 'businesses of passion' and are run by somebody who is very passionate about the arts and who is often driven by specific personal agendas. Even though dependent on sales to survive, galleries tread a fine line between an existence that is also defined by critical context, based on who they show and why. The reputation of a gallery is based on the success and content of its exhibition programme and gallerists are hugely conscious of the responses to each show, both critically and financially.

Commercial Galleries V's Public Spaces or Museums

Unlike public spaces or museums, commercial galleries 'represent artists' and these relationships form ongoing financial and creative working arrangements. These relationships vary in detail but broadly follow an established pattern with expectations and commitments from both sides that are well defined.

Public spaces and museums might hold solo and group exhibitions like commercial galleries, but generally they do not have ongoing relationships with artists in the same way. They do not (for the most part) sell art, but receive public grants that allow them to hold exhibitions.

Commercial galleries do not receive public money – they rely on sales to keep trading. Public spaces do not attend art fairs, which form a significant part of how a commercial gallery trades.

Being Represented by a Commercial Gallery

Representation by a commercial gallery is based on the principle that the artist makes the work for exhibition and the gallery sells the work. Commission taken as standard is 50-50% – i.e. 50 per cent of the sale to the artist and 50 per cent to the gallery. However, relationships are by circumstance much more complex.

Using their 50% commission, galleries pay for the gallery space, the gallery staff, the private view, the invitations and the promotion of the exhibition to the press. Artists make and fabricate the work and cover their own studio costs, as well as material costs.

As a rule of thumb, artists should never pay a hire fee to a gallery, and any suggestion that they should is simply wrong.

If an artist wishes to have a serious on-going working relationship with a gallery, then the 50% split of sales rule should always be used. Whatever the circumstances with discounts offered to collectors by the gallery, or any other reason, the artist should never receive less than 50% of the final sale price after tax and VAT has been accounted for. Discounts and tax are usually taken off the top of a sale before the 50/50 percent division is applied.

If the artist is seriously showing with a gallery then ALL sales should be made through the gallery and no sales made where the gallery does not share in its commission. This applies even for sales to friends, sales from the artist studio or to sales to collectors who approach the artist directly. This underlines how closely artist and galleries work together.

If a gallery has contributed any money to making costs and / or framing as is sometimes the case, then the gallery might ask for these costs to be deducted before commissions are calculated.

If the artist has special costs they would like to claim back 'off the top' such as printing costs with photography or materials costs, these must be declared before the sales are made so that gallerists have a clear idea of how the commission and costs might work.

Expectations of the Gallery

Galleries will have expectations about what makes up or constitutes a show. They will also have opinions about what they might be able to sell. It is important to remember that gallerists have close relationships with their collectors and walk-in visitors to galleries rarely buy work. Gallerists will know what the overriding theme of a collection might be, and what work might appeal to buyers.

As cynical as it may sound, the market shows us that painting, and by this I mean unique painted works on canvas, tends to be the most widely collected form of art, followed by drawing and works on paper, sculpture, then photography and editioned prints (except in rare cases) and then video and other forms of installation work.

It is worth noting that galleries are businesses and what kind of art you make, might affect your chances of achieving commercial representation. I think its worth looking at as many gallery websites as you can and listing:

- How many painters are represented?
- How many are women?
- How much video / media work in shown?
- How old are the gallery artists?

....and so on, so that you can get a real picture of the kind of artists that are usually represented by the majority of commercial galleries.

This exercise might not tell you what you want to know, but it is very important to be realistic and armed with as much information as possible before you approach any potential gallery.

Exhibitions and Art Fairs

The main aim of most good galleries is to hold serious solo (monograph) or group exhibitions (themed or subject-led) between seven and nine times per year. Galleries often have tight turn around periods for installation between shows and the average show lasts from between five to seven weeks.

Exhibitions are usually launched with a private view and oftentimes other events such as late openings or talks are held during the run of the exhibition.

Art fairs operate on a totally different footing. Galleries must apply to take part in art fairs by submitting a proposal. It is stipulated that all applying galleries must have an exhibition programme. Not all galleries get selected for the fairs they would like to attend.

It is generally better for galleries not to show too much work at art fairs and to keep their booth presentations as minimal as possible. This helps fairs appear as close to exhibitions a possible, though in essence they are not.

It is worth remembering that art fairs, especially international ones are very expensive for galleries to attend. Galleries are obliged to pay for their booths at fairs, as well as all shipping costs. If the fair is in a foreign country, then shipping and accommodation can be very expensive indeed.

Galleries will not show each artist that they represent at every fair they attend – they will be selective.

Art fairs also have a hierarchy, the best fairs internationally are considered to be Armory (New York) in March, TEFAF Maastricht (The Netherlands) in March, Basel (Switzerland) in June, Frieze (London) in October and Miami Basle (Miami) in December.

Artists and Art Fairs

In my view, art fairs are unpleasant places for artists as they often function as a great leveller of ideas. As a kind of Zeitgeist, they show internationally what artists are making and all at once. At fairs it is possible to make many more comparisons between international artists' work than in other circumstances.

Collectors, critics and curators like fairs a great deal as they can see a lot of work in a short period of time. There is also a large social element to fairs where collectors can meet each other as well as meet the gallerists and museums who they support. Because of this fairs have become very important to gallerists and many if not the largest percentage of their sales are made at fairs.

It is worth going to fairs to look and gauge the market if you are an artist, however the worst thing you can do is approach a gallery at a fair. Galleries attend fairs only to see three kinds of people: collectors, critics and curators. They are not there to see artists and will look on approaches from artists in this setting as an intrusion. It is worth remembering that they have spent a large sum of money to be present at the fair and are only there to work on the things they have in their booths.

How Do Galleries Find Artists?

Galleries find artists through a number of ways, which I will list below:

- 1. Through other artists. Most galleries listen intently to what their existing artists think as they are building a mutually supportive stable of artists.
- 2. Degree shows. Many dealers and gallerists will visit annual degree shows and MA shows, with a focus on particular colleges and institutions.
- 3. Particular selected shows. In the UK the most visited of these exhibitions are in no particular order: The New Contemporaries, EAST,Oriel Mostyn Open, The Royal Academy Summer Exhibition and so on.
- 4. Group exhibitions. Younger galleries often curate group shows by young artists. More established galleries often watch these shows to see who is up and coming. It is easier to become included in a group show rather than getting a solo show.
- 5. Through the press. Getting reviews or your works mentioned in any kind and every kind of magazine is a huge help as the art world reads copiously.

Approaching Galleries

Understanding the so-called pecking order in the art world is VERY important when considering approaching a gallery.

For example, if you are a recent graduate, who has never had a show, it is very unlikely that a gallery that only represents artists who have shown internationally for over a decade will be interested in your work.

Also, if you only paint kittens, and you find a gallery that already has a kitten painter, you might also find that they feel they have that ground covered.

Galleries have careers too and are all at different stages. Find out where the gallery you like is in the pecking order before you approach them.

The most important point is to find out as much as possible about the gallery and the person you are approaching before you approach them.

In my view sending unsolicited material to commercial galleries does not work. I also feel its VERY unwise to send anything to a gallery that you have not visited on a number of occasions. Gallerists can tell if you are aware of their programme and its good to have a strong working knowledge of what galleries show.

Attending openings is VERY important and cannot be underestimated. The art world is a large and varied place, and showing up and showing your face is important.

However if you are going to attend gallery openings a few words of caution. Do not arrive at somebody else opening and talk about your own work. Never ask to show you slides unless you have an appointment and never at a private view. Its better by far to talk about the show you are looking at, and express an opinion about that!

The short answer of how to approach a gallery is to get to know them as best you can, and think very carefully about if your work would fit the gallery you like best. For example, young artists stand better chances at younger galleries, and it's better to approach younger curators and writers to look at your work when you have just left college. Attending private views is a must, simply contact galleries by email and ask to be put on their email invitation list.

Applying to open submission exhibitions such as those listed above is also important as gallerists will see these and actually see your work if you are successful in getting in.

By Fred Mann

With Practicality comes a Practice: the Artist as Curator

Introduction

In France, 1648, a group of court artists sent a petition to King Louis XIV, who at the time was 10 years old, requesting the establishment of a Royal Academy of Painting, which would distinguish their work from the artisan trades. To make their case, they exhibited a grand display of works – all of which glorified the monarch and sought to demonstrate painting as a fine art solely dedicated to "the pursuit of virtue".* After much opposition from guilds and corporations, the _Académie Royale de Peinture et de Sculpture_ was secured alongside academies in Holland, England and Italy, and with it the status of the new academic artist as a professional distinct from the gilded tradesman.

This is the earliest example I can find of the artist as curator. I don't think it's a coincidence that it announces a time when art and its accessory occupations of criticism and curation were undergoing intense professionalization. Subsequent manifestations of the artist as curator, culled unsystematically from Europe and North America's art historical annals, are equally connected to moments when artists took it upon themselves to reform officially and socially decreed policies regarding their profession, and thereby redefine the cultural status of works of art. And with the awakening of artist as curator come more intricate, intelligent, and complex understandings of the ways that exhibitions mediate the public and private sphere beyond the mere display of objects.

To fully address the public and private, commercial and critical ways in which art exhibitions are intertwined, interpreted, absorbed and denied vis-à-vis a consideration of the artist as curator might actually require a re-writing of art history as we know it – too great a task for me – a non-historian. What I can do is posit the relevance of the artist as curator in art practice, and to offer some examples of how artists imagine this role today.

Salon-Style

When critics and members of the public in 1800s France were invited to view the new society exhibitions, they were entering a world dominated by artists – where artists selected the work on the walls and arranged every aspect of its presentation.

Consider for instance the Paris Salon – an annual exhibition juried by academy members to present the finest examples of classical French peinture. By 1830, fringe exhibitions known as Salons des Refusés – translated from French to mean "Salons of the Refused" – were being mounted by artists whose work the Paris Salon had refused official entry. Hosted in living rooms and small galleries, the artist as curator was an important component to these and other similar salon-style presentations, where groups of affiliated peers organised counter-exhibitions to the well-bridled Academy shows.

The most famous among the Paris Salons des Refusés occurred in 1863, when a group of artists interested in painting "everyday life" were outraged by the unprecedented number of works (over 3,000) the jury rejected that year. As usual, they organised an exhibition of refused work, yet in a controversial move they sought permission from the government to go above the jury's head and exhibit the Salon des Refusés in an annex alongside the regular Salon. In a decision that caused mayhem among Paris's art constabulary, Emperor Napoléon III granted permission and the 1863 Salon des Refusés became the first to be officially sponsored by the French government. Among other works, it included one of the most significant paintings of modern life, Édouard Manet's Le dejeuner sur l'herbe. The Impressionists continued to exhibit their works in successive Salons des Refusés, consistently dismantling the critical sway of the Paris Salon and allowing the public to judge their work. By 1881, the government had withdrawn official sponsorship of the Salon. In its place, a group of artists organised the Société des Artistes Français to take responsibility for the show. Soon after this another group that included Ernest Meissonier, Puvis de Chavannes, and Auguste Rodin seceded to form the Société Nationale des Beaux-Artsand in their newly founded association they organised their own exhibition, the Salon du Champs de Mars. Following in this vein, in 1903 a group of painters and sculptors led by Pierre-Auguste Renoir and Auguste Rodin organised the exhibition that would become the showpiece of 20th century European art, the Salon d'Automne. Jacques Villon, one of the artists who helped organise the drawing section of the first salon would later help the Puteaux Group gain recognition with showings at the Salon des Indépendants. Meanwhile, in North America the Association of American Painters and Sculptors organised the first Armory Show in New York in 1913, run by artists Arthur Davies and Walt Kuhn and critic Walter Pach. It displayed some 1,250 paintings, sculptures, and decorative works by over 300 European and American artists, including Marcel Duchamp who famously exhibited his Nude Descending on a Staircase No.2. The rest, as they say, is history.

The significance of the artist association in the development of the artist as curator persists today, for example in Dublin's Royal Hibernian Academy annual exhibition, a relatively unchanged descendant of the society exhibitions held in the late 19th century and early 20th centuries. As such they have done little to progress the role of the artist as curator beyond the salon-style show of a bygone era. While the context of these shows may be clear and the premise uncomplicated, at least on the surface, they exist primarily as an institutionalised reinforcement of values – to the exclusion of other ideas that might be present in the exhibition. Although more complex in origin and meaning, aspects of the end-of-year Fine Art degree shows or MA exhibitions also incorporate remote notions of the artist as curator. These shows are produced by and for the artists they represent, with the support of their 'member' organisation (school). A recognised lack of critical intent may be why many schools now commonly invite a guest-curator to oversee these shows.

Self-Organising

Self-organising is vital to any consideration of the artist as curator, and the ways in which the artist as curator has evolved through a cast of artist-initiated and run associations illustrates that artists (as early as 1648 France) have been deeply and actively involved in self-organisation as a form of curating.

Today artists continue to curate in ways akin to the salon-style, perhaps as a type of refusé in response to an official exhibition, or as a means to simply prepare an exhibition of recent work for a new audience. With the advent of artist-run spaces in the 1970s and 80s a new type of artist as curator emerges. Project in Dublin, founded by artists in 1969, and its counterparts in the US and London, directly positioned artists at the centre of their exhibition programmes. Artists selected the work, and instead of long-term planning for 6-8 week shows, exhibitions were usually in short, 2-3 week rotations. Flexibility, experimentation and support of unestablished artists countered both the institutional framework the museum and the commercial agenda of the gallery. Known in general terms as 'alternative' venues, gradually these spaces have morphed into variations of the organisations they sought to oppose, to become new hybrids of the museum and the gallery. Today, Project et al represent a prototype of a particular kind of arts organisation, working to complement established spaces rather than counter them, and the artist as curator has been replaced by a new creed of professional programme directors and curators.

There are art spaces where closely affiliated peer groups – for example Catalyst Arts in Belfast, Transmission in Glasgow, and Orchard in New York (which ran for 3 years from 2005-2008) – radically assign the role of artist as curator at the core of their activities. Initiated as self-organised venues, the responsibilities for planning and curating exhibitions falls upon a committee of individual artists who work together on all aspects of the programme, including fund-raising, administration and governance, and future planning. Here, modes of self-organising depend on an infrastructure that includes a physical space. Self-organising can also involve the artist as curator as the generator of events that expand beyond the exhibition – and beyond the exhibition venue – to off-site events, public gatherings, one-night performances, screenings, etc.**

The Artist-Curator

As artists tapped into and defined tasks now associated with curating, long before the role of the professional 'curator' was named or even imagined, the modern art exhibition also progressed from historic collections into the temporal, historic and thematic events we know today. By the 1920s artists were fully conscious of the exhibition as a revolutionary figure in the story of art, such that El Lissitzky aimed to exhibit an exhibition and Dadaist and

Surrealist activities explicitly re-imagined conventions in exhibiting. In a vivid description by curator Germano Celant...

"[Surrealist exhibitions] wanted to encourage all senses of the imagination, and they valued the interference of the outside world, whether it took the form of dirt, error, sex, disorder chance, disgust, fear, perversion[...]And so in their exhibitions, from 1938-1947, the space was inundated with pulsating sensations, involving the spectators" [emphasis mine].

It is precisely in the intensity of the viewer's experience that the exhibition begins to work against conventional directives for experiencing individual works of art and towards entire, spatial arrangements. Environments were filled to capacity – the work occupied the walls, the floors, the ceilings. And visitors reacted, usually to some level of psychological shock, the Surrealists preferred brand of audience participation.

But beyond theatrics, the Surrealist exhibition understood art in relationship to other cultural and social systems. And with these developments we can begin to recognise dimensions of the artist as curator that lead into the artist-curator – an individual whose practice exists in an expanded field, where the radical reworking of presentation, exhibition, display, and installation are fundamental to the practice of being an artist. By 1957, in an ambitious inhabitation of the artist-curator, Richard Hamilton made the now famous An Exhibit at the ICA in London. Hamilton's amalgamation of images, artworks and display techniques arguably created a new standard in both artistic and curatorial practice. Marcel Broodthaers' landmark 1968 project Musée d'Art Moderne, Département des Aigles is another key example of this kind of work.

As we jump through the 20th century and into the 21st, taking into account the artist-curator as a principle player, we can locate examples as diverse as Fluxus and the Situationists, to Gordon Matta-Clark's FOOD and Judy Chicago and Miriam Shapiro's Womanhouse, to the current practices of Liam Gillick, General Idea, Bik van Der Pol, Group Material, Pil and Galia Kollectiv, Gavin Wade, Atelier Van Leishout, Kathy Slade, Paul O'Neill, Nayland Blake, and many, many others.***

While the political and interpretive agendas may diverge (to the extreme), each of these examples prepares the exhibition as a discursive site, inextricably tied to the artist-curator as a proponent of collective work. Without entering into a narration of particular projects, what is important here is how these developments extend art-making beyond conservative, traditional ideas of medium or 'discipline'. These practices shift artistic practice and in doing so they move us, the audience, from a single understanding of 'art' towards a fuller terrain of creative practices in visual culture.

A Last Word about Professionalization

Politics, criticism and representation intersect in the exhibition perhaps more concretely than in other social and cultural manifestations – and for this very reason, the artist as curator embodies a link to the impact of

189

exhibitions on artistic production and reception. Indeed, the relatively modern awareness of 'audience' that is now integral to exhibition-making arises through the artist's – or artist as curators – cognizance of how artworks circulate and are introduced to the public. Without a doubt, a notion of the artist as curator precedes even a remote understanding of a 'curator' as the person charged with the tasks associated with exhibiting art.

As artistic practice continues to expand through Trans - and inter-disciplinary applications of the curatorial, it has become a worry (for some) to establish where artwork ends and curating begins. For the most part, I find these debates sorely limited. In thinking about situations or contexts where we find the artist as curator, it is important to remember that the curatorial evolves *through* artistic practice. The curator emerges in a history of art, bringing different sets of professional circumstances along the way. What it is *to curate* has shifted towards further participation in the production of meaning. These shifts have led to a blurring of the boundaries between the artist and the curator, thus the evolution of hybrid designations. How productive these designations are, who profits when we attempt to clearly define the artistic from the curatorial, and to what extent artistic production has internalized the criteria for 'being an artist' and 'being a curator', underlies the complexity of contemporary art. For certain, pinning down the artist as curator's work as somehow *different* has led to incredible insights, but it has also led to disparaging and conservative dismissals of certain types of cultural work. We need to be aware, as we heed the differences, what it at stake in the spaces where this work takes place.

* Art and Theory 1648 – 1815: An Anthology of Changing Ideas, Harrison, Wood, Gaiger, London: Wiley-Blackwell 1991, pp.13

** For a more expansive discussion of the potential for artists to self-organise and self-initiate projects, see Paul O'Neill's "Self-Organisation as a Way of Being" in the Professional Pathways section on the Info~Pool.

*** While there are multiple examples of the artist as guest-curator, I'd like to make a quick distinction between artists who occasionally curate once-off pursuits and those for whom the curatorial is integral to an art practice. In the present discussion, I am only interested in the latter.

By Sarah Pierce

Presenting Yourself

Documenting Your Work

Introduction – Basics of Photographic Documentation

For the past few years I have specialised in the photography of historical objects, documents and artworks. During this time I photographed items as varied as paintings, sculpture, and art installations. I have found that, while creating images that convey the atmosphere of an exhibition or installation can sometimes be difficult and challenging, the documentation of individual works can be a very straightforward process. In this piece I will endeavour to point out the minimum equipment needed to make adequate photographic documentation and most importantly the basic techniques to help you get consistent results. The following represents the minimum equipment needed to make a start:

- Manual SLR camera
- Tripod and cable release
- Spirit level
- Metering system
- Light source

Equipment You Will Need:

Manual SLR Camera: There is an abundance of 35 mm cameras available on the market – both new and used. I would recommend a second-hand model preferably a Canon, Minolta, Olympus or Pentax. Any of these models should be available either on the Internet or in camera shops for well below 200 Euro. A standard 50mm lens would be a good starting lens.

Tripod and Cable Release: My advice would be to allow the largest part of your budget for the purchase of a tripod. Do not buy a cheap lightweight tripod – it will not work efficiently and it will be difficult to position precisely. With a decent tripod soundly in position a cable release will trip the shutter without causing any vibration to the camera.

Spirit Level: Using a spirit level is the best method for levelling your camera. It is possible to buy a very small spirit level, which fits into the accessory shoe of an SLR camera. Alternatively a cheap decorator's spirit level will suffice.

Metering System: To meter accurately I would suggest the use of a hand held or 'incidental' light meter, which measures the specific light actually falling on the subject. However if working on a budget, your 'in camera' meter can be employed in conjunction with a grey card* (see 'Determining the Correct Exposure).

Light Source: Electronic flash would be my first choice as a light source for artworks, while tungsten lamps and even daylight can also be used. But one has to understand the limitation of each light source* (see the section on Photographing Installations and Exhibitions).The above 5 items are the absolute minimum that one would require to attempt to make any reasonable documentation of artworks. If you find yourself trying to document artwork without the above you should be aware from the start that you will not achieve consistently usable results. Your time will be wasted and the expense borne will be in vane.

Formats

Traditionally 35 mm slides, (or transparencies as they are also called) were all that an artist needed to promote their work as they where universally accepted by all galleries. Added to these there are now several more ways of communicating with galleries, institutions and organisations. Every day now we access websites, send e-mails, and write CDs and DVDs. These newer methods of communication are a perfect vehicle for digital photography. Once captured, an image can be infinitely copied at no extra cost, and can be sent by a number of mediums to an even greater number of people.

Digital cameras of sufficient quality with a reasonable level of control are still very expensive especially for the professional SLR models. The cheapest I can think of would cost roughly €1000. In addition to the cost of the digital camera you would also need to factor in the cost of a computer and software on which to download and edit images. If you are tempted to make the change to digital, do not be tempted by lower-priced models. Although offering high-resolution, lower cost point-and-shoot cameras cannot be controlled manually and therefore will not yield adequate results.

Determining a Correct Exposure

Determining a correct exposure for artwork can be tricky business. However, if the metering system employed is properly understood, the job of accurate metering can be made very easy and repeatable. The reflective metering system of an SLR camera works in the following way: Light reflected off the surface of the artwork passes through the lens of the camera and falls on a light sensitive cell. The intensity of the light determines the shutter speed and aperture set on the camera. Different tones and colours quite obviously have different levels of reflectivity where the darker colours reflect less light and lighter colours reflect more light.

Through their exhaustive research, camera manufacturers have determined that the average scene reflects only 18% of the light that falls on to it. All camera meters therefore are calibrated to reflect this discovery and so are only useful for average scenes. Over the years all kinds of additions have been made to camera meters to make them more accurate in a varied number of conditions, but still the most effective means remain the old faithful 'grey card'.

Kodak manufactures a piece of grey card which magically reflects only 18% of the light which falls on to it. So if we placed this card between the camera and our subject and take a reading using the in camera meter, set the shutter speed and aperture suggested on-camera and then make our shot (minus the grey card) and presto – we have an accurate exposure! Effectively what we have done is overcome the camera's inability to see differential tones within a scene and we have set an exposure that will definitely allow accurate reproductions of a predetermined grey tone (the camera meter is trying to measure for the scene that we have provided for it).

A separate hand held light meter (which meters the ambient light, i.e. the light falling onto the subject rather than that being reflected from it) is another alternative and proves in all cases to be far more accurate than any light meter situated within a camera. This would be my preferred tool for exposure readings.

Photographing Paintings and Prints

For copying two-dimensional items such as paintings or prints, align the camera so that it is perfectly parallel to the plane of your artwork. Use your spirit level to maintain levels on your artwork and your camera and lastly use your eye through the viewfinder to check that the subject is perfectly square.

The lighting needs to be even over the entire subject area and you do not want any part of the light source to be reflected back into the camera, as this will cause "flare". The best possible situation is to have two light sources each 45 degrees to the subject pointing to the opposite corners.

Use your light meter to determine the evenness of your lighting and adjust if necessary.

To determine an exposure setting using your meter or grey card, make the setting on your camera, depress your cable and there you have it, your copy.

If using daylight to capture your copy it is important to note that the value of light can rise and fall very quickly and must be constantly observed.

If working outdoors with flat artwork it must also be noted that colour of daylight can be affected by colour and reflections of the environment, only work in neutral coloured areas so as not to pickup colourcasts from colour walls, grass, etc. Also the colour of daylight changes through the day and can be colder in the morning then in the evening..

While working under a blue sky the blueness can be reflected in the artwork as a blue cast. A cloudy and overcast day may be the best choice for making images in daylight.

Photographing 3D Objects

Images of three-dimensional objects are easier to make indoors. If outdoors, I would advise that a background of some kind be employed. Black, white or a light grey paper backgrounds seem to work best in most cases but this is a matter of personal taste. They are available in 9ft rolls for large objects and 4.5ft rolls for small objects and can be purchased in large camera shops.

If using flash or other supplementary lighting, careful composition and positioning of lights to bring out the subjects character is important.

Shooting on large and medium format cameras should be considered if you are making work specifically for reproduction in high-quality publications. As the cost of cameras in this class is a lot higher I would suggest employing a photographer to make these images where necessary, unless of course you have already in your possession a large or medium format camera and you are able to use it easily. The reason I have chosen a 35 mm camera as a base level camera is because it can produce 35 mm slides, the stock in trade for visual artists.

Photographing Exhibitions and Installations

When working in a gallery space one has to take on a different approach and mindset to when undertaking straightforward documentation of individual works. You are no longer trying to make an exact copy of your work; instead you are now trying to make a reasonable representation of your work within a particular space. Paying attention to the particular 'feel' of an exhibition space requires that you consider a number of things:

The relationship between your work and the space

- Colour of lighting
- Level of lighting

Unlike our previous examples where we lit the work specifically for purposes of reproduction, we are now faced with the situation where the work is already lit for the viewers in the gallery. Introducing any additional lighting would create a false impression of how the work actually appeared in the gallery space.

In most indoor situations lighting levels are generally low and a tripod and cable release must be employed. After composing an image that shows the piece (or pieces) within the space in your viewfinder, consideration must be given to the colour of light which is predominant in the exhibition space. There are several possibilities:

The gallery is completely artificially lit with low-level tungsten background light and additional lighting to draw the viewer's eye to the pieces on exhibition.

The gallery is lit by daylight with supplementary tungsten light to highlight the objects on exhibition.

The gallery is lit by daylight with supplementary fluorescent strip lighting and tungsten lighting to highlight the objects on exhibition.

Case (A) is the easiest situation to cope with. As there is only one form of lighting (tungsten) we can choose a film that is balanced to this tungsten light source. My personal favourite would be a Fuji 64 tungsten balanced slide film. In a situation such as the above, the object to be photographed usually has the highest level of lighting by way of spotlighting. It is very important that the exposure is made for the highlight within the complete image. To ensure that this is the case the meter reading must be taken from the brightest part of the scene. Once a meter reading has been taken we are ready to make our exposure. Using available light usually means a slow shutter speed and this is where your tripod and cable release come into their own. The resulting image shot on tungsten film will have a very neutral tone with no sense of that yellow to orange glow we get when shooting on the daylight film under tungsten lighting.

Case (B) however presents us with the problem in that the piece to be photographed is illuminated with tungsten light, but the background light source is that of daylight. If we choose tungsten film in this instance the artwork may have a correct tone but the overall tone of the image will have an uncomfortable blue cast (the result of shooting daylight on to tungsten film). In this instance we must allow our artworks to look warm and choose a daylight film so that the overall effect will be much more pleasing to the eye.

Case (C) is a little bit tricky. We must use daylight film because of the daylight component in the overall lighting scheme. The best plan in this type of situation would be to make a multiple exposure on one frame of film. If the windows of the gallery space are shuttered or have blinds – the following would be possible. With the shutters or blinds open and all the other lighting switched off an exposure is made of the exhibition space. The shutters or blinds are then drawn. The camera shutter is cocked without advancing the film, and a second exposure is made with just the fluorescent strip-lights turned on. For this exposure a 0.5 magenta filter is placed over the lens to cancel out the green cast created by this type of light source. The camera is then cocked again without advancing the film and a third exposure is made with only the tungsten spotlight turned on, a blue filter is placed over the lens to cancel out cast created by the warm coloured light. To enable this method of shooting to be successful it must be possible for the photographer to make test shots and see them immediately – to facilitate this, a medium format camera with Polaroid back or a digital camera with computer is necessary. As you can imagine from the above, it can take some practice before one can accurately assess the lighting in any given exhibition space.

Video / Projections

Documenting video work and projections can also be tricky business, but there are three basic issues:

It is useful to create a screen grab (freeze frame) to work with

Remember that your projection is also a light source – it should be your primary exposure

To photograph outdoor artworks I would recommend a simple you must allow for these to be included in the exposure also.

These issues are addressed by making multiple exposures on one sheet of film. Finding a balance between all light sources is usually achieved by making several test Polaroid's or using some other instant test system.

Outdoors / In the Public Realm Approach.

Always use your tripod and cable release. Photograph at a time of day and when the sun is behind you illuminating your object to be photographed. It should be possible to photograph outdoor artworks at any time of day if the day is an overcast one (but try not to use sky as background). If you have purchased a hand held light meter – use it all the time. Camera meters can always be fooled, but not so your hand held light meter.

Digital Photography

I have used the image below as an example of how digital cameras can be employed to great effect. Again I have to say, use the best you can afford. An SLR type camera which can capture a RAW type file would be my preference. A RAW digital file is the actual data gathered from the sensor of the camera, and as such this data has not been processed or manipulated in any way. If you take a file like this into an image editing program you can work on the exposure, colour balance and contrast, with great ease and control ensuring that nothing is left to chance. A camera that produces a jpeg or similar type file processes the image in camera disregarding information that it regards as non critical. This is fine if the resulting image does not need any further adjustments. However if it does need further adjustments the missing information now becomes critical and any adjustments made have a degrading effect on some part of the image.

Colour correction would be the most important correction to be made on a file and I can safely say that if you colour correct a RAW file it has no noticeable effect on the quality of the file. To make a digital documentation of a space, as in the image above, I would suggest the following steps.

Make a test shot with a grey card or colour checker (this can be used as a colour correction tool later)

Multiple exposures can be made from the same tripodded spot.

After colour and exposure correcting, elements of each of the images can be composited together to make an image which would be close to a viewer's perception of the space.

- the overall environment.
- the video screen in the foreground.

196

- the items in the display cases and
- the illuminated panel right in the centre of the picture.

All of these items are correctly exposed in one of the four thumbnail images on the left and after careful colour correction they are composited together using layer masks in Photoshop.

This case is an extreme one but it proves the point that extremes do exist. If lighting is reasonably even overall in an exhibition space a single photo might suffice but it is worth mentioning that colour balance and exposure are crucial, and digital cameras make these particular variables very easy to capture.

By David Monahan

David Monahan graduated from the Dun Laoghaire College of Art and Design with a qualification in Photography in 1997. Since then he has worked for several National institutions including The National Library, National Museum and the National Photographic Archive. He recently worked on two major exhibitions for the National Library of Ireland (*James Joyce* and *Ulysses*, and *The Life And Works Of William Butler Yeats*) where he completed a large share of all photographic works. His general photographic practice has touched on areas such as artwork documentation, portraiture, architectural, and interiors His personal work has appeared in shows in the Gallery of Photography, Dublin and the National Photographic archive. He lives and works in central Dublin.

Preparing Proposals

Introduction

This document is intended to assist you prepare better proposals for funding opportunities, commissions, awards etc. In this article the term "commissioner" is used as a generic term for all people to whom you make a proposal.

Many artists have ambivalent feelings about preparing proposals. On one hand it is an essential skill because most funding opportunities require a formal proposal from an artist. On the other it can be seen as a time consuming exercise which takes the artist away from the "real" work of creating their art. If you want to secure funding (be that a commission, a residency or other) then you are going to have to prepare a proposal that outlines what you want to do, with whom and when in order to begin the conversation with a potential commissioner or funder. Preparing proposals is not rocket science but it is a skill and as such, requires time, patience and research. The common mistakes many artists make in approaching the task of preparing a proposal can be summarised in the following three points:

- Poor research
- A "one size fits all" approach
- Failure to view the process from the commissioner's perspective

Define Your Project

The first conversation you need to have is with yourself. Why do you want to embark on this particular project? It may seem like an obvious question but it's essential to know the answer. A project you are undertaking primarily for financial outcomes may require a very different decision to one which will offer you a once-off creative challenge. Ask yourself the following questions:

- What is the purpose of the project?
- What's the scope of the work?
- What are the broad objectives?
- Who will benefit? (particularly relevant if the work is in a community context)
- What's the outline time frame?

If you are clear about the intention of your project then it will be easier (a) to select the commissioning opportunities that are best placed to help you realise it and (b) convince the appropriate commissioner to partner you in that realisation.

The Commissioner's Perspective

The commissioner may have very complex social, political, community, aesthetic agendas that are informing their decision to offer funding or a commission at this time. For example, a commission may be offered because it enhances the social or physical profile of a particular community; their interest may be purely creative and aesthetic. These intentions may not compete with each other but a key question for consideration is – can your practice or idea live comfortably side by side with the intentions of the commissioner? Your idea may be very suitable for this process but it is at this point that you need to ask the first of a series of important questions – Is this the right commissioner or process for me? There's no point in trying to mould your idea around the availability of funding if there isn't a "fit". This generally results in a compromised project from the outset.

Research

Research is a central component of every artist's practice both as it relates to the artwork and the practice of seeking funding. Rather than seeing research as something that detracts from the work it should be seen as something that enhances opportunities for resourcing the work. All commissioning opportunities will have guidelines. In public commissions there will be a formal document available to you, which will outline essential information that you need to read and digest before you set about making a proposal. If the process is less formal then there are other ways of acquiring information about the commissioner.

- Look at their web site and see what kinds of projects or initiatives they fund; what sorts of communities do they work in and with? Has this person/organisation ever commissioned or funded an artist in the past? Has the commissioner any other sources of funding that might be more appropriate for the project you want to undertake?

- If there is no website then acquire copies of previous annual reports. Even a casual glance at the quality of the visual material will give you important information about the organisation and its interest in the arts.
- Look at local government county development and arts plans – this will give you important information on the strategies and priorities for funding at county wide level.
- Read the Arts Council's website and download the national arts plan 'Partnership for the Arts' and associated documentation outlining national objectives for the arts.
- Ask artists who have been successful in obtaining commissions or funding for their experiences of working with a particular organisation or commissioner.

If there is a formal process then the guidelines should tell you the following:

- Who the commissioner is
- What their motivation for commissioning/funding is
- The format for applying
- The level of funding
- Whom to contact
- Submission deadlines
- Eligibility
- Decision making process

Read the guidelines very carefully. Then read them again. Think of the commissioner as a resource and if you have questions then contact the relevant person in the organisation. It's important that the questions you ask are not seen to be an attempt to canvas on your behalf so be careful about what you ask and of whom. It may also be that you have identified a key question that the commissioner has forgotten to address and they may be grateful for your attention to detail.Now that you have done some research it's important to revisit your idea and clearly identify the fit between what you want to do and the funding and opportunities that may be available to realise it.

Preparing the Proposal

Commissioners generally require particular types of information. Many artists have a generic proposal that they submit more than once and this is a major mistake. One size does not fit all. Remember – if there is a selection panel there is every chance that someone on that panel may have seen your proposal on a previous occasion. That isn't going to instill confidence in the commissioner that this idea is unique and tailored to their particular context. If you have seriously considered your idea and undertaken your

199

research about the commissioner then you will know whether this commissioning opportunity is worth your time to apply for or not. Take a moment to view this situation from the perspective of the commissioner. They may have gone to considerable trouble to prepare a set of guidelines; perhaps they have also organised a site visit and there is also a contact person to whom questions can be directed. When an artist submits a generic proposal it means they haven't done their homework, the chance they will be unsuccessful increases and time is wasted by everyone. Sending generic proposals can damage your credibility and is bad professional practice.

In summary the kind of information a commissioner requires is:

Your Idea

Be creative, challenging and engaging about your idea. The commissioner will want to be excited about your proposal and this is your opportunity to distinguish yourself from the competition.

Curriculum Vitae

Make sure your CV is up to date and adjusted to fit the project you are proposing. Make it interesting and engaging for the reader by amplifying some of your experience as distinct from merely giving a list of dates and projects.

Artist's Statement

The statement gives you an opportunity to say more about you and your practice outside of the confines of a formal CV. It's important that an artist's statement is engaging, readable and interesting from the perspective of the commissioner who may (or may not) have a formal background in the arts so they may not know who you are or what your process and methodologies are. Help them out and make it easy for them to be curious about you, your idea and your practice.

Budget

The budget is an essential element of your proposal and is, in effect, the financial description of the project. A complete and realistic budget demonstrates to the commissioner that the idea is deliverable; you are a "safe pair of hands" to entrust with the resources and that you have considered the financial as well as creative aspects of the project. The budget outlines the prospective income and expenditure attached to the project; should also indicate any support in kind; and should be based on the most recent research you have done into costs of materials etc. Make sure that estimates you receive are VAT inclusive and indicate in your budget that the costings are for a fixed period of time (i.e. 12 weeks) after which they will have to be rechecked. (E.g. the recent increases in fuel costs would have had a significant impact on a budget which relied heavily on transportation). Keep an updated version of your budget on a spreadsheet (or a package like Quicken) on your computer and amend this as you get more information.

Visual Information

Have good quality visual material and make sure it is relevant to the application. The material should be good examples of your work that amplify your application. Make sure the images are in focus, correctly lit and are in the relevant and appropriate format. There's no point in sending a series of 35mm slides when the selection panel has a DVD player. Your proposal will look unprofessional and your slides will not give the selectors the information they need to assess your application in the same way as everyone else's. The visual information should be cued up and ready to go (if on video) and accompanied by the relevant applications for viewing. Depending on the project, it may be appropriate for you to produce models, maquetes, CAD drawings or other three dimensional material. If you are unsure, ask the commissioner before you submit your proposal.

The Selection Process

Selection processes vary depending on the commission but they are generally a one stage or two stage process. In the first case your proposal will be evaluated on the basis of what you submit, in the second case your proposal will be short listed and you will be invited to work up a more detailed proposal (including conceptual idea and realisation). In a two stage process you can expect a fee for the additional work involved in this more comprehensive proposal.

Selection panels, particularly for public art commissions, are generally comprised of a representative of all of the major stakeholders. In a local authority context for example this could include: The county architect, an engineer, an elected representative, a representative of the community context in which the work will take place/be sited, professional artists and the public art co-ordinator/arts officer or a professional curator.

The selection panel for any commission will check whether the proposals submitted meet the criteria for inclusion and the relevant material and documentation has been supplied. They will then go on to select the relevant artist to whom the commission will be awarded and will give feedback to those who have not been successful on this occasion.

You can imagine then the types of discussion that the selection panel will engage in – from the aesthetic purpose and value of the work to the practicalities of realising and siting it through to the political and community ramifications. It is a complex and sophisticated process and the more you can do as an artist to evidence the fact that you are cognisant of this complexity the easier it will be for your project to be a serious contender. I am not suggesting that you in any way downplay the creative and aesthetic considerations of your project – but I am suggesting that the context in which that work will be realised will be very present to the selection panel and if you can assist them in imagining its realisation then that can only been a positive contribution. Your ability to make that contribution is directly related to the quality of the research you undertake prior to submitting your proposal.

The important issues for an artist to consider are:

- Will there be professional arts expertise on the panel?
- How can I ensure that the quality of my idea and project are communicated clearly when there may be people on the panel who aren't familiar with the arts and in a way which won't compromise my idea?
- How can I help the panel imagine my work in situ?

Be Professional

You approach the creation of your work with a high degree of professionalism – approach the generation of proposals in the same way. What comes out of an envelope on a commissioner's desk should say as much about you as the work you produce so give yourself a psychological advantage by establishing your credibility as soon as that package is opened.

Make sure that the information you produce is typed, has been proof read, spell checked and is presented in a formal and appropriate way. All basic word processing packages offer templates to guide you but if you are unfamiliar with the relevant formats then ask for help from someone you know. Just because the deadline is next Friday week at 2pm doesn't mean you have to pull an all-nighter the night before. Aim to complete your proposal a week early, giving yourself enough time to have someone else read and edit for you. If you are applying online then make sure that the material you create can be read and seen on PC and MAC e.g. send written material as a PDF file and include a link to a site where a free Adobe reader can be sourced.

Make sure you put your name on everything and don't send original material unless you are specifically asked to do so. If you do send original material make sure it is insured; you get a signature on delivery and that you supply a mechanism for return.

Finally create a proposal checklist and go through it several times before you send the documentation.

Feedback

If you are successful in your proposal – congratulations! However, this is no time to be complacent. Keep a diary of the entire project (this is of particular importance if this is your first success). Log every call, email and journey you take. Keep detailed accounts of how much you spent and earned and log the time the project took from inception to completion. This is invaluable intelligence for the next proposal you write which will be based on fact rather than fiction.

202

If you have been unsuccessful then ask for feedback. If you don't know what didn't work this time then how can you improve on that the next time? It may be that your idea was superb but your budget was deemed to be unrealistic; it could be that your idea was seen before by the panel and not considered to be original or appropriate for this context; it could be that a key piece of information required by the commissioner was omitted by you from the proposal. Wouldn't it be a shame not to know what didn't work in your favour if it was something really simple you could amend immediately? Many artists don't ask for feedback and it is the single most important and relevant piece of information you can use to improve your chances of success next time.

Conclusion

Yes – preparing proposals is a time consuming process. If you build research into your practice then you will have a better idea of what a commissioner is looking for and you can then target those who will be a better fit. Artists can save a lot of time by throwing out the generic proposal and spending the time it would have taken doing mail shots researching a smaller number of potential commissioners who are interested in the work they create. Selection panels will know a bespoke proposal when they see it because it will address the guidelines they have published. Always remember that your proposal may be one of 50 that a panel will spend a day considering and you need to give yourself the best chance to be seen, understood and considered for the opportunity.

By Annette Clancy

Summary

Top Tips for Starting Out

Make use of the college facilities before you graduate!

It's very easy to take college facilities for granted but you'll have to pay for them when you graduate. So use the equipment to finish off works in progress. Use the photocopier to make copies of your CV. Avail of internet, computer and printer access to prepare submissions, proposals and job applications. It's also easy to take tutors and their valuable feedback for granted! So make the most of them too.

Document your work

Maintaining an organised, running history of your work for promotion, grants, reference, and exhibition purposes, is an important part of professional practice. Make sure to document your work carefully, especially your degree show and in particular if it's an installation, ephemeral, or transient work. Consider having the work professionally photographed – these photographs can be used for promoting your work and accessing future opportunities. You can find information on the best ways to document your work in the in the relevant section of this manual.

Prepare an Events Calendar

Set yourself goals for the coming academic year. Plan the year out with targets and submission dates in mind. You can find out about submission deadlines for public art commissions, gallery calls, residencies and funding opportunities by signing up for the twice weekly VAI eBulletin (www.visualartists.ie). You can also use the VAI website to keep a track of upcoming deadlines). This will help you allocate your time while identifying opportunities to which you can submit your work.

Network

Networking is one of the most effective ways to open up career opportunities in a competitive industry. Whether you're connecting at an art fair or getting to know your co-workers at an internship, you never know when that person might be able to help you. Get yourself on mailing lists for gallery openings and previews. You have to get out there and meet new people to get your work known. Networking might seem hard at first, but once you get the hang of it (and start recognising familiar faces at events) it becomes more natural.

Build a critical profile

Establish a list of contacts from college for collaborations, critique and support. Consider setting up a peer review group with other graduates to give critical feedback on each other's work. VAI runs regular peer critique sessions that you should join. The evaluation will help you understand how others view your work. Your peers bring a fresh perspective to bear and will often be able to point out whether something is clear or not. The input can be highly motivating.

Learn the art of writing Press Releases and the Artist Statement

The ability to write good press releases and artist statements is a key element in getting ahead. The written word is one of the most important elements that employers, galleries, museums, and graduate schools look for in an artist. The information you provide in a press release should be factual, clear and have some sort of edge that will attract critics / press to the show. Always avoid using superlatives in press releases. Write something interesting and engaging for the body of the release. The first two sentences are the most important you have to hook the viewers to make them want to know more.

An artist's statement is a living document that changes as your work progresses. Your statement could be updated at about the same rate that you might update a CV. A good statement will give you the ability to discuss and have confidence in your work.

Get your work reviewed

A conundrum for emerging artists is that you need a show to get reviews, but you need reviews to get a show. So initiate and curate your own show with your classmates and use this opportunity to get your work reviewed. There is no quick way of attracting curators, critics or other art professionals to shows. There are only really a small handful of writers and critics and there are hundreds of shows around the country each month. Develop a good contact list by researching all the major art publications, writers, press officers, galleries etc. Each contact should be sent a press release and a personal invite to the show. Tell them a bit about the show and invite them to meet you there for a glass of wine and a chat. Don't forget to advertise your show with Visual Artists Ireland's free eBulletin service. This is the primary way to let the wider art world know that your show is happening.

Reviews are beneficial not only because they bring your work to a wide audience but also because they are evidence that you are engaged with and part of the professional art discussion and dialogue. Reviews are recognition and acknowledgement by your peers. They can also come in very handy as supporting documents when making funding applications! Getting a review in the local press is a good way to start.

Price your work

In many professions unions tend to advise members on rates of pay, however most artists must take on this responsibility for themselves. There are many variables involved in establishing the price for your work, be it a painting, carrying out a public art commission, licensing a reproduction or giving a workshop. You will need to take into account your time, your profile, materials, overheads, provision for social insurance and income tax etc. Many artists start out on their career taking whatever jobs they can, and often for inadequate pay. Most people feel uncomfortable discussing money but a successful negotiation does not only affect the fees you will be getting – it will impact your self esteem and influence others perception and value of you.

Get Help!

You're not alone. Through Visual Artists Ireland you will find various local groups and networking events that will bring you into contact with your fellow artists. The best way to find out about the education or training provided by arts service organisations is to place your name on any eBulletin or similar notification lists available to you and/or to check their websites. VAI provides professional development courses (at a reduced rate for members) that are invaluable for helping you in your career development.

Join Visual Artists Ireland

Access the help desk along with numerous other benefits such as discounts on material suppliers and service providers, 6 copies of the Visual Artists News Sheet posted to your door annually, a reduction on fees charged for workshops and events, access to digital editing facilities and equipment hire, entry into the Living Artists Archive, your personal website listed on the VAI website. By joining you will also be strengthening our voice to advocate on your behalf.

The Writers

All articles have been commissioned by Visual Artists Ireland for distribution to the visual arts community.

Annette Clancy is an organisational consultant and psychotherapist with over 20 years experience working in and consulting to the cultural sector. Prior to establishing her consultation practice www.inter-actions.biz she was artistic director of Garter Lane Arts Centre in Waterford; worked with Dublin Theatre Festival and was administrator of the Soho Theatre Company (London). Annette is a graduate of Communications Studies, holds an MSc in Systemic Organisation and Management and is currently a Doctoral Candidate at the Management School at the University of Bath (UK).

Dr. Tina Fiske is co-director of Bracker Fiske Consultants, a consultancy specializing in the documentation of contemporary artworks. Tina received her PhD from the University of Glasgow, for her thesis on the acquisition and long term care of 'non-traditional' contemporary artworks by British public collections. She currently teaches undergraduate and postgraduate courses on 'Collecting and Conserving Contemporary Art' at the University of Glasgow, which introduce students to some of the philosophical, historical, and practical issues that attend the collection and conservation of non-traditional contemporary works of art. Tina has convened several conferences and workshops on issues of preservation in relation to digital and video media: for example, *The Preservation of Digital Art* (with Erpanet, October 2004) and *The Work of Video Art in the Age of Reproduction (with Streetlevel, April 2006), both at the Centre for Contemporary Arts in Glasgow. She has also organized workshops for Visual Artists Ireland (Dublin and Cork, 2006) on issues attending sales and management of new media / video artworks.* www.brackerfiske.com

Flannigan Edmonds Bannon is a Chartered Accountancy practice based in Belfast which offers a wide range of services, including: Management Accounting Services (bookkeeping, VAT returns, payroll services, and the preparation of management accounts); Compliance Services (annual accounts preparation, tax computations and returns, audit of company accounts, company secretarial function); Advisory Services (business development, taxation planning, corporate finance). If you believe that you could benefit from any of the services above you can contact: Flannigan Edmonds Bannon, 2 Donegall Square East, Belfast BT1 5HB, Northern Ireland

Sarah Glennie has been working as a curator both in Ireland and internationally for over 10 years. She moved to Ireland in 1995 to work at the Irish Museum of Modern Art where she curated a number of projects including solo exhibitions by Olafur Eliasson and Shirin Neshat and the major public art project GHOST SHIP by Dorothy Cross. In 2001, she moved to The Henry Moore Foundation Contemporary Projects where her curated projects included Paul McCarthy at Tate Modern, and Stopover: Graham Gussin, Hilary Lloyd and Richard Woods at the Venice Biennale 2003. In 2004, she co-curated Romantic Detachment, a Grizedale Arts project at P.S.1/MoMA and in 2005 curated a major new commission by Tacita Dean for Cork Capital of Culture 2005. She was the Commissioner of Ireland's participation at the 51st Venice Biennale 2005 for which she curated an exhibition of the largest number of artists to represent Ireland at Venice to date: Stephen Brandes, Mark Garry, Ronan McCrea, Isabel Nolan, Sarah Pierce and Walker and Walker. She is formerly Artistic Director of the Model Arts and Niland Gallery, Sligo; The Irish Film Institute, Dublin, and currently Director of The Irish Museum of Modern Art.

Kevin Kelly is the senior art handler at the National Gallery of Ireland and a practising artist and curator. He leads the art handling team at the Gallery and is responsible for the installation of temporary exhibitions and the movement and storage of the extensive collection of art held by Gallery. Kelly has completed the Art and Object handling course at West Dean College in England and has worked as an art handler in many contemporary art galleries in Scotland and Ireland. He holds a Masters Fine Arts degree from Glasgow School of Art and had his first solo show at the Project Arts Centre in 1997. Since then Kelly has participated in and curated many exhibitions both nationally and internationally.

Noel Kelly is a fellow of The Royal Society for the encouragement of Arts, Manufactures and Commerce (RSA); President of the International Association of Art Critics - Ireland (AICA Ireland); a board member of the International Association of Art Critics – International (AICA International); a member of IKT the International Association of Curators of Contemporary Art; a member of the British Society of Aesthetics; a board member of IVARO; Irish Visual Artists Rights Organisation; a member of The Institute of Directors; and a member of The Royal Dublin Society. In 2009 Kelly was curator for the Slovenian National Pavilion in the Venice Biennale. He has curated extensively on mainland Europe and Ireland, and has been curator for Temple Bar Gallery & Studios (2005 – 2007). Kelly was cultural programme director for the Slovenian Embassy in 2004 during the Accession process with exhibitions both of Irish and Slovene artists. He is a published writer and a commentator on broadcast media. His most recent publications are: Creative Ireland: The Visual Arts 2001 – 2011, and The Social, Economic, and Fiscal Status of the Visual Artist in Ireland. He currently holds the position of Chief Executive Officer/Director of Visual Artists Ireland.

Niamh Looney is Information and Research Officer with Visual Artists Ireland. In 2006, she successfully completed Managing Safely, a course validated by the Institution of Occupational Safety and Health

Jacinta Lynch is Director and founder of Broadstone Studios Ltd. 1997-2008. Arts Council Advisory Panel – Research on Visual Artists' Workspace, 2008. Director Roscommon Arts Centre, multi-disciplinary public venue 2001-2005. EU Culture 2000 Brussels – Visual Arts Selection Panel 2005. IETM – International Network for Performing Arts, Belgrade 2005. EU Culture 2000 Brussels – Visual Arts Selection Panel 2004. Danish EU Presidency – International Conference on Mobility in the Arts, Arhus, 2002. Assistant to International Architect & Designer Ron Arad, London, UK 1989 -1993. Craft worker with Fornasetti Srl, International Design Studio, Milan, Italy 1989. Artist-in- Residence, Villanuova de Jiloca, Zaragoza, Spain 1988. Masters Degree in Fine Arts, New University of Ulster, 1984.

Since leaving Brighton University where he studied sculpture, **Fred Mann** has been involved with Milch, the non-profit making London based arts space, 1993 – 2000, run a commercial gallery partnership, Rhodes + Mann from 2002 to 2005 and more recently Fred London Limited, where he represents the careers of 15 artists. He has attended many international and national art fairs, published many monographs and taught and lectured nationally and internationally.

Kerry McCall has been lecturing on Cultural Event and Project Management in the Business and Humanities Department of the Institute of Art, Design and Technology, Dun Laoghaire for the last 5 years. She also manages public art projects having most recently advised Dundrum Town Centre on the development of its public art strategy. Prior to 2001, she was Director of the Sculptors' Society of Ireland (now known as Visual Artists Ireland).

David McConnell is a consultant who provides corporate financial services to the arts sector – bookkeeping and accountancy services, in particular. He advises on grant applications and gives workshops. David is former chief financial officer to the Arts Council, Dublin. He also is an organist and choir director.

Jacqui McIntosh is an independent writer and curator based in London. Her writing has appeared in publications such as The Guardian, Irish Examiner, Circa, Magill, Contemporary, Art Review and in catalogue essays for galleries and artists. Curated shows include The mind was dreaming. The world was its dream (2012), Dig Down in Time (2010), The Marienbad Palace (2010), The World Needs A Narrative (2008) and Better is Something You Build (2008).

Paul O'Neill is an artist and curator researching curatorial histories at Middlesex University. He writes regularly for Art Monthly, The Internationaler and Contemporary. De Appel and Open Editions published his edited anthology of new writing on curatorial practice, Curating Subjects, in November 2006.

Alan Phelan studied at Dublin City University and Rochester Institute of Technology, New York. As an artist, his practice involves the production of objects, participatory projects, curating and writing. These all inform, combine and contribute to an interest in the narrative potential surrounding an artwork. This can be exploited or explored from actual and historical events, ideas, things and places as well as their fictional counterparts.

209

Working in the museum and archive sector has shaped this approach somewhat but more as a counterpoint than agency. He has exhibited widely internationally including Golden Thread Gallery, BOZAR, Brussels; Whitney Museum of American Art, New York; Chapter, Cardiff; SKUC, Ljubljana; Feinkost, Berlin; SKC, Belgrade; OK11, Helsinki; Eastlink Gallery, Shanghai; URRA/Galería Del Infinito Arte, Buenos Aires. In Ireland exhibitions include IMMA, Oonagh Young Gallery, mother's tankstation, Dublin; MCAC, Portadown; Limerick City Gallery of Art, Solstice, Navan and The Black Mariah, Cork. Screenings include Kevin Kavanagh Gallery; ÉCU Film Festival, Paris; Cinesonika, Derry and the Cairo Video Festival. Public art projects include projects for Dublin City Council, Dun Laoghaire Rathdown and the Department of Communications. Curated exhibitions at the RHA, Farmleigh Gallery, Project, Dublin. His work is represented in the collections of the Irish Museum of Modern Art, Limerick City Gallery of Art, The National Self-Portrait Collection and several private collections.

Sarah Pierce is an artist based in Dublin. Since 2003, Sarah Pierce has used the term The Metropolitan Complex to describe her project. Despite its institutional resonance, this title does not signify an organisation. Instead, it demonstrates Pierce's broad understanding of cultural work, articulated through various working methods, involving papers, interviews, archives, talks and exhibitions. Characterized as a way to play with the hang-ups (read 'complex' in the Freudian sense) that surround cultural work, one emphasis is a shared neuroses of 'place', whether a specific locality or a wider set of circumstances that frame interaction. Central to her activity is a consideration of forms of gathering, both historical examples and those she initiates. In 2011, solo exhibitions of her work will be held at the Schmela Haus, K21 in Düsseldorf, and Museet for Samtidskunst in Roskilde. Major projects between 2008-2010 include: Future Exhibitions, MUMOK, Vienna; QUEL CON, Centre Georges Pompidou, Paris; By now we share and affinity, Townhouse Cairo; The question would be the answer to the question 'Are you happy?', Van Abbemuseum, Eindhoven and Sala Rekalde, Bilbao; An artwork in the third person, Project Arts Centre, Dublin; and, It's time man. It feels imminent, ICA, London. Pierce regularly publishes The Metropolitan Complex Papers, and continues to collaborate with Annie Fletcher on the Paraeducation Department, which they began in 2004.

Gaby Smyth & Company is a chartered accountancy practice located in Ballsbridge, Dublin, which specialises in the music, theatre, film and visual arts. The firm offers taxation, audit and management accounting services. Gaby Smyth has delivered courses in taxation and accounting for Dublin Business School, the Institute of Bankers, AIB Corporate and Treasury, and Goodbody Stockbrokers. In addition, the firm has run courses specialising in accounting and tax in the arts for Music Network, Blackchurch Print Studio, Fire Station Artists Studios, Visual Artists Ireland and various county and city councils throughout the country.

Visual Artists Ireland is funded by:

Principle Funders

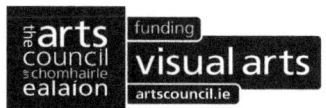 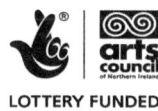

LOTTERY FUNDED

Project Funders

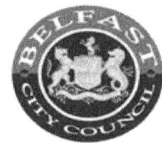 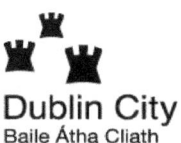